For Adrian Crapper
with the good wishes of
the author.

Edwin R. Harris

February 4, 1966

S

SHAKSPERE AND COMMON SENSE

SHAKSPERE

and

COMMON SENSE

By

EDWIN R. HUNTER

THE CHRISTOPHER PUBLISHING HOUSE
BOSTON, U.S.A.

TO MY STUDENTS
WHO
—UNSUSPECTING GUINEA PIGS—
HAVE THROUGH THE YEARS
HAD THESE IDEAS
FOR THEIR DAILY FOOD

PREFACE

For many years my occupation as a teacher of literature has made the plays of Shakspere one of my principal interests, and as a student of Shakspere I have become, perforce, an interpreter. As a member of this increasing tribe I claim no special distinction. I have thought, from time to time, that I have found a few new slants of exposition and that I have come upon a few glints of heretofore unnoted gold. In the main, however, I am simply one of the many who through familiarity and repeated reading and pondering have become increasingly convinced of the great playwright's insight and humanity and common sense.

It is around the growing realization of the element of common sense in his works and workmanship that my special philosophy of Shakspere interpretation has gathered and crystallized. This realization has in no way lessened my honor and appreciation for Shakspere. But it has led me to feel that there is a sense in which he is not to be stood in awe of. There is about him and his genius nothing occult; he is cloaked in no aura of infallibility. He is great but with a greatness that is solid and rational. It is to this quality which I am calling *common sense* as it appears in his works and in his workmanship that I direct the chapters which follow.

The first chapter sets the stage for the discussion. In it I endeavor to make clear what I mean by *common*

7

sense and to illustrate the manifestations of it, to show that he invoked it as a palliative against sentiment and with deft incision through pretense and affectation wherever they appeared. Also I undertake to show that in his handling of matters which naturally lend themselves to technical and specialized treatment, he employs rather a medium of treatment that is in terms of the intelligent layman whose understanding is clear and yet not specialized, whose approach is common-sensical and, in a proper degree, almost folkish.

In assuming this emphasis I do not for a moment seek to minimize the richness and even the profundity of much that there is in Shakspere. On the other hand, I would decry the tendency to find patterns of concealed meaning or hidden structures of topical reference placed in the plays by conscious design of the playwright for the benefit of—whom? Digging too deeply for allegory or searching too minutely for philosophical intent is to go beyond the warrant of the materials. The comedies are full of fun and the tragedies, though full of the basic truths of life and destiny, are built primarily to be dramatically effective. Reading too deeply Duke Theseus' discourse on the imagination or taking with too serious implications the melodrama of King Richard II is to go beyond what Shakspere intended.

This impression of Shakspere's common sense comes not alone through what is in the plays but also through his shrewd, almost elfish refusal to involve himself, his ability to hold himself so completely out of the matter as to be able to give it always the benison of his cool judgment and discerning eye. This is *par excellence* Schiller's ideal of the naive artist, Keats's formula for "negative capability."

The final chapter, "Some Observations Regarding the

Processes of the Creative Mind," is intended to suggest
in a somewhat more general fashion how the creative
mind goes about its work. Illustrations are taken from
Shakspere mainly, but also a few from Chaucer, to point
out that the mind of the artist functions in a normal,
orderly way like yours and mine, the one difference being in the quality of the product. The chapter concludes
with a special defense of those of us who pore over the
literary man's work in the study, seeking thereby to
come closer to an understanding of what went on in his
creative processes.

The eleven chapters between the first and the last may
seem, on surface consideration, to be unconnected, a
sort of miscellany. But my intention has been to bind
them all with the strand of emphasis on this same common sense. I have written into each of them—risking
repetitiousness for the sake of making their essential unity
clear— suggestions of how each subject treated illustrates
the common sense of the great playwright.

To be able to read the book one does not need to be
a deeply-stored Shaksperean, but to understand it one
does need to know the plays. Only the *Comedy of Errors*, the three *Henry VI* plays, *All's Well*, *Timon*, and
Pericles are not referred to somewhere in the pages which
follow. References to the text assume that the reader
knows the plays familiarly. There is little effort to
accommodate a reader whose knowledge of Shakspere
is scanty.

The citations from the text are from the *Complete
Works of Shakespeare* edited by G. L. Kittredge (1936).
The reference data for each quoted passage follow it immediately and are to act, scene, and line—I, ii, 3-4. They
have been kept as simple and unobtrusive as possible. If
a second passage is from the same act and scene as the

one immediately preceding, all data are omitted except the line numbers.

Notes of acknowledgement are relatively few. Actually I am indebted consciously to much Shakspere scholarship that is not specifically credited, and unconsciously to a great deal more. I have special debts of gratitude to the following persons for encouragement and help. My friend and former student, Dr. John H. Fisher of New York University and the Modern Language Association, was the first to read the manuscript and to give useful suggestions. My colleague, Miss Elizabeth Hope Jackson and my son, William Harold Hunter read the manuscript with great care and gave me a wealth of helpful criticism. My young colleagues, Miss Carolyn L. Blair and Mr. Arthur S. Bushing, read it and were helpful and encouraging. I am also grateful to my friend and neighbor, Dr. Alwin Thaler of the University of Tennessee and to my friend and former colleague, Dr. Hill Shine of the University of Kentucky for valuable counsel.

I have special cause of gratitude to President Ralph Waldo Lloyd of Maryville College not only for his encouragement over the time in which the book was taking shape, but also to him and to the Committees of the Directors of the College who gave me generous and necessary financial help in bringing it into print.

Far from least of all, my wife has been constantly encouraging and when effort has flagged has supplied always a gentle spur to prick the sides of my intent.

Maryville College
Maryville, Tennessee
1954

TABLE OF CONTENTS

Shakspere and Common Sense

CHAPTER I

SHAKSPERE AND COMMON SENSE

The concern of this chapter is not with common sense *about* Shakspere. Much of what has been said and written about him has had that quality; much, also, has departed not alone from common sense but from sense altogether. From such extreme deviation may good angels guard us here. For we are to deal with Shakspere *and* common sense; with his relation to common sense in two aspects: (1) with the credit and value he consistently sets upon this quality in his plots and in his characters; and (2) with the common or popular or every-day sense in which he deals with situations which have their developed significances and techniques for the specialist but which, for the ordinary man—one of whom William Shakspere was—have a well-received common or popular understanding.

I

In developing the first aspect, that Shakspere gives credit and place to sound common sense in his plots and characters, I should like to take as a principal illustration the whole situation of *As You Like It*. Surely, of all the plots, this is one of the most romantic and fanciful, filled with unreal and fantastic situations and sentimental motivations.

13

A ruling duke is supplanted by his unscrupulous
younger brother, who drives him from his dukedom
out to exile in a forest, not wild and inhospitable but
exotic and friendly, where, attended by an equally romantic coterie of followers, he basks in the sun, rhapso-
dizing about how sweet are the uses of adversity, spread-
ing picnic lunches beneath greenwood trees, and at the
sight of houseless poverty and broken age breathing
piously:

> Thou see'st we are not all alone unhappy.
> This wide and universal theatre
> Presents more woeful pageants than the scene
> Wherein we play in.
>
> II, vii, 136-139

With this there is the story of the usurper's daughter
Celia, who for love of her cousin, the banished duke's
daughter Rosalind, leaves the court where it seems she
is now first lady, and, disguised as a country wench, goes
out to exile with this cousin, who, in turn, is metamor-
phosed into a young man by doublet and hose.

Thus far the elements of the story are very humane
and idyllic. They tax our credulity mainly because the
usual exiled duke is not so comfortably philosophical and
the usual young lady, raised to the quality of a duchess
with the leadership of a court just opening to her, does
not so readily take to the woods even for the love of a
cousin.

But there is more. Once in the forest, Rosalind, who
came there to seek her father, finds him, but perversely
does not reveal her identity. Then the young Orlando
comes, who had, before she left the court, already cap-
tured her heart in record time as she had his. Now he
goes sighing like a furnace about the forest, desecrating
the young trees with sonnets made to his mistress' eye-

brow, and riming ever on one theme: Rosalind. For
her part, despite the many fathoms deep she is in love
with him, she does not reveal her identity. Rather she
invents a fantastic game of having him address his
speeches of love for Rosalind to her—to him—that is, to—!
The very confusion of the pronouns of reference is eloquent of the fantastic confusion of the plot. In the course
of this masquerade, Rosalind—or Ganymede, to use the
forest name of the youth—is seen and sighed for by a poor
sentimental shepherdess named Phebe, whom Ganymede
must fend off, for he cannot reveal his disguised condition; that would spoil the Rosalind make-believe which
he is playing with Orlando. This may be good pleasant
comedy but it is not life nor like life.

But there is still more. There are two conversions of
cruel-minded villains, one, most fantastically managed,
has accompaniments of palm trees and lionesses in a
forest somewhere in France, the other, most frailly motivated, has the usurping duke coming into the forest with
threatenings and slaughter against his brother. At the
edge of the forest he unexpectedly meets a holy hermit,
who in short order turns him about into the ways of a
contrite penitent.

Moreover, there is much marrying and giving in marriage as the play draws to an end. This is the sentimental
comedy of *As You Like It*.

But Shakspere redeems this comedy from the fanciful
and sentimental by the introduction of two, if not three,
spokesmen of common sense and reality. To this service
he devotes the melancholy Jaques and Touchstone, and,
in certain passages, Rosalind. (1) Jaques' consuming
interest is in the oddities and vagaries of human behavior.
He is an early recruit to the ranks of those who make
case studies. To him the philosophical senior duke is a

lovable but boresome old Pollyanna; Orlando is an insufferable sentimental nuisance; the youthful Ganymede-Rosalind is too alert and sharp to be overlooked, but being so is not comfortable company; Amiens is a charming singer but his romantic pastoral song draws from Jaques a cynical parody; and Touchstone is to him an unfailing joy. "Motley," he cries, "motley's the only wear!" (II, vii, 34).

When the old duke falls upon the metaphor of the world as a theater, *Yes*, says Jaques, *and what a theater! Everybody has a role; seven acts,*[1] and as he parades them we see them as so many facets of the disillusioned realist's view, from the infant "mewling and puking" (144) in unlovely aspect, to the picture of senility at the end: "sans teeth, sans eyes, sans taste, sans everything" (166). At the end of the play we find Jaques still stage-managing Touchstone, first into a position at the center of the stage in the scene of the multiple weddings—which scene, by all the canons of romance ought to have been reserved solely for sentiment and fantasy—and thence he leads him into his burlesque about the seven degrees of the lie. And we hear him, from lungs that crow like Chanticleer, shouting:

> Is not this a rare fellow, my lord?
> He's as good at anything, and yet a fool.
> V, iv, 109-110

(2) Touchstone is *par excellence* the pricker of sentimental bubbles. His is the flat, crass parody of the verse about Rosalind:

> If the hart do lack a hind,
> Let him seek out Rosalinde.

---

[1] The style adopted in this book for paraphrase of this sort to distinguish it from the large amount of direct quotation is italic type.

If the cat will after kind,
So be sure will Rosalinde. . . .
                III, i, 107-110

and eight lines more. Hearing Silvius in his love-sick pleas to Phebe, Rosalind, in Touchstone's presence, remarks of her own lover's pain:

Alas, poor shepherd! Searching of thy wound,
I have by hard adventure found mine own.
                    II, iv, 42-43

And Touchstone says, blubbering and sniffling in clownish caricature:

And I mine. I remember, when I was in love I broke my
sword upon a stone and bid him take that for coming
a-night to Jane Smile; and I remember the kissing of her
batlet and the cow's dugs that her pretty chopt hands
had milked; and I remember the wooing of a peas-cod
instead of her, from whom I took two cods and giving
her them again, said with weeping tears, 'Wear these for
my sake.' We that are true lovers run into strange capers.
                        44-54

Under such treatment how can sentiment remain fully self-complacent?

Note also the Fool's attitude toward marriage for himself. He finds Audrey in the forest and leads her to an improvised altar with only the non-conformist Martext to officiate, but when Jaques interferes because the priest is not a good priest, Touchstone is only partly pleased, muttering aside:

I am not in the mind but I were better to be married of
him than of another; for he is not like to marry me well;
and not being well married, it will be a good excuse for
me hereafter to leave my wife.
                        III, iii, 91-96

In a later scene (V, i) he belabors her local suitor with

the valor of words and drives him trembling from the scene. And still later we see him coming in that procession of couples which calls to Jaques' mind the pairs of creatures coming to the ark, and Touchstone is the expositor:

> I press in here, sir, amongst the rest of the country copulatives, to swear and to forswear . . . A poor virgin, sir, an ill-favour'd thing, sir, but mine own. A poor humour of mine, sir, to take that that no man else will.
>
> V, iv, 57-62

And as he launches into his analysis of the lie circumstantial, his eye catches the slatternly Audrey slouching in the foreground, and he interjects: "Bear your body more seeming, Audrey" (72).

(3) Though Rosalind is most of the time so enmeshed in that net to snare the moonlight, which is the main plot interest, as to have little time for anything else, she does, better than the rest of her group, maintain her common sense, and in a few instances falls into step with Jaques and Touchstone as a deflater of sentiment. The best instance of her basic sensibleness is in the situation in which Orlando protests that unless his Rosalind love him he will die, and the disguised Rosalind answers like a true skeptic:

> No, faith, die by attorney. The poor world is almost six thousand years old, and in all this time there has not any man died in his own person, vidilicet, in a love cause. Troilus had his brains dash'd out with a Grecian club; yet he did what he could to die before, and he is one of the patterns of love. Leander, he would have lived many a fair year though Hero had turn'd nun, if it had not been for a hot midsummer night; for (good youth) he went but forth to wash him in the Hellespont, and being taken with the cramp, was drown'd; and the foolish chroniclers of that age found it was 'Hero of Sestos.' But these are

all lies. Men have died from time to time, and worms
have eaten them, but not for love.

                                        IV, i, 94-108

Thus a play, running heavily to the romantic and the
sentimental, is shot through with the cool incisive cyni-
cism and burlesque spirit of Jaques and Touchstone and
Rosalind until one is forced to conclude that a work
that bears on its surface the blazon of fine romance may
have become, in part at least, a semi-serious parody on
romance. Certainly if you don't like too much sugar
in your tea, you can still find your pleasure in *As You
Like It,* for Jaques and Touchstone and young Ganymede
are abroad in the forest, and they, like you, prefer their
tea not too sweet.

As You Like It is the capital case in point of an entire
play in which the hard base of common sense saves the
sentimental from becoming oppressively dominant.
Other plays, in their degree, present the same diffusion
of emphasis. A quick inspection reveals the difference
that would emerge if we had the basic plot of *Much Ado
About Nothing* unconvoyed by the brittle but merry
wit combats of Benedick and Beatrice or the fantastic
adventures of the lovers in a *Midsummer Night's Dream*
without the delightsome improvisations of Robin Goodfellow and the incongruous behavior of Bottom the Ass
in the refined atmosphere of Queen Titania's court.
Other plays would yield similar illustration but our point
is made so far as entire plays are concerned.

But I do wish to note four or five instances of characters who are marked by a strong common-sense hatred
of cant, pretense, and false sentiment. You recall the
Bastard Falconbridge in *King John,* who, hating the
Austrian Archduke for good cause and estimating him
for what he is—an affected, pompous braggart—listens

with great pleasure as Queen Constance mercilessly berates the Austrian for perfidy. Coming to the end of
her tirade, she exclaims:

> Thou wear a lion's hide?   Doff it for shame,
> And hang a calve's skin on those recreant limbs.
> *John* III, i, 128-129

"O," says the ostensibly aroused Austrian, "O that a man
should speak those words to me." And immediately, and
after that frequently, Falconbridge obliges:

> And hang a calve's skin on those recreant limbs. . .
>
> *   *   *
>
> And hang a calve's skin on those recreant limbs.
> 131; 133; 199; 220; 299

Empty pretentious speech draws his scorn. Before
the walls of Angiers the English and French kings rant
and boast. King John:

> Twice fifteen thousand hearts of England's breed —

And Falconbridge interjects, "Bastards and else." Then
the French king:

> As many and as well-born bloods as those —

"Some bastards too," comments Chorus (II, i, 275-279).

In the street brawl in Venice occasioned by the hue
and cry over the marriage of Senator Brabantio's daughter to the Moorish General, the various small bombastious
fellows of the factions are thrusting and parrying fiercely in the half light of the street when the Moor himself,
seasoned poised veteran, quiets and shames them with one
cool common-sense word:

> Keep up your bright swords, for the dew will rust them.
> Good signior, you shall more command with years
> Than with your weapons. . . .

> Hold your hands,
> Both you of my inclining and the rest,
> Were it my cue to fight, I should have known it
> Without a prompter.
>
> *Oth.,* I, ii, 59-61; 81-84

In the opening scenes of *I Henry IV*, young Henry Percy tells King Henry why he replied with what sounded like refusal to the King's demand for his prisoners. It was, he said, his hot but honest reaction to the appearance on the battle field of a strutting, affected, snuff-taking popinjay, who came as the King's messenger. We get the picture of a tired, wounded, chilled soldier pestered and vexed by the dandy's inept comments and affected manners, and we have another demonstration of sturdy common sense:

> He questioned me, amongst the rest demanded
> My prisoners in your Majesty's behalf.
> I then, all smarting with my wounds being cold,
> To be so pest'red with a popinjay,
> Out of my grief and my impatience
> Answer'd neglectingly, I know not what—
> He should, or he should not. . . .
>
> *   *   *
>
> I answered indirectly, as I said,
> And I beseech you, let not his report
> Come current for an accusation
> Betwixt my love and your high majesty.
>
> *I H IV,* I, iii, 47-53; 66-69

This same Percy's literality could not brook the fantastic self-conceit of Owen Glendower, the Welsh mystic. The Welshman boasts:

> At my nativity
> The frame and huge foundation of the earth
> Shak'd like a coward.
>
> III, i, 13-17

And Hotspur replies:

> Why, so it would have done at the same season, if your
> mother's cat had but kitten'd, though yourself had never
> been born.
>
> 18-20

After more of this, Glendower shifts the ground of his
boast: "I can call spirits from the vasty deep." "Why,
so can I," rejoins Hotspur, "or so can any man; But will
they come when you do call for them?" (54-55).

Many examples come to mind of Hamlet's hatred of
affectation and duplicity. The pompous indirections of
Polonius enrage him. The latest recruit to the coterie of
the obsequious, Young Osric, draws his scorn. Guildenstern, who tries to wheedle Hamlet into self-revelation
but who cannot play upon the box-flute he offers him,
is withered for his presumption, and at the grave of
Ophelia the Prince is offended by Laertes' overdone display of grief and mockingly attempts to outdo it. Explaining his behavior to Horatio, he says:

> [T]he bravery of his grief did put me into a tow'ring
> passion.
>
> *Ham.,* V, ii, 78-79

I conclude this part of the discussion with a hasty
mention of Horatio. I take first Hamlet's address to Horatio on the qualities of character which led him to admire
and trust him:

> Horatio, thou art e'en as just a man
> As e'er my conversation cop'd withal.
>
> *   *   *
>
>   Dost thou hear?
> Since my dear soul was mistress of her choice
> And could of men distinguish, her election
> Hath seal'd thee for herself. For thou hast been

As one, in suff'ring all, that suffers nothing;
A man that Fortune's buffets and rewards
Hast ta'en with equal thanks; and blest are those
Whose blood and judgment are so well commingled
That they are not a pipe for Fortune's finger
To sound what stop she please. Give me that man
That is not passion's slave, and I will wear him
In my heart's core, ay, in my heart of heart
As I do thee.

III, ii, 59-60; 67-79

This is Horatio, the man to tie to, to depend upon. When poor demented Ophelia gets out of hand and all the rest are helpless to deal with her, Horatio is the one person who can quiet and divert her troubled mind, not because he is a trained psycho-therapist, but because he is one

Whose blood and judgment are so well commingled
That they are not a pipe for Fortune's finger
To sound what stop she please.

So common sense shows itself as a counteractive to sentiment and also, in instance after instance, is demonstrated in the contempt and disdain with which strong balanced persons view affectation and pretense.

II

We turn now in the second aspect of this discussion to suggest that Shakspere's knowledge and view of situations, which was clear and broadly based, was nevertheless not technical or specialized. I pointed out earlier in this chapter that his view was the ordinary view or in line with the common sense in which matters are taken, because he was himself an ordinary man. I am sure you do not misunderstand me, for I do not mean to disparage the most extraordinary mind as to clarity and scope and understanding that our race has produced. I mean only that his knowledge was, in the main, ordinary every-day knowledge and his interpretations and applications the common, popular interpretations and applications. Chaucer is the logical contrast, Chaucer, who knew so many branches of knowledge technically—astronomy, astrology, alchemy, medicine, dream lore, philosophy, rhetoric, physiognomy, and many more.

Let me suggest a few incidental examples of the ordinariness of Shakspere's treatment of matters for which technical treatises were at hand. Shakspere's ghosts are fundamentally for dramatic effect. He is at no pains to place them in their relation to the world of spirits, to devils on the one hand and to angels and ministers of grace on the other. The ghost of King Hamlet walks at midnight and tells his story with kingly dignity, but also he shifts his position beneath the platform like a mole in the earth. One wonders how Mr. Dover Wilson's erudite explanation of this beneath-the-platform work would have impressed Shakspere.[2]

Another instance is that of the apparitions in the last act of *Richard III*, where Richard sleeps fitfully at one side of the stage and Richmond sweetly at the other, and Shakspere thriftily makes the same set of spirits serve simultaneously to curse and threaten Richard and to bless and assure Henry. By the canons of no known school of spirit or dream lore can such a situation be supported, but, after all, it saved an extra scene and released the cast for other roles and was, on the whole, a common-sense thing to do.

In the *Winter's Tale*, Antigonus, the unwilling caster-away of Queen Hermione's baby girl on the sea coast of Bohemia, on the night before he came to shore, had

---

[2] J. Dover Wilson, *What Happens in Hamlet*, "The Cellerage Scene," 78-86.

a dream in which Queen Hermione appeared to him as
a ghost. He is not surprised to see her a ghost, for when
he left home her health and fortunes were most low.
And we think she is a ghost, for we saw her "die" and
saw the arrangements for her burial. But she is not dead;
as we learn later, she was not at any time dead, and so
was not at any time a ghost either in Antigonus' dream
or otherwise. But the same dramatic effect is served as
if she were a ghost, and Shakspere is not interested in
the hair-drawn distinctions among dreams as Chaucer
is in the "Nuns' Priest's Tale" with its discussion of
dreams, swevens, and *avisiouns.*

Let us glance at one subject of philosophical discussion
which comes up in a number of Shakspere's plays in his
mid-period. It is the question of free will, which in
Chaucer the poet himself and the Nuns' Priest and
Chanticleer and Troilus discuss after the learned manner
of the schools. First among Shakspere's people it is Cassius who broaches the subject:

> Men at some time are masters of their fates:
> The fault, dear Brutus, is not in our stars
> But in ourselves, that we are underlings.
> *Caesar,* I, ii, 139-141

Then Iago:

> I have look'd upon the world for four times seven years;
> and since I could distinguish between a benefit and an
> injury, I never found man that knew how to love himself.
> Ere I would say I would drown myself for the love of a
> guinea hen, I would change my humanity with a baboon.
> . . . Virtue! a fig! 'Tis in ourselves that we are thus or
> thus.
> *Oth.,* I, iii, 312-318; 322

And Edmund:

> This is the excellent foppery of the world, that, when we

are sick in fortune . . . we make guilty of our disasters
the sun, the moon, and the stars; as if we were villains
on necessity; fools by heavenly compulsion; knaves,
thieves, and treachers by spherical predominance; drunk-
ards, liars, and adulterers by an enforc'd obedience of
planetary influence; and all that we are evil in by a divine
thrusting on. An admirable evasion of whoremaster man,
to lay his goatish disposition to the charge of a star! . . .
My nativity was under Ursa Major, so that it follows I
am rough and lecherous. Fut! I should have been that I
am, had the maidenliest star in the firmament twinkled on
my bastardizing.

Lear, I, ii, 128-145

And there is all this strange insistence on the theme of
free will with not a technical word, not a scholastic citation, nothing but the simplest common-sense terms in
which intelligent minds anywhere might understand it.

A capital example of this sort is found in the effort of
the Doctor and Cordelia to restore the distraught mind of
old King Lear. In it there is no display of any specialized
knowledge, but merely the employment of the simple
practical services which you and I know. Sleep is the
great restorer.

Says the Doctor:

Our foster nurse of nature is repose
The which he lacks.

IV, iv, 12-13

To help in inducing sleep there are herbs and drugs:

That [sleep] to provoke in him
Are many simples operative, whose power
Will close the eye of anguish.

13-15

Next come clean garments. (Our modern sense cries
out for a bath for the old man, but this is only the early
seventeenth century; we must be patient):

> In the heaviness of sleep
> We put fresh garments on him.
>
> vii, 21-22

Then sleep (13); then music:

> Louder the music there.
>
> 25

Then a loved face and voice to greet him on his first awaking. The Doctor says to Cordelia, "Be by, good madam, when we do awake him. I doubt not of his temperance." As Lear stirs, she says to the Doctor, "He wakes. Speak to him." But the Doctor insists, "Madam, do you; 'tis fittest" (22-23; 42-43). And as Lear comes fumbling through the fog of his last days and nights to try to comprehend Where and When and How, the Doctor enjoins Cordelia to caution:

> Be comforted, good madam. The great rage
> You see is kill'd in him; and yet it is danger
> To make him even o'er the time he has lost.
> Desire him to go in. Trouble him no more
> Till further settling.
>
> 78-82

Thus are employed the common practical means of restoration with no technical jargon and not a single invocation of any of the standard anatomies of the passions which Shakspere's generation knew. It is all as ordinary and as practical as the wisdom of kindly and intelligent and untrained folk: simples, sleep, clean garments, music, a loved face and voice, and patience.

When Gertrude, seeing Hamlet's distracted behavior at the appearance of the Ghost which was present to him but unseen by her, calls it ecstasy, Hamlet cries:

> Ecstasy?
> My pulse as yours doth temperately keep time
> And makes as healthful music. It is not madness

That I have utt'red. Bring me to the test
And I the matter will reword; which madness
Would gambol from.

Ham., III, iv, 139-144

That is, *give me a form of words to say, and after I have
said it, have me repeat it. Madness can't do that.* That
is the test; how striking an instance of a simple, tradition-
al, common-sense test of sanity.[3]

Examples stretch out before us and must be denied.
If I have made clear my point, you have it as an impression gained from reading the plays that Shakspere took
things and situations in their common every-day light
as ordinary men took them.

The researches of scholars in our generation have carefully and with real learning reminded us of the availability and currency in Shakspere's time of many technical works: such books as *The French Academie*, available
in English after 1594; Thomas Wright's *The Passions of
the Mind in General*, 1604; the venerable *Bartholomeus de
Proprietatibus Rerum*, revised and expanded by Batman
in 1582; Thomas Rogers' *Anatomie of the Mind*, 1576; Sir
Thomas Elyot's *Castel of Health*, 1547; Thomas New-
ton's *The Touchstone of the Complexions*, 1581; and
Lavater's *Of Ghosts and Spirits Walking by Night*, 1572.

But so far as Shakspere was concerned, treatments of
such technical sort were of only indirect service. It may
have been to a degree a feeling on his part that drama
would be hampered by the inclusion of such specialized
materials. But we should recall that Chaucer cited au-
thorities, both ancient and modern, and split hairs, both
scientific and metaphysical, with no detraction from the

---

[3] It is likely that Jaques' suggestion that Touchstone repeat his
rigamarole about the degrees of the lie is essentially the same thing
in a slightly different application. *A. Y. L.*, V, iv, 92-93.

charm of his tales. It seems much more likely that Shakspere's approach to scientific and philosophical matters
was not by direct knowledge through specialized treatments but was by virtue of being intelligently alert and
alive in a generation served by them as our day is served
by Locke and Kant and Croce.

Down from the upper reaches of philosophical specu-
lation the systems of thought come filtering through
from mind to mind and from generation to generation,
losing much of the impedimenta of exact terminology in
the process but keeping the great body of their value for
the service of the practical mind. One does not have to
have read Hume to be a skeptic, or Spinoza to be a rationalist, or Berkley or Croce to be an idealist. Indeed one
does not need to know that he is a rationalist or a tran-
scendentalist in order to be one and to talk and write like
one. Of such sort I consider Shakspere to have been.

Does it not seem clear that he honored ordinary common sense, that he liked to see affectation deflated and
sentiment reduced to absurdity, and that his own system
of thought was not directly drawn from specialized and
esoteric sources but that it was rather the ordinary or
common sense of things, breathing out of the vital and
questioning air of that Renaissance time?

The chapters which follow take up various topics, but
each in its own way has at its center this concept of
Shakspere as the champion and exemplar of common
sense.

CHAPTER II

SHAKSPERE'S INTENTIONS REGARDING KING RICHARD II

The story of how nervously Elizabeth and her partisans felt the parallel of Richard II and his times with her and her times is well known. The earlier studies of Miss Evelyn Albright[1] and more lately studies by Miss Lily B. Campbell[2] have pointed out many pertinent connections between the Hereford faction in Richard's time and that of the Earl of Essex and his associates (one of whom was the Earl of Southampton, Shakspere's patron) in Elizabeth's time.

There is much support for Miss Albright's assumption that John Hayward's pamphlet history of the deposition of Richard and the accession of Henry IV was available to Shakspere and was influential in coloring his handling of these events. In any case it seems clear that there was little, if any, reason for treating the personality or the career of Richard II with respect.

Two hundred years is ample warrant for scanting the reverence due even to a king, and the likelier so if a descendant of his supplanter is on the throne. If we may judge by his treatment of Henry IV and Henry V, on the one hand, and of Edward IV and Richard III, on the other, Shakspere, in any matter involving the conflicting claims of Lancaster and York, is decidedly Lancastrian.

[1] Evelyn May Albright, "Richard II and the Essex Conspiracy," in *PMLA*, XLII, 686-720.
[2] Lily B. Campbell, *Shakespeare's Histories*.

Thus we may believe with Miss Albright that Shakspere was a well-wisher of the Essex attempt, which depended for its justification so far as genealogical claims are concerned on the Earl's descent from Richard's uncle and victim, Thomas of Gloucester.[3] Or we may believe the dramatist was a good Queen's man with orthodox loyalty to the dynasty as represented by Henry Bolingbroke and Henry of Richmond. In either case we have small reason to expect from him any defence of the character of the second Richard or any idealization of the third.

My intention here is to indicate that Shakspere conceived as the dominant trait of Richard II a bent for self-dramatization, a theatrical habit of mind, and that in a few scenes this comes dangerously near to the grotesque. There is, it must be admitted, much to qualify and mitigate this trait. There are references to Richard's beauty and grace of person. A number of people are fond of him—the young Queen, some servants, his uncle York. York's reaction to the deposition scenes was not alone one of shock that the sanctity of the crown had been violated, but also one of genuine regret for the personal humiliation suffered by Richard. And there is, in his last scene (V, v), the flash of manly vigor on Richard's part where he snatches an axe and kills two of the assassins before he is himself struck down. But when all this is considered, there is still an unfavorable balance against him.

During the past century and a half students of this play have rather generally agreed that Richard's character is marked by weakness, and that he is much more impressive in word and gesture than he is in act. None of them has, I think, given enough notice to the bulk of material

[3] Albright, 695-696.

which piles up to make this the principal fact about his presentation. Nor has any one of them quite admitted how close the King's behavior comes, in a few places, to the grotesque and foolish.

Coleridge lists Richard's traits as "insincerity, partiality, arbitrariness, and favoritism," and goes on to say that the persistent feature of Richard's character is "his attention to decorum and high feeling of the kingly dignity."[4] Perhaps a more incisive statement from Coleridge is his calling Richard "a man with a wantonness of spirit in external show."[5] "Richard," Coleridge says, "is not meant to be a debauchee; but we see in him that sophistry which is common to man, by which we can deceive our own hearts, and at one and the same time apologize for, and yet commit the error."[6]

Hazlitt's attitude differs mainly in the phrasing. "We feel neither respect nor love for the deposed monarch," he says, "for he is as wanting in energy as in principle; but we pity him, for he pities himself."[7]

Walter Pater is emphatic in his praise of the poetry of Richard's speeches, which he characterizes as "that royal utterance, his appreciation of the poetry of his own hapless lot, and eloquent self-pity."[8]

Dowden has a number of happy phrases regarding this quality in Richard. "Richard," he says, "to whom all things are unreal, has a fine feeling for 'situations'. . . . Instead of comprehending things as they are, and achieving heroic deeds, he satiates his heart with the grace, the

[4] S. T. Coleridge, *Lectures on Shakespeare*, Ev. Lib. Ed., 112.
[5] *Ibid.*, 117.
[6] *Ibid.*, 115.
[7] William Hazlitt, *Characters of Shakespeare's Plays*, Ev. Lib. Ed., 138.
[8] Walter Pater, *Appreciations*, 205. It is Pater (201) who calls Richard "an exquisite poet if he is nothing else."

tenderness, the beauty, or the pathos of situations. Life
is to Richard a show. . . . He is an amateur in living; not
an artist." In another passage Dowden refers to Richard's ineffective eloquences as "rhetorical piety." He
cites, also, Kreysigg's phrase (*Vorlesungen über Shakspeare*, 1874) which he translates as "pseudo-poetic
pathos." Another Dowden comment refers to "the aes-
thetic satisfaction derivable from the situation of a van-
quished king." "There is," he says, still speaking of
Richard, "a condition of the intellect which we describe
by the word 'boyishness.' The mind in the boyish stage
of growth 'has no discriminating convictions and no grasp
of consequences'. . . . The talk of a person who remains
in this sense boyish is often clever, but it is unreal."[9]

Stopford Brooke speaking with special regard for the
Castle scene comments on "the inability of the passion,"
and continues, "Richard unlades his heart in fluent feebleness." Referring to the mirror episode as "that spectacular scene with the mirror which is quite unnecessary,"
he goes on to say of that scene, that it "worst of all . . .
lowers our pity for Richard because it exhibits his theatrical folly in public."[10]

George Brandes makes an interesting parallel between
Richard of England, in the play, and King Frederick William IV of Prussia, in real life, because, says Brandes,
they "displayed just the same mingling of intellectuality,
superstition, despondency, monarchical arrogance, and
fondness for declamation."[11]

Hardin Craig, speaking of the spectacular collapse of
the Coventry tourney, says, "At Coventry, Richard,

[9] Edward Dowden, *Shakespeare, his Mind and Art*, 173-178. The
internal quotation regarding boyishness is from Newman's preface
to his "The Idea of a University."

[10] Stopford A. Brooke, *On Ten Plays of Shakespeare*, 91-95.

[11] George Brandes, *William Shakespeare*, 124.

who spent his life, not living, but playing parts, partici-
pates up to the crucial moment in a great spectacle."[12]

Mark Van Doren attributes Richard's tragedy to his
poetic bent. "What explains his failure to oppose Bolingbroke at all, his sudden collapse, as soon as the threat of
deposition becomes real, into a state of sheer elegy, of
pure poetry? The answer is simple. Richard is a poet,
not a king. Surrounded by favorites and deceived by
dreams of his utter safety, he can strut in the high style
awhile. But an acute ear detects the strut even at the
brave beginning."[13]

Note again this array of phrases: "attention to decorum," "wantonness of spirit in external show," "he
pities himself," "eloquent self-pity," "Life is to Richard
a show," "rhetorical piety," "pseudo-poetic pathos,"
"boyishness," "fluent feebleness," "theatrical folly in public," "fondness for declamation," "spent his life not living but playing parts," and "strutting in high style." Any
one of these would make an effective label for the quality in King Richard's character which is the subject of
the remainder of this chapter.

The scene in the lists at Coventry (I, iii) is the first
instance in point. Shakspere has very decidedly changed
the element of time as it is in Holinshed, speeding up the
action, as often elsewhere, to heighten dramatic impression; but here, in particular, the dramatic impression
takes the form of a show of the King's bent for arbitrary
action and flashy display of royal caprice. Both in his
selection of details and his alteration of details found in
his source, Shakspere is playing up this impression.[14]

[12] Hardin Craig, *An Interpretation of Shakespeare*, 128.
[13] Mark Van Doren, *Shakespeare*, 89-90.
[14] The dramatic gesture of halting the fiery knights in the very
act of charging, Shakespeare keeps substantially as it is in Holinshed,
but for Holinshed's statement that after this there were two long

When Richard arbitrarily clips four years from Hereford's sentence of banishment, the banished Duke himself remarks it and points with ironic emphasis to the very quality of the King's act of which we are speaking:

> *Boling.* How long a time lies in one little word!
> Four lagging winters and four wanton springs
> End in a word, such is the breath of kings.
>
> I, iii, 214-216

The next outstanding instance of this theatrical and over-rhetorical trait comes in Richard's speech and action upon his return from Ireland:

> I weep for joy
> To stand upon my kingdom once again.
> Dear earth, I do salute thee with my hand
> Though rebels wound thee with their horses' hoofs.
> As a long-parted mother with her child
> Plays fondly with her tears and smiles in meeting,
> So, weeping, smiling, greet I thee, my earth,
> And do thee favours with my royal hands.
>
> III, ii, 4-11

Let us scan this for a moment. With all necessary allowances for the conceitfulness of the age and of Shakspere's early manner, this is worse than the customary— worse with a badness which argues the author's intent to color the character of the speaker. Note the forced parallel of:

> I do salute thee with my *hand*.

and

> Rebels wound thee with their horses' *hoofs*.

Moreover, the similitude of Richard in relation to England as a parted mother reunited with her child is not

---

hours of conference, Shakspere substitutes the immediate pronouncement of sentences of banishment on Mowbray and Hereford. Holinshed, *Chronicles*, Ev. Lib. Ed., 28.

merely inappropriate as a symbol of a king's relation to
his country, but is particularly inept and ironic here in
view of his negligence and trifling in his royal office. But
worst of all, what is he doing with his hands?

> I do salute thee with my hand.

and

> So weeping, smiling, greet I thee, my earth,
> And do thee favours with my royal hands.

What is he doing? For, after all, this is a stage direction
and the actor must fall in with it. (1) Is he patting the
face of a cliff-like shore, (2) or is he letting beach sand
run through his fingers, (3) or is he down on the ground
stroking or patting the earth with his hands?[15] But
enough! It cannot at its best be a very kingly spectacle,
and to ponder it longer leads us toward grotesquerie.

> And do thee favours with my royal hands (!)

The next twelve lines of this speech are given over to
the conjuration of the earth to do *disfavors* to his enemies:

> Feed not thy sovereign's foe, my gentle earth,
> Nor with thy sweets comfort his ravenous sense;
> But let thy spiders that suck up thy venom,
> And heavy-gaited toads, lie in their way,
> Doing annoyance to the treacherous feet
> Which with usurping steps do trample thee.
> Yield stinging nettles to mine enemies;
> And when they from thy bosom pluck a flower,
> Guard it, I pray thee, with a lurking adder
> Whose double tongue may with a mortal touch
> Throw death upon thy sovereign's enemies.

[15] I am told by one who saw *Richard II* performed by the Stratford players that their Richard followed the third alternative suggested above; he got down and patted the ground. Maurice Evans
played it so. It is the most grotesque way, therefore, probably the
best way to do it.

Mock not my senseless conjuration, lords.
This earth shall have a feeling, and these stones
Prove armed soldiers ere her native king
Shall falter under foul rebellion's arms.
                                        III, ii, 12-26

Let us note first regarding this speech the close literalness
of its figures. This is a prayer to the earth for earthly
disfavors, and the matter of it is all hewn to the exactions
of this pattern; there is no mistaken call for thunderbolts,
or torrents of rain, or baleful influence of planet or star.
It is all of the earth. If one takes the passage from this
point of view together with the speech in V, v in which
Richard, in Pomfert Prison, is hammering out similes
just for pastime, we are tempted to conclude that Shakspere conceived as one facet of Richard's theatrical folly
this strained and conceitful attention to the devices of
rhetoric.

But the most significant line in the speech just cited is
the fourth line from the end. After the invocation to
English earth to disfavor Bolingbroke, comes this line:

Mock not my senseless conjuration, lords.

Who is mocking? Are we not once more dealing with
an implied stage direction? Recall the conclusion of
Hamlet's speech about the recent loss of his accustomed
zest for life. "Man delights not me; no, nor woman neither, though by your smiling you seem to say so." Rosencrantz replies, "My lord, there was no such stuff in my
thoughts." "Why did you laugh then," Hamlet insists,
"when I said 'man delights not me'?" And the reply is
not a denial of laughing but only another reason for having laughed. (*Ham.*, II, ii, 321-326). Is Richard's situation different from this to the degree that one can claim
there was no mockery in the lords' faces? The scenes
come to mind, also, of Cloten surrounded by attendants

taking scant pains to conceal their disdain for his stupidi-
ties. (*Cym.*, I, ii and II, i). If Cloten had had but the wit,
he, too, would have seen mockery on lords' faces. Richard's situation is, of course, more decorous, but that fact
aside, there is much suggestion of similarity. Indeed this
line—"Mock not my senseless conjuration"—reads like a
very index to the dramatist's conception of how the
King's behavior is being taken by his associates and of
how it is to be taken by us.

Another instance almost as gross in its flouting of the
practical and the kingly is the sequence of images (III,
iii, 144-186) in which first he develops the idea of for-
swearing all the symbols and trappings of royalty in
favor of the humble properties of a religious hermit. The
last of these forswearings is the logical and poetic last—
the giving up of his large kingdom for a little grave. Seeing tears in his cousin Aumerle's eyes, he goes on to propose that they two weep themselves out a pair of graves:

> And my large kingdom for a little grave,
> A little little grave, an obscure grave;
> Or I'll be buried in the King's highway.
>
> *   *   *
>
> Aumerle, thou weep'st, my tender-hearted cousin!
> We'll make foul weather with despised tears;
> Our sighs and they shall lodge the summer corn
> And make a dearth in this revolting land.
> Or shall we play the wantons with our woes
> And make some pretty match with shedding tears?
> As thus — to drop them still upon one place
> Till they have fretted us a pair of graves
> Within the earth; and therein laid — there lies
> Two kinsmen digg'd their graves with weeping eyes.
> Will not this ill do well?
>
> III, iii, 153-170

And just as had been the case in the scene of the patting

of the earth at the landing place in Wales where he had
caught the deprecatory smiles of mockery on his lords'
faces, so here he ends this speech:

> Well, well, I see
> I talk but idly and you laugh at me.
>
> 170-171

This surely is enough underscoring to make the point
clear. As a rule, Shakspere does not leave us confused,
but on few points is he clearer than on this. Richard
is a prolific and incurable poet, and because he will indulge his fancy while other necessary matters go undone,
he is totally ineffective as a king.

> I see
> I talk but idly and you laugh at me.

Probably some Shaksperean somewhere has called this
wept-out-grave speech one of Shakspere's sublimest passages. It would be most errant and wanton understanding to take it so. It is one of the worst of his poetic
passages; it seems clear that he intended it to be so. As
Professor Kittredge so well says of another passage in
another play, "If the speech were better, it would not
be so good."[16] But to make assurance surer Shakspere
has Richard add four lines which are wretched as poetry
and completely insane as the speech of a man with any
notion of kingship or any sense of responsibility. He is
still king, but he can not remain so long if he persists
thus in talking his crown away:

> Most mighty prince, my lord Northumberland,
> What says King Bolingbroke? Will his Majesty
> Give Richard leave to live till Richard die?
> You make a leg, and Bolingbroke says ay.
>
> 172-175

[16] G. L. Kittredge, *Complete Works of Shakespeare*. Introductory
article to *Winter's Tale*, 432. A remark about the speech of Father
Time as Chorus.

Even those who are deserting him credit the collapse of
his fortune to this habit of poetizing and grandiose
prattle. After he has gone out, Bolingbroke and Northumberland sum it up soberly:

> *Boling.* What says his Majesty?
> *North.*   Sorrow and grief of heart
> Makes him speak fondly, like a frantic man.
>   185-186

Two other notable scenes remain for attention. The
one is the scene of Richard's surrender of the crown.
In the midst of the deliberations, suddenly Richard conceives a bit of dramatic business—a sort of royal tug-of-
war in which he and Henry are to pull to see which gets
the crown. How far to go with this on the stage is a
director's problem. But its outlines are surely quite clear.
Here is the crown on a table. Richard on one side directs
Henry, who is standing opposite, to seize the other side
of the crown and they will pull:

>   Here, cousin, seize the crown.
> Here, cousin.
> On this side my hand, and on that side yours.
>   IV, i, 181-183

Henry, obviously, has no disposition to play at this, and
it is well, for, put into execution, this would have been
a most undignified business. Accordingly Richard is
forced to something else, and his image-making faculty
plunges on into a similitude of the well with the two
buckets, one down, one up.[17] And across this flow of
poetry there falls the flat prose of the usurper.

> I thought you had been willing to resign.
>   190

---

[17] George Brandes, *William Shakespeare*, 125, calls this crown-seiz-
ing speech one of the most beautiful passages Shakspere ever wrote.

For many centuries among Christian men it has been a well-received convention that no one who thinks reverently, no matter how he may suffer or be beset, thinks other than that the sufferings of our Lord are unique among experiences of suffering. No one, in good taste, likens his sorrow to that of Christ. One who does so is either loose of thought and tongue or has an inflated notion of his own woes. Richard does it, and Shakspere's taste, which in such matters is impeccable, is fully aware of what he is making Richard do:

Yet I well remember
The favours of these men. Were they not mine?
Did they not sometime cry 'All hail!' to me?
So Judas did to Christ; but he, in twelve,
Found truth in all but one; I, in twelve thousand none.
IV, i, 167-171

Though some of you, with Pilate, wash your hands,
Showing an outward pity, yet you Pilates
Have here deliver'd me to my sour cross,
And water cannot wash away your sin.
239-242

Shakspere has surely marked this character well. Here is pathos, but it is false and shallow.

What a contrast the glib pathos of these scenes makes with the tragic depth of feeling in Romeo's speech in the Capulet's tomb, with Hamlet just before the sword play, with Othello to the Venetian emissaries, with Macbeth and Cleopatra face to face with death.

There is another scene for which a word is required. It is the soliloquy of sixty-five lines in the last act, scene v. An interesting discussion of this passage is that by Mr. G. Wilson Knight under the title "The Prophetic Soul."[18] With great respect to Mr. Knight's gift in the

[18] *The Imperial Theme*, 351-367.

field of imaginative interpretation,[19] I have to report my total inability to follow through with his subtle processes in analyzing this speech. Shakspere, in the opening lines, plainly marks it as of a piece with the rest of the fluent feebleness and theatrical folly which we have been noting. Richard, alone in a dungeon in Pomfert Castle, soliloquizes:

> I have been studying how I may compare
> This prison where I live unto the world;
> And, for because the world is populous,
> And here is not a creature but myself,
> I cannot do it. Yet I'll hammer it out.
>   V, v, 1-5

What is this? It is simply the old rhetorical flair. A simile—one to be built up by close literal parallels— a practical difficulty arises in the process, but the rhetorician resolves to hammer it out. If lords were present, would there not again be mocking glances?

He does proceed to hammer it out. In the remaining lines of it Mr. Knight sees what, I fear, Richard and Shakspere did not see, *viz.*, the whole sequence of Shakspere's tragic themes laid out in prophetic symbol. What a less gifted sight sees is another chain of similes, link after link of empty rhetoric, for the forging of which the best word is *hammer,* and in which the King's self-pity and fondness for declamation are displayed for the last time. Theodore Spencer comments on this passage. "To the last, he is an inveterate seeker of correspondences, and when he is alone in prison just before his death, he is still hunting for parallels, trying in vain to turn his prison into a macrocosm."[20]

---

[19] My warrant for the use of "interpretation" in this sense is Mr. T. S. Eliot's introduction to G. Wilson Knight's *The Wheel of Fire.*
[20] *Shakespeare and the Nature of Man,* 76.

Many persons in life, some in literature, dramatize themselves. Some do it better than Richard, but, when the mask is lifted, it is never a very creditable role. One recalls notable literary instances: Becky Sharp, the Signora Neroni, and, in her dumb fashion, Hetty Sorrel. Readers of Booth Tarkington will remember that this is a frequent element in his novels. Its best exemplification is in the title role of *Alice Adams* and there is a fine demonstration in a less-known novel, *Claire Ambler*. Let me cite a page from this novel for what it is, a really remarkable demonstration of the self-dramatizing faculty. The scene requires no context so far as our point is concerned:

> Then the bride came down the aisle, alone. She walked with her head a little advanced but her face uplifted; and about her grave and tender eyes, and upon her lips, there appeared the faintest foreshadowings of an ineffable smile. . . . Never had she been so graceful; never had she looked so lovely. And when she passed through the coloured light of the great window, and her bridal white became a drifting rosiness in aureoles of amber and softest blue, a breathed "Ah!" of pleasure was multitudinous upon the air. For she seemed then just such a glimpsed vision of angelic beauty, wistful, yet serene. . . .
>
> She suspected this herself, for she had seen her bridesmaids passing through the light before her. "I hope it's doing as well by me," she thought. "With this beautiful cream-white it ought to do even a bit better. . . . I shan't begin to let my smile be more definite just yet—not till I reach the third pew from the end—and I mustn't forget to turn my head to the right and let a gentle little corner of a smile go to poor Mother after I've given Walter that look. He's there waiting, of course. . . . I'm getting married to him and this is my wedding—my *wedding!* . . . Why don't I realize it? How on earth does it happen? How does it come to be my wedding—if it really *is!* Am I in

love with him? Is it because of that? . . . And that
"double" sense of hers was never more strongly with her
than then, as she came down the aisle to be wedded. As
audience, she saw herself distractedly asking these belated
questions and at the same time stage-directing her every
movement and expression.[21]

Other factors than this bent for self-dramatization
contributed their part in bringing about the loss of his
kingdom for Richard. He made errors of judgment and
committed crimes against responsibility such as his rude
treatment of the dying Gaunt, the farming out of the
realm, and the cold-blooded seizure of the estates of
Lancaster. But when one counts them all and lets them
weigh as heavily as they will, one comes back to the
Shaksperean emphasis on his habit of making poetic
images while his antagonist is taking castles and recruit-
ing friends and making himself master of England. If
there were a world or even an England where the current coin were metaphor and the chief traffic the emotional and the dramatic, then Richard should be king in that
country. But England was no such fairy realm in his
day, nor has it been since. Especially pertinent is Professor Stauffer's word for this: "The play is a succession
of situations . . . that show Richard's inability to square

---

[21] Booth Tarkington, *Claire Ambler*, 250-252.
There are men of this sort, but those we have named as notable
are all women. Is that significant regarding an understanding of
Richard? Is it any part of what Coleridge saw in the King of an
affinity to the feminine character? In two not widely separated
passages he has these statements: "It [Richard's] is a weakness . . .
of a peculiar kind, not arising from want of personal courage . . .
but rather an intellectual feminineness, which feels a necessity of
ever leaning on . . . others." *Lect. on Shakes.*, Ev. Lib. Ed., 115.
And "It is clear that Shakespeare never meant to represent Richard
as a vulgar debauchee, but a man with a wantonness of spirit in
external show, a feminine *friendism*, and intensity of woman-like
love of those immediately about him." *Ibid.*, 117.

circumstances with his own emotional distortion of them."[22]

If Richard had been something else, he might have done his office better, and it would have been vastly better for England. Professor Campbell makes this point well: "Richard's weaknesses, though disastrous to a monarch, would have been attractive traits in a poet or in a playwright, for he has an irresistible impulse to dramatize himself and to act and speak what he thinks theatrically effective in the situation in which he finds himself."[23]

What stands out then in our conclusion as to Shakspere's intentions regarding the character of King Richard II is that he does not expect him to be taken as contemptible or vulgar, but as ineffectual, and in developing this complexity of his character he projects situations which come dangerously close to the ridiculous. Richard does not sense the seriousness of situations but takes them as opportunities for grandiose and labored simile. Even —or perhaps, particularly—his followers sense the ineffectiveness of his poses and the ornate emptiness of his words. "Such is the breath of kings," says Bolingbroke with contemptuous irony of his cousin's arbitrary word. His lords *do* mock his senseless conjurations. Northumberland reports him as speaking fondly like a frantic man. Henry curtly humors his theatrical whim for a mirror, "Go some of you and fetch a looking glass," and the last pathetic view shows him in Pomfert dungeon, hammering dully through sixty-five lines of strained simile, while just outside, down the dark prison corridors, death comes striding.

Richard II is the tenth or eleventh play in Shakspere's

[22] Donald Stauffer, *Shakespeare's World of Images*, 93.
[23] Oscar J. Campbell, *The Living Shakespeare*, 38.

growing record of accomplishment as a playwright. Already three or four really interesting character creations have appeared—Richard III, the Bastard Falconbridge, Berowne, Bottom the Weaver—but, well done as they are and delightful as they are, they are not yet of the full flight of Shakspere character creation. It is surely proper to say that Richard II is the first real Shaksperean character in the sense that he is complex, highly individualized, and to be gauged properly only by the measuring tools of psychology. His kinsmen, to name a few of the foremost, are Henry V, Brutus, Hamlet, Iago, Antony.

Richard is not precisely novice work, for, as we have said he has some very creditable predecessors, but he is the first in the sense that his conduct, his passions, his decisions all lend themselves to psychological analysis. This, I contend, cannot be accidental nor is it an *ex post facto* imposition of nineteenth and twentieth century criteria on sixteenth century materials. It is clearly there, and put there consciously by the young dramatist, now beginning with maturing confidence to read more authoritatively from the book of life.

The question I should like to be able to answer is, how much psychology did Shakspere know and by what means did he come by it?

Within our own generation much scholarship has been devoted to the answer to a parallel question, what was the state of psychological knowledge in Shakspere's day? Miss Lily B. Campbell's *Shakespeare's Tragic Heroes, Slaves of Passion,* and Professor Walter Clyde Curry's *Shakespeare's Philosophical Patterns* are notable compendia of material regarding sixteenth century psychology and its literature. Other studies of the sort abound. But still we do not know how much and specifically what of all this Shakspere knew. I am bold to say that I think he knew little of it directly, that he had most probably read few of the books and more probably did not so much as know that there were such books as the most specialized and technical of them.

To understand human behavior one does not need to know psychology technically, but one does need to be attentive and observant and to catch the temper of the time. It is out of such knowledge as this, a common-sense realization of humanity, that Shakspere created Richard II and the rest. If Richard's *passion* is self-love carried at an exaggerated level, Shakspere can anatomize that passion incisively, with common sense, without recourse to the learned treatises on the passions. That he was indebted to them as all intelligent men are always in debt to the accumulated lore and culture of the ages is, of course, to be admitted, but his sense of humanity bears no musty smell of the library; his is a psychology of common sense.

CHAPTER III

FALSTAFF'S HEIR

It is one of the commonplaces of the study of Shakspere to call attention to the freedom with which he repeats character types, usually with delightful variations, but still with strong marks of similarity. Such roles as those of Hotspur, Casca, Kent, Enobarbus, and Menenius Agrippa are of unmistakable identity of pattern and so are such others as Malvolio, Polonius, Oswald, and Alexas. The very repetition of clownish characters, of disguised ladies, of pert designing wenches such as Julia, Nerissa, Margaret, and Maria is testimony to this point.

Once, at least, he emphasizes a repetition within a play when Young Osric comes on almost immediately after Polonius is safely stowed as if to say that their species of superserviceable, pompous, affected ass is indestructible—let the old one be killed, the young ones come on.

Much of this repetition, of course, must have come because the company afforded a limited but highly capable group of actors, and Shakspere wrote, as playwrights have always done, for the special talents of individual actors. Hence, in part, repetition of types. But there is also the fact that some types of character are dramatic and some are not, and from that it comes that certain types are called up with frequency. Moreover, there was in the near background of Shakspere's practice the strong revival of interest in classical comedy with its store of stock comedy types: the braggart, the gull, the parasite, the garrulous gossip, the fair shrew, and others.

In the handling of the greatest characters this practice of repetition is not so evident. Iago, indeed, is of
a line of villains, and Edmund and Iachimo follow him in
many particulars, but there is no duplicate of Hamlet,
and there is only one Lear, only one Cleopatra, and one
might remark that even her Antony is no more than
faintly reminiscent of the Antony of the funeral oration
and the battle field of Philippi. In like fashion Sir John
Falstaff has no clear successor in kind. Only Sir Toby
Belch suggests him, and that but partially. They are both
huge drinkers, but Toby becomes inebriated and Sir John
never does. They are both parasites, but Toby gives
back little in the way of *quid pro quo* as compared with
the great fund of entertainment provided by Falstaff.
Sir Toby cannot, therefore, be called Falstaff's heir.

In this chapter our concern is with a character who is
not made by Shakspere in Falstaff's image, but who is
so placed as to be laid liable to being shaped and impressed
by the quality of Falstaff's personality and character, one
who is in a fair way to become his spiritual heir, the
inheritor of the Falstaff tradition. It is the diminutive
page boy placed in Falstaff's service by the Prince. This
boy appears first at the beginning of *II Henry IV*, and
his role runs through that play and through *Henry V*
with at least a titular appearance in the *Merry Wives of
Windsor*.

In one sense we are entitled to say that Prince Henry
gave the little page to Falstaff. This is the emphasis of
the first scene in which the boy appears (*II H IV*, I, ii).
It is in many ways the most amusing of all the devices
called up to emphasize Sir John's huge bulk to set beside
him this mite of a boy, to go with him from tavern to
tavern through the London streets and to stand beside

him a constant living reminder of his huge hill of flesh.

Fal. If the Prince put thee into my service for any other reason than to set me off, why then I have no judgment.

II H IV, I, ii, 14-16

So says Sir John, and with characteristic quickness of turn he proceeds to credit himself with being the inspiration of the Prince's device:

The brain of this foolish-compounded clay, man, is not able to invent anything that intends to laughter, more than I invent or is invented on me. I am not only witty in myself, but the cause that wit is in other men.

8-12

So he admits the boy to his company and keeps him beside him to give life to the jest and to give credit to the jester.

There is another sense, however, in which one must say that *Shakspere* gave the little page to Falstaff. It is surely not too much to imagine that in the interval between the appearance of *I Henry IV* and *II Henry IV* there came one day to the theater the tiniest imaginable boy that could play, a saucy, pert boy but infinitely small, and all at once there flashed into Shakspere's mind his possibilities as a living physical foil for Falstaff, and from that inspiration grew the many quick, sure touches which mark the sequel. But whatever else we find, and whether we think of the designing mind as being directly Prince Henry's or indirectly Shakspere's, the basic use of the boy is for physical contrast. That is Sir John's own realization of it:

I do here walk before thee like a sow that hath overwhelm'd all her litter but one.

12-13

There is no Shaksperean creation—although one remembers misshapen Richard, the slatternly posturings of Audrey, and the fish-like aspects of Caliban—that depends so on the eye for its full realization as does Falstaff. He fills the stage. If he is silent, he is nevertheless there, and his every movement is an aspect of his hugeness. Many scenes come to mind, but one stands out above all the others. It is *II H IV*, V, v, where at the beginning of the scene the Coronation Procession has just entered Westminster and the great doors close upon it. It is just at that moment that, blown and spent, disheveled and stained from their wild ride down from Gloucestershire, arrive Falstaff, Justice Shallow, Pistol, Bardolph, and the Page. The problem now is a director's problem how to line up this company. Huge swollen Sir John, Shallow, who is infinitely long and thin, Pistol with his ill-sorted garb and bantam strut, Bardolph in his rags and with his everlasting bonfire light of a nose, and the diminutive Page boy. The text leaves the arranging almost entirely to the director.[1] Perhaps as a first choice, I think I'd line them up with Falstaff nearest the great portal, Shallow beside him, Bardolph and Pistol next, and the boy last of all. But it would also be good to put the boy beside Sir John, for they are both marvels, and no matter where they are on the same stage, they set each other off.

But it is characteristic of Shakspere's handling of characters that, while he may design them for dramatic purposes which can be served by nothing more than mere presence on the stage, he more often goes on to gather and develop other aspects of behavior until the figure comes to assume qualities of its own and to become what we call a character. This he does with the boy, and after Falstaff's death he follows him on through the scenes

[1] Falstaff's speech, *II H IV*, V, v, 5, places Shallow next to himself.

of *Henry V* in a fashion that has suggested to me the propriety of calling the boy Falstaff's heir.

In this treatment Shakspere suggests the development of his mind and also of his moral being. Mentally the boy shows quickness and a sort of singleness of resource. The quickness, while his, stems to a degree from the fact that he is a page in this sixteenth century tradition of the drama. There is Dobinet Doughtie in *Ralph Roister Doister*, Epiton in Lyly's *Endymion*, and Moth in Shakspere's own *Love's Labour's Lost*. All are quick, pert, and capable in retort. But the other quality of the boy is peculiarly his; this quality I have called a limitation of resource, a sort of singleness of mind. What I am pointing to particularly is that out of all the witty devices and subjects of invention which he had again and again observed coming from his Master's brain, one jest alone sticks in the boy's mind, and that is an extension of Sir John's hilarious and unfailing delight in Bardolph's flaming red face and swollen fiery nose. Everyone recalls especially Falstaff's declamatory speech about that nose, certainly one of the best specimens of his fluent pseudo-eloquence:

> I never see thy face but I think upon hellfire and Dives that lived in purple; for there he is in his robes, burning, burning. If thou wert any way given to virtue, I would swear by thy face; my oath should be 'By this fire, that's God's angel.' But thou art altogether given over, and wert indeed, but for the light in thy face, the son of utter darkness. When thou ran'st up Gadshill in the night to catch my horse, if I did not think thou hadst been an ignis fatuus or a ball of wildfire, there's no purchase in money. O, thou art a perpetual triumph, an everlasting bonfire-light! Thou hast saved me a thousand marks in links and torches, walking with thee in the night betwixt tavern and tavern; but the sack that thou hast drunk me would have bought me lights as good cheap at the dearest

> chandler's in Europe. I have maintained that salamander
> of yours with fire any time this two-and-thirty years.
> God reward me for it!
>
> *I H IV*, III, iii, 34-55

Of course, the boy has no speech to match this in quality
but he has four speeches of his own on this subject which,
taken together, are his most ponderable body of speech
and are all obviously an inheritance from his Master.

In *II Henry IV*, II, ii, the Prince and Poins are joined
by Bardolph and the boy, and, as usual the cue is for
someone to begin to comment on Bardolph's flaming
complexion. In this case, Poins is the commentator, taking up the conceit that Bardolph's flushed face is in reality
a perpetual blush of shame. This device the Prince had
used once earlier (*I H IV*, II, iv, 345), and on the basis
of Poin's opening jest the boy invents:

> 'A calls me e'en now, my lord, through a red lattice, and
> I could discern no part of his face from the window.
> At last I spied his eyes, and methought he had made two
> holes in the alewive's new petticoat, and so peeped
> through.
>
> *II H IV*, II, ii, 85-89

And the Prince leads the applause. "Has not the boy
profited?" he gloats.

Bardolph, in the proper degree of drink to be irritable,
says, "Away, you whoreson upright rabbit, away!" and
the Page's next speech is his second invention on the red-
face-and-nose theme: "Away," he says, "Away, you
rascally Althea's dream, away!" The Prince clamors
now for construction, "Instruct us, boy, What dream,
boy?" "Marry, my lord," says Falstaff's heir, "Althea
dreamt she was delivered of a fire brand, and therefore
I call him her dream." At this, once more, the Prince
is delighted, delighted a crown's worth, and Poins six-

pence worth, and there is not a word of question about the boy's twisted mythology (*II H IV*, II, ii, 83-102).

The next two instances of this, his perennial jest, come in connection with the sickness and death of Sir John. In the first the boy runs in calling, "Mine host Pistol, you must come to my master—and you, hostess. He is very sick, and would to bed. Good Bardolph, put thy face between his sheets and do the office of a warming pan. Faith, he's very ill" (*H V*, II, i, 85-89). So he's still at it. In bad taste, you may say, but still in good fettle of invention. As for taste, if the boy had it, would he not have to inherit it from someone other than John Falstaff?

Finally, after Sir John is dead and Mrs. Quickly has told her loquacious old wives' tale of his last hours, the boy perversely chips away at her determination to keep the story respectable with his last word on the Bardolph theme. "Do you not remember," he says, " 'a saw a flea stick upon Bardolph's nose, and 'a said it was a black soul burning in hellfire?" (II, iii, 42-44), which recalls what Sir John had said once of Bardolph's face, "I never see thy face but I think upon hellfire and Dives that lived in purple; for there he is in his robes, burning, burning." So the boy has learned at least one lesson well.

It remains to speak of the moral inheritance of the boy and of what he made of it. In a scene we cited for another purpose, when the drunken Bardolph and the boy enter to the Prince and Poins, the Prince exclaims upon the boy's appearance: "And the boy I gave Falstaff. 'A had him from me Christian, and look if the fat villain have not transform'd him ape" (*II H IV*, II, ii, 73-77). Take this however you may, it at least hints at deterioration in the boy, and, I think, deterioration in the moral realm. From Christian to ape. It is, of course, no part of my notion that the boy was an untouched

cherub when the Prince found him and gave him to
Falstaff, but at least he has now been sadly transformed
in appearance and, no doubt, also in manners and character by Sir John's caprice and example.

The boy lacks tenderness. All the other people of the
tavern mourn for the dead Knight—Mrs. Quickly and
Bardolph deeply—but not the boy, as witness his crass
jests in the presence of death, and his insistence on bringing out the less than savory truth about his Master's final
delirium. Says Nym, "They say he cried out of sack."
"Ay," says the Hostess, reluctantly, "that 'a did."
"And," says Bardolph, "of women." "Nay," says Mrs.
Quickly, seeking to save Sir John's last hours from
scandal, "that 'a did not." But the boy insists, "Yes,
that 'a did, and said they were devils incarnate." Still
trying hard, the Hostess says, " 'A could never abide
carnation, 'twas a colour he never lik'd." But the boy
sticks to the perverse realities, " 'A said once the devil
would have him about women" (_H V_, II, iii, 29-36). At
that point Nym calls out, "Shall we shog?" (47) and
shog they do off to France and the wars and King Henry's glory. The boy goes along, but always takes his
independent way, analyzing his associates, and ticking
off as so many casual incidents with no sentiment and
no memory of old associations—Bardolph, Pistol, Nym—
whose thieving ways have landed them in the clutches
of martial law.

> As young as I am, I have observ'd these three swashers.
> I am boy to them all three; but all they three, though they
> would serve me, could not be man to me; for indeed
> three such antics do not amount to a man. For Bardolph,
> he is white-liver'd and red-fac'd; . . . For Pistol, he hath
> a killing tongue and a quiet sword; . . . for Nym, he hath
> heard that men of few words are the best men, and there-
> fore he scorns to say his prayers, lest 'a should be thought

a coward; . . . I must leave them and seek some better
service. Their villainy goes against my weak stomach, and
therefore I must cast it up.

III, ii, 29-37

So we see this boy has a great gift for incisive analysis,
but he has no personal loyalties and none of the warmth
of companionship of his Master, neither attracting nor
wanting anyone's love.

There is just one more speech from him that is an
echo of the fat Knight's voice and spirit. You recall
Falstaff far back in the story, after a King's Council at
which he had heard spoken plain cannon fire and smoke
and bounce about the on-coming war as if they were
words of every day. Left alone with Prince Henry at
the end of the Council, he breathes almost plaintively,
"I would it were bedtime, Hal, and all well" (*I H IV*, V,
i, 126). And on the battle field at Shrewsbury there is
his quick prayer, "God keep lead out of me" (iii, 35).
And so one ill day over in France, with the sounds and
sights of battle all about us, we come upon Falstaff's
boy and hear him saying—do you catch the echo?—
"Would I were in an alehouse in London! I would give
all my fame for a pot of ale and safety" (*H V*, III, ii,
12-14).

Of Falstaff's strong points the boy has inherited only
his wit, and that almost alone in the exercise of a single
jest. There is in him nothing of the amazing freshness
and fertility of Sir John's invention. The boy is a sort
of discreet coward after the pattern of his Master, but
he has none of the Falstaffian charm which drew almost
all who knew the fat Knight to love him. Indeed, the boy
seems stolidly unaware of his master's real quality, taking
it almost as if all it contained was a perpetual jape about
a sodden drunkard's flaming nose.

Of Falstaff's points of weakness he inherited his un-
reliable taste and his fragile sense of propriety. But he
has more independence than Sir John because he is so
constituted socially as to need people less. Watch him as
he goes his way into the shadows of the French War.
He will never be loved or famous, but also he will never
be hanged.[2]
Here as everywhere, Shakspere's art is well-nigh infal-
lible. It is again a triumph of common sense. He might
have used the romantic method of having the boy develop
into a replica of his Master. That would have been amusing and might have seemed proper and probable, but it
is much more like reality to have it otherwise. So the
playwright has not used here any pattern of like beget-
ting like or of Falstaff perpetuated in the personality
and the career of the boy. He knows better than that.
He knows that pupils do not become living replicas of
their teachers, that children develop strange unaccount-
able deviations from their parents. Accordingly, in his
hands, Falstaff's heir exhibits his own unpredictable
pattern of inheritance, with parts of his Master reflected
in him, with parts altogether missing, and all in a new
and individual design.

[2] The terms of Captains Fluellen and Gower's prize atrocity story
about Agincourt seem to say that Falstaff's boy was one of the
victims:

> *Flu.* Kill the poys and the luggage? 'Tis expressly against the
> law of arms. 'Tis as arrant a piece of knavery, mark you now,
> as can be offert. In your conscience, now, is it not?
> *Gow.* 'Tis certain there's not a boy left alive; and the coward-
> ly rascals that ran from the battle ha' done this slaughter.
>   IV, vii, 1-7

When I said, "He'll never be hanged," I meant, of course, that
given a chance he'll take care of himself, but there is no escape
from cowardly French rascals.

CHAPTER IV

MACBETH AS A MORALITY [1]

Shakspere's early environment was in no sense circumscribed or limited in opportunities for seeing and hearing dramatic performances. It was only twelve miles from Stratford to Coventry, and in Coventry was to be seen one of the fullest and finest of all the cycles of scripture plays in England. Here and, no doubt, elsewhere the youthful Shakspere saw Herod rage and rant upon the stage and listened with exquisite terror to the raucous voice of the stage Pilate such as had furnished Chaucer, two centuries earlier, with his apt metaphor for the hoarse boisterousness of Robin the Miller, and here he saw Judas in red wig setting the pattern for later depictions of villainous Jews.

In 1575, when Will Shakspere was eleven, the Earl of Leicester presented the magnificent revels at Kenilworth, only ten miles from Stratford-on-Avon, in honor of his royal visitor, the great Queen. The account of these revels as set forth in George Gascoigne's *The Princely Pleasures of Kenilworth Castle*, indicates a great variety of display: fireworks, water pageantry, allegorical presentation, and poetic addresses. Professor Cunliffe is of the opinion that Shakspere at eleven likely did not attend these festivities but got his idea of them later when, as a young man, he came upon a copy of Gas-

---

[1] Reprinted with alterations from *Shakespeare Association Bulletin*, XII, No. 4 (Oct., 1937), 217-235.

coigne's book.[2] For my part, I am not quite willing to
give up the picture of little eleven-year-old Will tagging
along and weaving his way through the motley crowd at
Kenilworth to see

> [A] mermaid on a dolphin's back.
>
> *Dream,* II, i, 150

and looking up with wide eyes as the manipulators of the
fireworks brought it about that against the darkening
Warwickshire sky

> [C]ertain stars shot madly from their spheres.
>
> 153

But even if he did not go to Kenilworth himself, many
and many a Stratford man did, and for days the streets
and loitering places of the little town were full of reports of the wonders seen at Kenilworth, and Will Shakspere, we may be sure, missed none of this talk and certainly did not have to wait twelve or fifteen years to
read about it in a book. Dramatic display was most popular in these later years of the sixteenth century, and
young Shakspere's whole environment must have been
particularly conducive to a direct acquaintance with
plays and the conventions of playing.

Among the various types of play which he would have
opportunity to see were the moral plays or moralities
as they were called. Such plays as the *Castle of Perseverance, Everyman, Wit and Science, Mundus et Infans,
Nice Wanton,* and *Mankind* were still current and were
widely known.[3] The type had degenerated sadly by
Shakspere's day so that the antics of the devils and the

---

[2] Brooke, Cunliffe, MacCracken, *Shakespeare's Principal Plays,* 35.
[3] For details regarding the persistence of the morality plays into
and beyond the reign of Elizabeth see Ward, *English Dramatic Literature,* I, 99-143. I call particular attention to the performance of the

farcical carryings-on of the Vice had crowded out much of the moral emphasis and had superseded the didactic intent of the earlier moralities by a degenerate form of horseplay.

A very interesting side light on Shakspere's opportunities for seeing morality plays and becoming familiar with their conventions is given us by a man named Willis, who, born within a year of Shakspere, has left an account, written in 1639 when he was seventy-five years of age, of a play to which his father took him as a boy in Gloucester, in the very near neighborhood of Stratford. As we follow Willis' account, may we not, without difficulty, imagine the boy Shakspere at many such a performance?

After telling of the arrangements for the play, Willis' account proceeds:

> At such a play my father took me with him, and made me stand between his legs as he sat upon one of the benches, where we saw and heard very well.
>
> The play was called the *Cradle of Security*, wherein was personated a King or some great Prince [named Wicked-of-the-World] with his courtiers of several kinds, amongst which three ladies [Pride, Covetousness, and Luxury] were in special grace with him; and they, keeping him in delights and pleasures, drew him from his graver counsellors, hearing of sermons, and listening to good counsel and admonitions, that in the end they got

Contention between Liberalitie and Prodigalitie before the Queen in 1600.

It is also of more than passing interest that in the *Book of Sir Thomas More* (conjectural date between 1586 and 1596; *v.* Brooke, *Shakespeare Apocrypha,* xlix), in IV, i, 40-47, a player reports to More that his company has in its repertory the *Cradle of Securitie, Hit Nayle o' th' Head, Impacient Povertie,* the *Play of Foure Pees, Dives and Lazarus, Lusty Juventus,* and *Marriage of Witt and Wisdome.*

Three of these, perhaps four, are clearly of the morality type. More chose the last-named play, a typical morality. An excerpt from it is presented later in the same scene.

him to lie down in a cradle upon the stage, where these three ladies joining in sweet song rocked him asleep. . .

Whilst all this was acting, there came forth of another door at the farthest end of the stage two old men, the one [End-of-the-World] in blue with a sergeant-at-arms' mace on his shoulder, the other (Last Judgment) in red with a drawn sword in his hand and leaning with the other hand upon the other's shoulder. And so they two went along in a soft pace round about by the skirt of the stage, till at last they came to the cradle when all the court was in greatest jollity; and then the foremost old man [End-of-the-World] with his mace struck a fearful blow upon the cradle, whereat all the courtiers, with the three ladies . . . all vanished; and the desolate Prince, starting up . . . and finding himself thus sent for to judgment, made a lamentable complaint of his miserable case; and so was carried away by wicked spirits. . . .

This sight took such impression in me that when I came toward man's estate it was as fresh in my memory as if I had seen it newly acted.[4]

I quote thus at length from Willis' account not alone to show the nearness of opportunities for seeing moralities of the conventional sort in the time and vicinity of Shakspere's youth, but also because this apparently rather crude morality, the *Cradle of Security*, is obviously such a good representative of the stock morality treatment. It contains very clearly two of the three accepted themes of the morality. These three themes are: (1) the conflict of the vices and virtues, (2) the coming of death, and (3) the debate of the heavenly virtues. Willis' well-remembered play apparently contained in clear form the

[4] Cited by J. Q. Adams, *A Life of William Shakespeare*, 46-47, from R. Willis, *Mount Tabor, or Private Exercises of a Penitent Sinner—Published in the Year of his Age 75, Anno Dom.* 1639, 110.

It is altogether likely that this play reported by Willis is the same play which stands first on the list submitted to Sir Thomas More.

first two of these, for he recalls that the three ladies, Pride, Covetousness, and Luxury, three of the seven deadly sins, drew the Prince from his graver counsellors, who may very well have been Meekness, Charity, and Abstinence, the three directly opposed virtues, thus supplying the conflict of the vices and virtues.

In the second movement of the play we have the coming of death announced by old End-of-the-World's fearful blow upon the cradle. As in the typical morality in general, so here there is the arousal to fear and lamenting on the part of the human figure and his carrying off to Hell by attendant devils.

The debate of the heavenly virtues, sometimes called the four daughters of God, is not so familiar as the other themes. It appears in fullest form in the *Castle of Perseverance*, where the four daughters debate the judgment to be meted out to mankind. The *Castle of Perseverance* is the only extant morality which contains all three of these themes. The deservedly best-known of the moralities, *Everyman*, deals entirely with the coming of death.

But in practically all the moralities which we know or know about the central theme is the conflict of the vices and virtues for the soul of man, or, as in the unique *Nice Wanton*, for the soul of woman. Often there is only one evil solicitor and only one agent of goodness. In Marlowe's *Dr. Faustus*, they are called simply Evil Angel and Good Angel. In all, however, the formula is essentially one: a human figure—Mankind, Infans, Wit, or Everyman—is besought in quick alternation by the agencies of evil and the agencies of righteousness to take his course of life under their direction. Invariably he goes the way of evil. Ultimately death comes. Sometimes he repents in time to escape damnation. Sometimes the debate of the daughters of God prevails in his behalf. But often his realization of his desperate plight comes too late and he is given over to the tortures of Hell.

It is surely pertinent to remark here that the history of the development of the morality play shows a trend toward tragic ending. In the introductory article in his edition of Skelton's *Magnifycence*, Mr. Robert Lee Ramsey points out that even from as early as 1450 there was a steady development within the conventional framework of the morality, and that particularly after 1450 there was more and more a turning toward tragic outcome. Of the thirteen extant moralities dating before 1520, as Mr. Ramsey shows, all end in the redemption of the central figure, but after 1520, with increasing frequency, the outcome is tragic.[5]

Notable instances of the fatal outcome are *Nice Wanton*, the *Cradle of Security*, and Marlowe's *Faustus*. Also, more and more in these later moralities the figures are becoming personalized. In *Nice Wanton* the central figure is Delila, and Marlowe's pivotal figure is not an abstraction but an individual named Dr. Faustus.

Before we pass on to the serious consideration of the moral problems presented in *Macbeth*, may we turn aside for a brief inspection of a very interesting bit in a much earlier play, the *Merchant of Venice*, in which it seems clear that Shakspere is burlesquing the stock theme of the conflict of the virtues and vices so familiar in the morality plays.

I refer, of course, to the monologue of Launcelot Gobbo (*Merch.*, II, ii), in which he clownishly exhibits himself as in the throes of a struggle as to whether he shall run or not run away from his Jew master, Shylock.

[5] J. Skelton, *Magnifycence*, ed. Robert Lee Ramsey for EETS (1908).

As he capers back and forth, plucked now, as he would have you think, at one elbow by his conscience, and now at the other by the fiend, what else than the conflicting solicitations of good and evil in the morality plays can Shakspere be thinking of? This, I would suggest, is not ridicule of the morality convention, not even satire of the cruder forms of the morality; it is merely easy and pleasant burlesque of something easy to burlesque because it is well and familiarly known, just as nowadays we are confronted with utmost frequency by burlesque versions of the balcony scene from *Romeo and Juliet* or innocent parodies on the "Charge of the Light Brigade" or the "Psalm of Life." And all this not with any desire to make these well-known pieces ridiculous but simply taking advantage of their familiar forms in order to make inapt materials appear grotesque in their well-known dress.

My point in citing the Launcelot monologue, then, is to add further, if that is necessary, to the indications that Shakspere had familiar acquaintance with the moralities and with their stock themes.

At the close of the third act of *Romeo and Juliet,* when the Nurse has so coolly counselled Juliet to forget Romeo and to marry Paris too, she goes out, leaving her young mistress alone. In her soliloquy which follows, Juliet's terms of reference are remindful of the stock morality convention of the solicitations of good and evil. Even though the reference may be subconscious, it is clear, for, after all what other terms are so familiar to the girl and to the theater audience?

> Ancient damnation! O most wicked fiend!
> Is it more sin to wish me thus forsworn,
> Or to dispraise my lord with that same tongue
> Which she hath prais'd him with above compare

So many thousand times? Go, counsellor!
Thou and my bosom henceforth shall be twain.
                                  Romeo, III, v, 237-242

In the respect that Juliet defies evil and cleaves to good,
this is unlike the moralities. In all other respects it is
suggestive of the pattern and of the terms of that convention, and we see once more how naturally the devices
and the terminology of the morality come to the dramatist's mind and hand.[6]

Before we turn to an examination of the theme of
Macbeth, one other matter of contemporary import
remains to be noted. Soon after Shakspere's arrival in
London, his greatest predecessor in the field of dramatic
composition, Christopher Marlowe, brought out his
Tragical History of Dr. Faustus, which, there can be

---

[6] I offer another fragment of suggestion as to Shakspere's accus-
tomedness to the symbolic drama. Lady Macbeth is telling her
husband that all is in readiness for the bloody deed. She has taken
care to close up the sense of the grooms of the King's chamber:

> I have drugg'd their possets,
> That death and nature do contend about them
> Whether they live or die.
>   II, ii, 6-8

It would be folly to insist that this passage argues a present and
conscious sense on Shakspere's part of the patterns and conventions
of the morality or of the "Body and Soul" or "Life and Death"
debates. But with his background of familiarity with these conventions—as familiar as ours with the conventions of the Words-
worthian nature lyric or of the O. Henry short story, what more
likely basis for this than a vivid image of personalized figures of
Death and Nature standing over the deep-drugged grooms, as on a
stage, contending as to which is to have them?

For the connection between the debate and the morality, see W.
H. Schofield, *Eng. Lit. from the Norman Conquest to Chaucer*,
(1925), 424-430. Schofield suggests specifically that such interludes of
Heywood as *Wit and Folly* and *Pardoner and Friar* are probably
directly developed from the debates of *Vices and Virtues*, the *Soul
and the Body, Death and Life*, etc. Mr. Ramsey (*op. cit.*, cxlviii),
lists the Body and Soul debate theme as one of the stock themes of
some of the earlier non-extant moralities.

little doubt, was a conscious return on his part to an established form and a familiar basic theme. Marlowe's artistic powers were adequate, however, to breathe new life into the form and to give new potency to the theme so as to make the play not only the greatest of the moralities but also one of the great pieces of dramatic writing in our literature. It is in some such fashion that Keats's "La Belle Dame sans Merci," written long after the day of the popular ballad and by a sophisticated hand, is nevertheless one of the best of our ballads.

The young Shakspere, of course, knew Marlowe's play.[7] He recognized its powerful retouching of the old theme of the conflict between evil and good for the soul of a man, and he must have been powerfully attracted by the stupendous lines in which Marlowe depicts the coming of death and the agony of soul of the self-condemned scholar as he soliloquizes:

Ah, Faustus,
Now hast thou but one bare hour to live,
And then thou must be damn'd perpetually!
Stand still, you ever-moving spheres of Heaven,
That time may cease, and midnight never come;
Fair Nature's eye, rise, rise again and make
Perpetual day; or let this hour be but
A year, a month, a week, a natural day,
That Faustus may repent and save his soul!
O *lente, lente, currite noctis equi!*
The stars move still, time runs, the clock will strike,
The Devil will come, and Faustus must be damn'd.
O, I'll leap up to my God! Who pulls me down?
See, see where Christ's blood streams in the firmament!
One drop would save my soul—half a drop; ah, my Christ!
Yet will I call upon him: O spare me, Lucifer! —
Where is it now? 'Tis gone; and see where God

---

[7] Observe his use of one of its most spectacular lines, thrice repeated in *Richard II* (1595), IV, i, 281-286. "Was this the face . . . ?"

Stretcheth out his arm, and bends his ireful brows!
Mountains and hills, come, come and fall on me,
And hide me from the heavy wrath of God!
                              Dr. Faustus, xiv, 74-94 [8]

My point, therefore, is that when about 1606 Shakspere came to take up the writing of *Macbeth* he was thoroughly accustomed to the morality play tradition. It was a part of the atmosphere of the period. If, in writing this play so fraught with moral struggle, he uses the morality play method of treatment, it will not be in any way surprising. But I do not undertake to call *Macbeth* a morality play even in the sense in which *Dr. Faustus* may well be so called. *Macbeth* is unlike the conventional morality in too many salient features for that. Its persons are individualized human characters not abstractions, its events are precise happenings, and its plot is woven closely out of the very stuff of human motive and contriving. But in other respects, as I shall try to show, its basic theme and the working out of its catastrophe are so similar to the theme and the outcome of the morality as to suggest more than merely chance resemblance.

First, let us note the similarity of its theme to that of the morality. Barely stated, that theme is: I. Good and evil solicit the allegiance of mankind. II. Man, yielding to the enticements of evil, is led to judgment.

I

Whatever understanding you may prefer regarding the witches in *Macbeth*, the point of view of the play itself and of the chief actors in the play identifies them with the solicitors to evil in the morality. Macbeth, following

---

[8] Neilson, *Chief Elizabethan Dramatists*, 95.

their announcement of his elevation in rank and of coming kingdom, refers to their speech as, "This supernatural soliciting" (I, iii, 130), and Lady Macbeth, after reading his letter telling of the appearance and speech of the witches, eagerly wishes for his coming to add her words of urgency toward his reaching out for what she calls

> the golden round
> Which fate and metaphysical aid doth seem
> To have thee crown'd withal.
>
> I, v, 29-31

In his letter to her, Macbeth says:

> I have learn'd by the perfect'st report, they have more in them than mortal knowledge.
>
> 2-3

Macbeth's later attitude is clearly one of blame toward the witches for having solicited him to evil as well as one of blame of himself for having yielded. Following Banquo's murder, he seeks them and learns from them how much farther the stream of blood stretches out before him, and he exclaims with passionate bitterness:

> Infected be the air whereon they ride,
> And damn'd all those that trust them!
>
> IV, i, 138-139

and almost with his last breath he cries:

> And be those juggling fiends no more believ'd,
> That palter with us in a double sense,
> That keep the word of promise to our ear
> And break it to our hope!
>
> V, viii, 19-22

The degree to which we are to identify Lady Macbeth with the party of the evil solicitors is difficult to determine. But it is principally because the dramatist's genius

for characterization has individualized her and human-
ized her that this is difficult. She is, as I see her, wholly
and entirely unselfish. Her wish is for her husband's
advancement. She must, if she is to do what is to be
done, be transformed, for she is feminine and possessed
with womanly instincts. Even before she can begin her
work of urgency upon Macbeth, her seemingly necessary prayer is:

Come, you spirits
That tend on mortal thoughts, unsex me here,
And fill me, from the crown to the toe, top-full
Of direst cruelty!

I, v, 40-43

Her young motherhood is a precious memory to her:

I have given suck, and know
How tender 'tis to love the babe that milks me.

I, vii, 54-55

She is strangely wrought upon in the very hour of her
direct inhumanity by the memory of a happy daughter-
hood, for even as she clutches the dagger to slay the
kindly, innocent, sleeping King, a flash of fond memory
comes over her:

Had he not resembled
My father as he slept, I had done 't.

II, ii, 13-14

How ironic as an admission of her need of some means
of keeping her courage screwed to the sticking place,
is her naive confession that she has taken a portion for
herself of the stuff which she has given so liberally to
the grooms to make them sleep:

That which hath made them drunk hath made me bold;
What hath quench'd them hath given me fire.

1-2

Then observe her particularly in the bitter pathos of the
sleep-walking — heart broken, mind broken, broken by
the weight of guilty knowledge and the inner gnawings
of remorse. Hear her, as her mind glances from one
shadowed depth of association to another, but always
back to the blood:

> Yet who would have thought the old man to have had
> so much blood in him?
>
> V, i, 44-45

> What, will these hands ne'er be clean?
>
> 48

> Here's the smell of the blood still. All the perfumes of
> Arabia will not sweeten this little hand.
>
> 56-58

> Wash your hands. . . . I tell you yet again, Banquo's
> buried. He cannot come out on 's grave.
>
> 69-71

Surely one who feels guilt so keenly was once sweetly
innocent; surely such a one is not unmixed and incarnate
evil!

But with all this insistence upon the womanly quality
of the Lady, the fact remains that Lady Macbeth *is*
consciously and actively the ally of the supernatural
solicitors. She seizes eagerly upon Macbeth's report of
the witches' prophetic words and is impatient for his
coming:

> Hie thee hither,
> That I may pour my spirits in thine ear
> And chastise with the valour of my tongue
> All that impedes thee from the golden round
> Which fate and metaphysical aid doth seem
> To have thee crown'd withal.
>
> I, v, 26-31

Throughout the scenes which precede the murder of

Duncan, Lady Macbeth is the principal driving force in getting Macbeth into the stream of the action. Caught and deterred as she is by feminine impulses and girlhood memories, she can, in a crisis, cry out upon Macbeth, the valiant warrior:

> Infirm of purpose!
> Give me the daggers.
>
> II, ii, 52-53

Gradually, as he commits himself more fully to his course of violence, he needs her less and less, and she drops back into the gloom of remorse and troubled memories. He might, no matter how ingenious the lure of the solicitations of the Weird Sisters, never have become a criminal without the impulsion of her words, but is it not significant that, though he blames the witches bitterly, he has nowhere a word of blame for her?

Thus far I have attempted to point out the presence in the groundwork of the plot of *Macbeth* of the element of solicitation to evil by the agents of evil. But that is not enough to make it a morality play; there must be, also, a conflict between evil and good. And that conflict in this play, as is always true in the old moralities likewise, is centered in the inner being of the principal character. No point about the play seems clearer than that the idea of achieving the kingship by violence was already alive and active in Macbeth's mind before he met the witches. Note his behavior upon being hailed by the Sisters and his meditation upon their foretellings, which he calls

> that suggestion
> Whose horrid image doth unfix my hair
> And make my seated heart knock at my ribs
> Against the use of nature.
>
> I, iii, 134-137

Farther on in the same speech is a reference which is to dark imaginings of dreadful deeds—not a matter just sprung up in his mind, but a subject of long pondering:

> My thought whose murther yet is but fantastical,
> Shakes so my single state of man that function
> Is smother'd in surmise.
>
>   139-141

Then note especially the entire colloquy of I, vii, 31-61, in which Lady Macbeth seems so definitely to be talking of a specific time (pre-play) when Macbeth had boasted of his desperate purpose and had sworn hugely to its performance:

> What beast was't then
> That made you break this enterprise to me?
>
>   *   *   *
>
> Nor time nor place
> Did then adhere, and yet you would make both.
> They have made themselves. . . .
>
>   47-48; 51-53

All of this points to the element of responsibility of choice. It is completely antipathetic to Shakspere's method of dealing with character to set up a hero who is irresponsible. So the struggle is between the innate sensitiveness and nobility of Macbeth's nature and his growing impulse to win falsely. What the witches say and what Lady Macbeth says and does are simply added pressures on the side of evil.[9]

This conflict in *Macbeth* is assumed, on the part of good, by the noble instincts in Macbeth's own nature, by common-sense considerations and by the dictates of the ordinary claims of human decency. The conflict is

---

[9] Bradley's treatment of this point is especially strong and well supported. *Shakespearean Tragedy*, 343-344.

in Macbeth's own mind. Note how it sways back and
forth. Hear his first soliloquy after the meeting with the
witches and after Ross has acclaimed him from the King,
Thane of Cawdor:

> This supernatural soliciting
> Cannot be ill; cannot be good. If ill,
> Why hath it given me earnest of success,
> Commencing in a truth?   I am Thane of Cawdor.
> If good, why do I yield to that suggestion
> Whose horrid image doth unfix my hair
> And make my seated heart knock at my ribs
> Against the use of nature?
>
> I, iii, 130-137

And at the close of this phase of the conflict, good wins,
for we hear Macbeth saying:

> If chance will have me king, why chance may crown me
> Without my stir.
>
> 143-144

But this is before he joins Lady Macbeth, and so, after
his return home and after Duncan comes and is feasted
and has gone to his safe rest for the night, Macbeth,
alone, renews the conflict. This time it is common
reason, the dictates of personal well being, the conventions of society that move in on the side of good, but it
is still a conflict:

> If it were done when 'tis done, then 'twere well
> It were done quickly. If th' assassination
> Could trammel up the consequence, and catch
> With his surcease, success; that but this blow
> Might be the be-all and the end-all here,
> But here, upon this bank and shoal of time,
> We'd jump the life to come. But in these cases
> We still have judgment here, that we but teach
> Bloody instructions, which, being taught, return
> To plague th' inventor. This even-handed justice

Commends th' ingredience of our poison'd chalice
To our own lips. He's here in double trust:
First, as I am his kinsman and his subject—
Strong both against the deed; then, as his host,
Who should against his murtherer shut the door,
Not bear the knife myself. Besides, this Duncan
Hath borne his faculties so meek, hath been
So clear in his great office, that his virtues
Will plead like angels trumpet-tongu'd, against
The deep damnation of his taking-off;
And pity, like a naked new-born babe,
Striding the blast, or heaven's cherubin, hors'd
Upon the sightless couriers of the air,
Shall blow the horrid deed in every eye,
That tears shall drown the wind. I have no spur
To prick the sides of my intent, but only
Vaulting ambition, which o'erleaps itself
And falls on th' other side.

                                        I, vii, 1-28

And, once more, may we not suppose, honesty and common decency are about to win, but Lady Macbeth enters and the balance of his decision is forced over to the side of evil.

There is another strong indication that Shakspere has in mind the existence of conflict between vice and virtue. This is furnished in the person of Banquo. Twice in the course of the first two acts Macbeth suggests to Banquo a private conference on the matters contained in the sibylline words of the witches.[10] Each time Banquo assents with something like eagerness. "Very gladly," he says to Macbeth's first suggestion; the second time, "At your kindest leisure."

It is, I think, significant to note in addition to what has been said already regarding the witches as spokeswomen of evil, that Banquo is very quick to identify

[10] I, iii, 152-156 and II, i, 22-28.

them with the evil kingdom. When Ross announces
Macbeth's elevation to the thaneship of Cawdor, confirming thus the second article of their words, "What,"
says Banquo, "can the *devil* speak true?" (I, iii, 107).
And a little later when Macbeth is pointing out to him
that the witches' words carry also much of promise for
himself, he quickly replies in an argument very familiar
to Shakspere's auditors:

> But 'tis strange!
> And oftentimes, to win us to our harm,
> The instruments of darkness tell us truths,
> Win us with honest trifles, to betray 's
> In deepest consequence.
>
> I, iii, 122-126 [11]

After Duncan is abed on the night of the murder, we
find Banquo with his son Fleance in a state of mind
which bears all the marks of inward conflict. He is
heavy with sleep but he fears to trust himself to sleep:

> A heavy summons lies like lead upon me,
> And yet I would not sleep. Merciful powers,
> Restrain in me the cursed thoughts that nature
> Gives way to in repose.
>
> II, i, 6-9

What are these cursed thoughts if not thoughts prompt-
ing him, too, toward violent deed to aid the bringing in
of his promised good fortune before its time? Indeed,
within five minutes after this speech about the "cursed
thoughts that nature gives way to in repose," he tells
Macbeth:

> I dreamt last night of the three Weird Sisters.
> To you they have show'd some truth.
>
> 19-20

This gives us not only a fairly clear notion of what he

[11] *Cf. Ham.,* I, iv, 69-76; II, ii, 626-632.

means by "cursed thoughts," but also shows clearly that the meeting with the witches and their words have been very much on his mind. He suggests, moreover, by his remark to Macbeth, "to you they have show'd some truth," his willingness to open the subject. Whereupon Macbeth proposes for the second time that they confer. "At your kindest leisure," says Banquo, and Macbeth continues:

> If you shall cleave to my consent, when 'tis,
> It shall make honor for you.
>
> 25-26

and honest Banquo, holding stoutly to the course of righteousness, answers:

> So I lose none
> In seeking to augment it but still keep
> My bosom franchis'd and allegiance clear. . . .
>
> 26-28

Speaking from the standpoint of dramatic construction, Banquo is a foil for Macbeth. Both are caught in the meshes of the conflict between vice and virtue. Macbeth yields to the solicitings of evil. Banquo behaves as Macbeth should have done.

So far we have traced the first part of the formula of the morality as it appears in *Macbeth*: *Good and evil seek the following of mankind*. The witches and Lady Macbeth and, most important of all, Macbeth's own evil impulses and imaginings have the role of the agents of evil; Macbeth's common sense, the sanctions of society, and the claims of every-day decency supply the good influences. There is a conflict, spurred on but not determined by the witches and the Lady, but waged chiefly within Macbeth's own spirit. His first inclinations are to follow the counsels of good; ultimately he yields to evil. But this is not over with and done at the first encounter. It sways back and forth like a tossing sea. This conflict is further emphasized by the circumstances of a similar conflict with a contrasted outcome in the case of Banquo.

II

It remains for us to observe the working out of the second phase of the theme: Mankind, yielding to evil, is led to judgment.

Scarcely is his course of evil set out upon before Macbeth begins to indicate the arousal of regret and remorse. Almost immediately after Duncan is murdered comes the fearful knocking at the gate with all of its suggestions of the inevitable coming in of the business of the world and of the questioning eyes of men and the full shining of the sun upon the dark and secret places of these two guilty souls.[12] Knock! knock! knock! and Macbeth, now committed to evil, is astonished at his fearfulness.

"Whence is that knocking?" he exclaims. "How is't with me when every noise appals me?" (II, ii, 57–58). And then, in the imminent presence of discovery, he sees his blood-stained hands:

> What hands are here? Ha! they pluck out mine eyes!
> Will all great Neptune's ocean wash this blood
> Clean. from my hand?
>
> II, ii, 59-61

Following this comes the nervous haste of preparation for the opening of the door and for confronting the

[12] For my statement here about the Knocking at the Gate, I am greatly obligated to Sir Arthur Quiller-Couch's article, "The Workmanship of *Macbeth*," in the *North American Review*, Oct., Nov., Dec., 1914. Of course, he and all other Shakspereans are chiefly indebted to DeQuincey.

inquiring eyes of men. Hands are washed; sleeping apparel is donned; faces are composed; and still, Knock! knock! knock! till from the depth of his spirit, new-sold to evil, Macbeth exclaims:

> Wake Duncan with thy knocking! I would thou couldst!
>   74

Thus, from the beginning, Macbeth seems aware of the spiritual consequences of his deed. By spiritual consequences I mean more than a mere feeling of guilt for having committed sin. There is present a sense of the irretrievable and final in his attitude toward his deed; a suggestion that his act is of the nature of a bargain or contract with evil in the same fashion as that with which Faustus bound himself, cutting a vein and writing the fatal compact in his own reluctant blood.[13] It is true that there is no single point or situation in *Macbeth* which we can identify as the moment of the signing over of his soul to Lucifer, but there are clear references to the matter throughout the last three acts in words which plainly indicate that Macbeth looked upon his case in such terms.

One of the most dramatic elements from this point of view is Macbeth's strong realization of his inability to pray, which comes just after the murder of the good King. Coming down stairs from the doing of the bloody deed, he passes a chamber where two are lodged together. As he passes, they stir restlessly in their beds as if aroused from a troublous dream—perhaps, so Macbeth thinks, a dream of a man with bloody hands standing just outside their door. Rousing enough to realize the source of their fears to have been but a dream, they

---

[13] Neilson, *Chief Elizabethan Dramatists*, "The Tragical History of Dr. Faustus," v, 48-75, p. 85.

cross themselves, say their prayers, and address themselves again to sleep, one saying, as their prayers are
ended, "God bless us," and the other, "Amen."

"List'ning their fear," Macbeth tells his wife with
dawning horror at the spiritual import of it all, "I could
not say 'Amen!' when they did say, 'God bless us!' "

"Consider it not so deeply," she cries, fearful of his
fear, but he persists:

> But wherefore could not I pronounce 'Amen'?
> I had most need of blessing, and 'Amen'
> Stuck in my throat.
>
> II, ii, 31-33

How striking and suggestive is the comparison of this
with the stark fatality of Faustus' realization that he cannot call upon Christ and that not even half a drop of
Christ's blood is available for him. And, in the same
way, how vividly it recalls the fatal realization of Mankind in many a morality that his evil choice has led him
to a point beyond the reach of mercy.

But the most convincing statement of the case of
Macbeth as of a compact with the Devil is in his analysis
of his spiritual situation as he ponders the plot to kill
Banquo. The two prophetic articles of the witches'
salutations to him have been fulfilled. He is Cawdor;
he is king. Proved true prophets in two particulars, may
the Weird Sisters not be supposed also to be reliable as to
their word to Banquo? They had hailed Banquo as
father to a line of kings. Banquo! If this, also, be true,
then Macbeth's whole slaughterous course has been for
only a trifling return. He will be king himself for only
the short remaining span of his own days. No son of his
is to succeed. All the benefits of the bloody deed will
be for Banquo's profit. At what bitter cost, then, has

he purchased Banquo's good! Hear him as he counts
this cost:

> If 't be so,
> For Banquo's issue have I fil'd my mind;
> For them the gracious Duncan have I murther'd;
> Put rancours in the vessel of my peace
> Only for them, and mine eternal jewel
> Given to the common enemy of man
> To make them kings.
>
> III, i, 64-70 [14]

Note, please, three phrases here: "fil'd my mind,"
that is *de*filed my mind; "Put rancours in the vessel of
my peace." The first two are statements about the
present condition of his soul. They indicate remorse,
regret, bitter disappointment. The third is the clearest
of all the references to a compact with the Devil: "and
mine eternal jewel Given to the common enemy of
man." That is, my soul and its salvation given to the
Devil. This is Macbeth's own disillusioned statement
of his case. What clearer word might we expect regarding the fatal transaction?

From the time of the murder of Banquo, Macbeth is

---

[14] Assuming with most students of the play, that the scene in which
Hecate reprimands the witches (III,v), is not by Shakspere but by
another, say, Middleton, we have a very interesting side light on
how an intelligent contemporary read Shakspere's intentions. Hecate
says:

> How did you dare
> To trade and traffic with Macbeth
> In riddles and affairs of death?
>
> 3-5

which seems clear indication that Middleton thought of the affair
as having involved some occult transaction darker and more sinister
and more binding than a simple resolve to do an evil deed. If
Middleton, reworking the play and handling its occult elements
in the light of general renaissance understanding of such matters,
saw it so, is it not logical to assume that intelligent spectators in
the theaters saw it in the same light?

harder, more bloody, more resolved. There is no indication that he hopes for success, much less for happiness,
but he does resolve upon a heroic attitude for himself.
He apparently knows the futility of the thought of repentance. After the banquet and his distraught conduct
in the presence of the blood-boltered ghost of Banquo,
he may consider passingly the possibility of repentance,
but he turns from it saying:

> I am in blood
> Stepp'd in so far that, should I wade no more,
> Returning were as tedious as go o'er.
>
> III, iv, 136-138

His major responsibility now, he seems to feel, is to carry
his role with as strong a hand as possible for as long as
he can. He is no longer to be deflected or delayed by
any slightest considerations of conscience. He hesitated
for a moment, and in that lost moment Macduff escaped
and fled to England. Macbeth hears of it and takes his
resolution:

> From this moment
> The very firstlings of my heart shall be
> The firstlings of my hand.
>
> IV, i, 146-148

But it would be altogether false to the spirit of the
closing scenes of the tragedy to suppose that Macbeth
loses his sense of regret and that he passes beyond remorse.

Close upon the time of his death, he is found lamenting
his course of life, especially regretting what it has cost
him in human friendships and loyalty. He begins by
speaking of his present military enterprise, his last stand
of resistance, and drifts on into some of the bitterest and
most poignantly regretful words about life which were

ever given a man to say. He says, speaking of his military plan:

> This push
> Will cheer me ever, or disseat me now.
> I have liv'd long enough. My way of life
> Is fall'n into the sere, the yellow leaf;
> And that which should accompany old age,
> As honour, love, obedience, troops of friends,
> I must not look to have; but, in their stead,
> Curses not loud but deep, mouth-honour, breath,
> Which the poor heart would fain deny, and dare not.
>
> V, iii, 20-28

Almost immediately the doctor enters, and, responding to Macbeth's inquiry regarding the Queen, reports her more troubled in mind than body. With the bitterest irony Macbeth cries:

> Cure her of that!
> Canst thou not minister to a mind diseas'd,
> Pluck from the memory a rooted sorrow,
> Raze out the written troubles of the brain,
> And with some sweet oblivious antidote
> Cleanse the stuff'd bosom of that perilous stuff
> Which weighs upon the heart?
>
> 39-44

And Macbeth, surely still conscious of the irony, plunges on to demand the cure of Scotland's ills:

> If thou couldst, doctor, cast
> The water of my land, find her disease,
> And purge it to a sound and pristine health,
> I would applaud thee to the very echo
> That should applaud again.
>
> 50-54 [15]

[15] This passage is too slight to prove a point, but it at least raises a question in view of Bradley's remark (*Shakes. Tragedy*, 350), regarding the Macbeths: "We observe in them no love of country."

Just before the final battle begins, a cry of women is heard inside the castle, and Macbeth comments:

> I have almost forgot the taste of fears.
> The time has been, my senses would have cool'd
> To hear a night-shriek, and my fell of hair
> .Would at a dismal treatise rouse and stir
> As life were in't. I have supp'd full with horrors.
> Direness, familiar to my slaughterous thoughts,
> Cannot once start me.
>
> V, v, 8-14

Once more, at least, there is a surging up of regret and the sense of loss, when in the press of battle he suddenly finds himself face to face with Macduff, who bids him turn and fight. Macbeth cries out:

> Of all men else I have avoided thee.
> But get thee back! My soul is too much charg'd
> With blood of thine already.
>
> V, viii, 4-6

We conclude this phase of the study by an examination of Macbeth's speech which follows upon the report of Lady Macbeth's death. It is most clearly the speech of a man who has not only found life empty and futile but who looks also with no hope to the life beyond death. All the hopes he may once have had have gone the way of his eternal jewel into the possession of the common enemy of man. It is just after the cry of women which we heard a moment ago:

> Wherefore was that cry?

Macbeth asks, and the messenger says, "The Queen, my lord, is dead," and the King goes on:

> She should have died hereafter;
> There would have been a time for such a word.
> Tomorrow, and tomorrow, and tomorrow

Creeps in this petty pace from day to day
To the last syllable of recorded time;
And all our yesterdays have lighted fools
The way to dusty death. Out, out, brief candle!
Life's but a walking shadow, a poor player,
That struts and frets his hour upon the stage
And then is heard no more. It is a tale
Told by an idiot, full of sound and fury,
Signifying nothing.

V, v, 15-28

I have sought to show that this and the passages cited just before it are the utterances of a man sickened not primarily by military defeats and reverses but of a man sickened by the effects upon his spiritual being of an evil course of life, sick, if you will, of a most filthy bargain. Macbeth never loses his physical courage. He is strong and fierce and valiant down to the very end, but his whole joy in life, his whole satisfaction in the exercise of power, his pride in his own devisings—all of these have become the very ashes of bitterness in his mouth because of what has happened to his soul.

Macbeth and Lady Macbeth stand out among Shakspere's great human creations as the only ones to exhibit great spiritual sensitiveness. No other major character, with the exception of Hamlet's uncle, is troubled by deeply spiritual concerns. Brutus, Hamlet, Othello have free souls so far as any cause for personal sense of guilt is concerned. Antony and Cleopatra are rather amoral than immoral. Richard, Iago, and Edmund are native plants in the seedbed of iniquity and possess no conscience. The heroes and heroines of the great comedies live for the most part happily and always innocently.[16]

---

[16] The moral patterns in *Measure for Measure* seem to me too much involved in the fantastic tangles of the plot to have any real value as moral problems.

But Macbeth and Lady Macbeth are, from the beginning, spiritually sensitive. Their problem is a spiritual one; the outcome of their tragedy is a spiritual catastrophe. Their loss is greater than the loss of a kingdom, or the loss of the whole world, or even the loss of life: it is loss of soul.

III

In conclusion, may I gather up the threads of suggestion which I have sought to lay down in this chapter? I have not presumed to say that this play is a morality play in the same sense that *Everyman* is, or even that Marlowe's play is. I have already suggested that it is much more than that, for it is full of the concerns of a pair of remarkably interesting and convincing personalities and its plot is made out of the stuff of life. But, on the other hand, it is like the moralities in the basic handling of the moral issues. Practically the entire plot of *Macbeth* is made up of two of the conventional situations of the morality. The conflict of the vices and virtues occupies us almost to the murder of Duncan. After the commitment of Macbeth to evil, we are occupied with the coming of death, as throughout the remainder of the play Macbeth rouses to the fatality of his evil bargain, to the futility of life, and to the hopelessness of life after death. To my mind the situation is not that Shakspere, setting his hand to this play, said: *I will now compose a modernized and personalized morality play as Kit Marlowe did in "Faustus," only mine will be still more modern and personalized.*

Rather I should suppose that, determining to take up the Macbeth story, and finding it a story involving spiritual problems and the very issues of salvation, naturally,

because of his own early and continued familiarity with
them, and because of their complete familiarity to his
audience, he fell back upon the basic formulae of the
morality play. By using its stock situations, emphasizing
particularly the elements of the debate between good
and evil, the closing of the doors of mercy, and the
coming of death he made a perfectly natural common-
sense appeal to the understanding of his audience.

To have passed this morality convention by in favor
of a pattern of more dignity, say a pattern from Æschy-
lus or Sophocles or the Comedy of Job would have been
to make it less effective for his purpose. It is true that
in execution he goes far beyond the best that had been
done in the morality tradition but only in quality. The
fact that it was written in the terms of the dramatic
experience of his contemporaries, that he thus used the
pattern best adapted to his own audience, has not made
against its continuing as one of the greatest of all works
of art. No matter how Shakspere might, at this stage of
his creative powers, have done it, it was predestined to
greatness, but the pattern he chose attests not only to
his artistic judgment but also—if it is something different—to his artistic common sense.

CHAPTER V

SHAKSPERE'S POETS

There is much to note and much to say about Shakspere's poetry. It is one of the four or five aspects of his work—plot, characterization, moral content, breadth of interest and observation, and poetry—for which he has been praised. In this chapter we shall say practically nothing about the poetry of his plays. There is also much that might be said regarding the estimation he set upon poetry and his references to poetry and the poetic. That, also, we shall no more than barely touch upon and then only as the treatment of some other phase may bring it in. It is our purpose here to deal rather with Shakspere's treatment of poets and of those who deal in poetry as they appear as persons in the plays. There are six sorts of these: (1) lovers, (2) a group I shall call anti-poets, (3) persons designated in the text as bad poets, (4) a group of connoisseurs of poetry and song, (5) those whose habits of poetizing draw unfavorable comment, and (6) persons who draw favorable notice for their poetic expression.

I. Lovers

It is not needful to develop at any length the fact that, although most lovers in actual life manage to get along very well without song and verse, the literatures of all ages have called them prominently into service in the business of love making. The literature of the courtly convention throughout the later Middle Ages and of

the Italian Renaissance in Italy and later in its trans-
plantation to France and England made great use of verse
as a means to the wooing of fair ladies. The development
of the sonnet as a vehicle and the practice of putting
scores and scores of them together in praise of a real
or imagined lady well-nigh exhausted the invention of
a generation of poets. Shakspere made his own enigmatic
and wry contribution to this growing volume of love
poetry. And in his plays, as men go wooing, he makes
great use of verse and song.

In two plays serenaders appear and sing beneath ladies'
windows. These plays, the *Two Gentlemen of Verona*
(1591) and *Cymbeline* (1609), are at the extremes of
his writing career, and the two songs are among the
most acceptable of the many songs in the plays. They
belong in this discussion because they are used by lovers
in the furthering of their wooing. But it is ironic to discover that they are both promoted by two of the least
attractive of Shakspere's lovers. Each in his doltish way
has certain comments to make upon the songs which
affirm the propriety of songs as a means to wooing and
which are in the way of treating them critically as pieces
of expression. The song in *Two Gentlemen* is sponsored
by the slow and inept Sir Thurio. Sir Proteus has told
him that he must use verse to win Lady Sylvia:

> You must lay lime to tangle her desires
> By wailful sonnets, whose composed rhymes
> Should be full fraught with serviceable vows.
>   III, ii, 68-70

And the Duke of Milan, who is as naive and serious in
this matter as Thurio, chimes in:

> Ay!
> Much is the force of heaven-bred poesy.
>   71

So Proteus, who knows much more than these two of what is going on, and whose view of things, if not so honorable, is much more intelligent, urges Thurio on both as to the content of the song and as to the manner of its delivery:

> Say that upon the altar of her beauty
> You sacrifice your tears, your sighs, your heart,
> Write till your ink be dry, and with your tears
> Moist it again; and frame some feeling line
> That may discover such integrity.
>
> * * *
>
> After your dire lamenting elegies,
> Visit by night your lady's chamber window
> With some sweet consort. To their instruments
> Tune a deploring dump. The night's dead silence
> Will well become such sweet-complaining grievance.
> This, or else nothing, will inherit her.
>
> III, ii, 73-87

Sir Thurio is completely convinced, for he agrees to everything:

> And thy advice this night I'll put in practice.
> Therefore, sweet Proteus, my direction giver,
> Let us unto the city presently
> To sort some gentlemen well skill'd in music.
> I have a sonnet that will serve the turn
> To give the onset to thy good advice.
>
> 89-94

When two scenes later the musicians come on, the "sonnet" is the much-admired "Who is Sylvia?" Thurio's "I have a sonnet" suggests the possibility that he thinks he made it himself, but that would have to be in the way in which persons do sometimes think of things they have begged for or paid a great deal of money for as being really theirs. Obviously, Thurio never made this song. It is too lovely, and for our purpose, perhaps that is just the point: That such a lovely bit of song should be the instrument of a stupid gull such as Thurio and the device of a deceitful rascal such as Proteus. Beauty, like misery, often finds itself with strange bed-fellows.

The situation in *Cymbeline* is that, at dawn, after a night of dicing, Cloten is waiting for a "consort" of musicians to come to serenade the Princess Imogen. Cloten speaks:

> I would this music would come. I am advised to give her music a-mornings; they say it will penetrate.
>
> Enter *Musicians*.
> Come on, tune! If you can penetrate her with your finger-ing, so. We'll try with tongue too. If none will do, let her remain; but I'll ne'er give o'er. First, a very excel-lent good conceited thing; after, a wonderful sweet air with admirable rich words to it—and then let her con-sider.
>
> *Cym.*, II, iii, 12-21

The song is the beautiful "Hark, hark! the lark at heaven's gate sings." And just as surely as Sir Thurio did not make "Who is Sylvia?" so Cloten did not make "Hark, hark! the Lark." Surely Shaksperean irony is working well to give two such lovely songs into the sponsorship of two such stupid fools. It is a part of this ironic emphasis that the Cloten song with all its skyey and earthly lovliness is set in the text between his rough, uncouth speeches. We have just heard his crude prelude to the song; when it is over he hurries the musicians away with:

> So, get you gone. If this penetrate, I will consider your music the better; if it do not, it is a vice in her ears which

horsehairs and calves' guts, nor the voice of unpaved
eunuch to boot, can never amend.

31-35

In *Love's Labour's Lost* is to be found the most profuse employment of wooing verse. The profuseness is
due in large measure to the profuseness of lovers in the
population. Four wooers, all poets! The first poem in
point of appearance in the text is Berowne's, intended
for Rosaline, committed to Costard to be delivered to
her, and mistakenly given by said Costard to Jaquenetta,
who goes about to find some one who can read it to her.
The reading person turns out to be the Curate, Sir
Nathaniel, whose reading is apparently very bad, for
the pedant Holofernes is learnedly critical of it as
reading:

You find not the apostrophas, and so miss the accent.

IV, ii, 123

Is it a good poem? It is a fourteen-line poem with
the rime pattern of the English sonnet. The lines are
hexameter iambics. It has the customary conceitfulness:
*If I forswear myself, it is only to swear my troth to thee,
my love. If I leave off studying to con your eyes, I become truly and fully learned; to do otherwise would be
to remain foully ignorant.*
Is it a good poem? How can one know, for all its
initial intent and whatever amorous beauty it may have
had are smothered beneath the incongruities of the situation. Delivered to the sluttish Jaquenetta, read out aloud
in the presence of those who have no feeling for its
tender purposes, read vilely by a silly sycophantic priest,
criticized learnedly by a pompous, pedantic ass, and at
last, just in the nick of time, falling into its author's own

hands, it is torn to bits before it is ever put beneath a really qualified eye. This is its fate. It is the sort of wild irrational treatment that no love missive should ever have, but that's what happened to this one. Once more, is it a good poem? I don't know. How, in such circumstances, could one know?

In IV, iii, Berowne is pacing alone in the park in meditation on the fortunes of his poem. "The clown bore it, the fool sent it, the lady hath it," he broods. "By the world, I would not care a pin if the other three were in." And at that juncture, a figure appears down the path, and Berowne slips into the shadows, for it is the King bearing a paper in his hand with a poem on it which he proceeds to read. Following this, the King slips also into the shadows, and Longaville comes on with a paper and a poem, and almost immediately thereafter Dumain with a paper and a poem. So the plot is almost wound up. Berowne knows all; the King is in love and a vow-breaker. Berowne and the King know that Longaville is in love and a vow-breaker, and all three of them know that Dumain is so. Only one more piece remains to complete the pattern. For just a moment of brief triumph, Berowne steps forth to berate the recreants and to boast his own unflawed integrity, but his triumph is like a breath, for now Jaquenetta and Costard enter with the letter which Nathaniel's reading had not made clear to Jaquenetta. She seeks another reader. So she thrusts the letter upon Berowne. It is, as we know, his own sonnet to Rosaline. So he tears it, but his confreres suspect him, study the hastily assembled pieces, and the pattern of the plot is complete.

Once more, are these poems—the King's, Longaville's, Dumain's—good poems? The King's is a sixteen-line poem in iambic pentameter. Its first fourteen lines are

the regular English sonnet rime pattern. The two remaining lines are a couplet. It, too, has the customary
conceits of the Elizabethan sonnet: *The loved one's face
shining on the tear drops of the lover's cheeks reflects her
bright beauty in every tear as the sun is reflected in every
dew drop on the rose.*

Longaville's poem is a regular English sonnet with the
conceit that: *He is not forsworn since he has not broken
the specific terms of his vow. He had sworn not to love
a woman, but this creature whom he addresses as "O
most divine Kate," is a goddess and no woman.* Dumain's
poem is, in like fashion, characteristically conceitful:
*He, like Love, has espied a beautiful flower; the air can
bathe this flower in its very being. Oh, to be that air!
To love a thing so beautiful would not be to be forsworn, or if it were it would be a god-like kind of for-
swearing. Did not Jove often leave off divinity to become mortal for such a love?* Dumain's poem, formally,
is altogether unlike the others. It is trochaic in meter,
tetrameter in line length, and is made up of ten couplets.
The fact of its being so different may be the reason why
it seems better, fresher. But who knows—or greatly
cares—about the merit of these poems? The plot is
moving fast. The consternation of each lover at his own
exposure and his delight at the ensnaring of the others,
the intrusion of Costard and the wench to seal up Berowne's discomfiture are all too much to give us time
or concern for the judging of the poems. They are, let
us say, not remarkably good; also, they are not hope-
lessly bad. They are good enough to serve the purpose
of the plot, and their ordinariness of form and content
may well be taken as another sly protest from Shakspere
against the worn-out tradition of the courtly sonnet.

The best comment on this sort of wooer's device not

only in this play but almost the best anywhere is Berowne's vehement repudiation of it:

> O, never will I trust to speeches penn'd
>   Nor to the motion of a schoolboy's tongue,
> Nor never come in vizard to my friend,
>   Nor woo in rhyme like a blind harper's song!
> Taffeta phrases, silken terms precise,
>   Three-pil'd hyperboles, spruce affectation,
> Figures pedantical—these summer flies
>   Have blown me full of maggot ostentation.
> I do forswear them; and I here protest,
>   By this white glove (how white the hand, God knows!)
> Henceforth my wooing mind shall be express'd
>   In russet yea's and honest kersey no's.
> V, ii, 402-413

In a hurried passage in *Much Ado About Nothing*, we
almost come to grips again with this business of verse
used for lovers' purposes. In V, ii, Benedick, who to
everyone's observation, and even to his own bewilderment, is transformed of late, asks Margaret to carry a
message to the Lady Beatrice. This Margaret will do,
but not without consideration:

> Will you then write me a sonnet in praise of my beauty?
> 4-5

she asks:

> *Bene.* In so high a style, Margaret, that no man living
> shall come over it; for in most comely truth thou deservest
> it.
> 6-8

This lends weight to the deep-lodged feeling that love-
making and poetizing go together, for Margaret knows
—has known from the beginning—what goes on. She
knows that Benedick is in. And knowing that, she assumes that he will be in poetic vein.

While Margaret is delivering Benedick's message, he hammers away at a poem—whether one for his own purposes or the one in praise of Margaret's beauty does not matter. It does not go right. The rimes are unsatisfactory: lady, baby; scorn, horn; school, fool—very ominous endings, he concludes, and almost in the spirit of Berowne's vigorous renunciation of taffeta phrases, he declares:

> No, I was not born under a rhyming planet, nor I cannot woo in festival terms.
>
> 39-40

So far in this survey of Shakspere's poets the use of rhyme for lovers' purposes is not faring well. Two loutish lovers have used two lovely songs for wooing purposes completely ineffectively, and two of Shakspere's most brilliant young gallants have turned disgustedly against poetry as a means of love-making.

Before there is any lovers' poetry on the trees in Arden, the subject of the use of verse by lovers comes up for review and estimation. In Jaques' review of the seven acts which are the seven ages of man, the third actor is the lover:

> Sighing like furnace, with a woful ballad
> Made to his mistress' eyebrow.
>
> A.Y.L., II, vii, 148-149

This is a small bit but within its slim confines it does two things very well: (1) It is one of seven in a list of unlovely and unwinsome aspects of life, the emphasis in this one being upon the social uselessness and the utter selfishness of the lover for so long as he is in love. (2) The other points to the fatuity of the subjects to which, in search of something new to say, the lover-poets have been driven: "his mistress' eyebrow" in good faith!

At the beginning of III, ii in this play, we come upon
Orlando hanging a poem on a tree. From what we
gather in the succeeding scenes, this is only one of a
multitude of such displays of verse. It is most interesting that his speech spoken as he fastens the poem to the
sapling—it must be a sapling—is in rime. It is the last
ten lines of an English sonnet. All is there except the first
quatrain. Is it being too subtle to suggest that Shakspere
conceives a youth so saturated in the tradition of love-
making by means of verse that he not only writes verse
but, in the prosecution of his amorous purposes, thinks
it and speaks it? It is only fair to recall that the first
exchange of speech between Juliet and Romeo takes the
form of an entire sonnet plus four lines of another
(*Romeo*, I, v, 95–111).

Most of what *As You Like It* has to say about lovers'
poetry comes in the remainder of III, ii. Rosalind
(Ganymede) enters shortly with a poem. She reads
eight lines of it. It may or it may not be Exhibit A
which we saw Orlando hanging on the bush a while
ago. All of its lines rime on Rosalind's name. It says
little and that rather poorly. Touchstone catches its
measure and pattern and in a ribald parody of twelve
lines reduces it to absurdity, exclaiming at the end:

> This is the very false gallop of verses! Why do you
> infect yourself with them?
>
> 119-120

"Peace, you dull fool!" says Rosalind; "I found them
on a tree" (121).

Ponder that speech a moment. It is, if I mistake not,
a most revealing speech. As we remarked above, the
verses are far from good. If that needed any demonstration to Rosalind's quick perceptions, Touchstone has

more than provided it. But, at the same time, there is more here in this little speech than meets *our* eye. Look for a moment at the matter with Rosalind's eye. Here is paper with matter upon it in the form of verse, in the name of love, with her name in it. A girl cannot afford to be over-hasty in closing the door upon such a matter. So Rosalind neither judges the verses nor does she commit herself:

> Peace, you dull fool! I found them on a tree.

But the next episode is still more amazing, and revealing. Celia (Aliena) enters now reading. Thirty lines this time, also with *Rosalind*[1] in them and much hyperbole of praise. Touchstone and the rustics are dismissed, and there is frank discussion of the situation:

> *Cel.* Didst thou hear these verses?
> *Ros.* O, yes . . . some of them had in them more feet than the verses would bear.[2]

> 172-175

Celia says, "That's no matter," and perhaps she's right, but it is still Rosalind's quick judgment catching on the technical flaws even when she is so many fathoms deep involved in love. Celia, it seems is all for discussing the wonder of the thing; so is Rosalind—but *would that the verses were better!*

Before the scene closes Jaques and Orlando meet and Jaques in the interest of forest preservation and other matters says:

[1] If we had to depend on the evidence of the rimes in these poems and in Touchstone's parody, we should pronounce this heroine Rosa*lajnd*.

[2] Rosalind has in mind, no doubt, line 147:
> The quintessence of every sprite
and line 161:
> Heaven would that she these gifts should have.

Jaq. I pray you mar no more trees with writing love
songs in their barks.
Orl. I pray you mar no more of my verses with reading
them ill-favouredly.

276-279

When, if it is not too trivial a question, had Jaques read
any of Orlando's verses at all, much less ill-favoredly?
He should be thankful that Sir Nathaniel is in another
play. Touchstone, to be sure, may have read his Rosalind parody for Jaques' criticism. Or they may have had
a session of putting their gatherings from the trees together. If so, we may rely on it that it was a ribald and
boisterous time and would be talked about and word of
it would have come to Orlando's ears. Jaques himself
is a parodist, as we know, from his additional "stanzo"
for Amiens' song (II, v, 52–59). So, although we must
go on not knowing when Jaques read any of Orlando's
verses, perhaps some such conjecture will serve.

Once again, it seems, we must say that the credit of
verse as a means to love-making is not running very high.
Rosalind herself says, partly—but only partly—in the
spirit of play-acting:

> There is a man haunts the forest that abuses our young
> plants with carving 'Rosalind' on their barks; hangs odes
> upon hawthorns and elegies on brambles; all, forsooth,
> deifying the name of Rosalind. If I could meet that fancy-
> monger, I would give him some good counsel. . . .

III, ii, 377-383

Let us be mindful of one thing. Shakspere is mindful
of it, although many of his interpreters forget it. As a
general thing, the personal literature that passes between
lovers is less than good stuff to any eye but theirs. These
poems we have been dealing with are well enough for
Rosaline and Katherine and possibly for Beatrice and

Rosalind, but when they fall into other hands and are
read by Sir Nathaniel without the giving of the accent
or by Jaques ill-favoredly or are parodied by Touchstone, they seem flat and insipid. One might expect for
a moment that a love letter written by Prince Hamlet
would be a veritable gem of beauty—but it is not so.
It is personal and for the loved one, but to other eyes
and ears, vapid and silly.

What a sport it was in school days to intercept a missive passing between two love-sick adolescents, its ten-
derest protestations within an hour becoming the by-
words of the school ground. And one knows how stale
and empty love letters become when introduced as evidence and read into the record of a court of domestic
relations. It is surely with this as a major emphasis, this
private personal preciousness of the love lyric which so
readily becomes the sport of irreverent and unsympathetic outsiders, that Shakspere makes the use of verse
by lovers a device of not altogether kind comedy:

> to your ears, divinity;
> to any other's, profanation,[3]

and a good deal of hilarious fun.

II. The Anti-poets

There is a small group of characters, for the most part
brilliant and active fellows, who in one way or another,
some seriously and some as a part of a sort of professed
humor of theirs, speak out against poetry and the poetic.

The first of these is the Bastard Falconbridge in *King
John*. He is quick to scent out affectation and pretense.
As it develops, his instinctive distaste for the Duke of
Austria becomes a thing of beauty. His realization that

---

[3] *Twel.* I, v, 233-234.

his elevation to bastardhood has made him a man of the
world is finely expressed in his soliloquy beginning:

> Well, now I can make any Joan a lady.
>
> I, i, 184-216

In this speech he probes the vanities and pretenses of the
travelled man and the empty fop. But this is not quite
to the point. The point comes in II, i, when the man of
Angiers suggests a marriage as a means to prevent a war.
It is a matter of wonder to Falconbridge that mere words
can be so potent. To this man of deeds the substitute of
words for valiant act seems less than brave and manly.
The Angiers man speaks his specious proposal, and Falconbridge takes up the comment:

> Here's a 'Stay!'
> That shakes the rotten carcass of old Death
> Out of his rags! Here's a large mouth indeed,
> That spits forth death, and mountains, rocks and seas;
> Talks as familiarly of roaring lions
> As maids of thirteen do of puppy-dogs!
> What cannoneer begot this lusty blood?
> He speaks plain cannon-fire and smoke and bounce;
> He gives the bastinado with his tongue.
> Our ears are cudgell'd; not a word of his
> But buffets better than a fist of France.
> Zounds! I was never so bethump'd with words
> Since I first call'd my brother's father dad.
>
> II, i, 455-467

This, of course, does not mean that Falconbridge
would react so violently against all talk. In the presence
of good or stirring talk he would surely be stimulated.
But this is diplomatic talk, and its speciousness does not
deceive him.

In a moment Lewis, the Dauphin, who is following
eagerly the Angiers man's suggestion, speaks a reply in
the style of the conceits of the love sonnets, and Falcon-

bridge wrings out a bitter extension of the conceit which, better than anything else he says, can be taken as his dictum against poetry. Lewis is urged by his father to look in the lady's face:

> I do, my lord, and in her eye I find
> A wonder, or a wondrous miracle—
> The shadow of myself form'd in her eye;
>
> *   *   *
>
> I do protest I never lov'd myself
> Till now infixed I beheld myself
> Drawn in the flattering table of her eye.
>
> *Whispers with Blanch.*

> *Bast.* [Aside] Drawn in the flattering table of her eye,
> Hang'd in the frowning wrinkle of her brow,
> And quarter'd in her heart.
>
> II, i, 496-506

There are a few phrases more, but this is enough to show how thorough a contempt our stout man of deeds holds for mincing and conceitful verse, especially when it shoulders its way in where the cue, he feels, is not words at all but brave deeds.

In *A Midsummer Night's Dream*, IV, i, the scene is a hunt, and the great Duke Theseus and his prospective bride, Hippolyta, are awaiting the unleashing of the Duke's hounds in the next valley. Hippolyta says she was a-hunt once with Hercules and Cadmus and recalls a particularly great pack of their hounds in full cry, and Theseus takes up the tale in behalf of his own hounds:

> My hounds are bred out of the Spartan kind;
> So flew'd, so sanded; and their heads are hung
> With ears that sweep away the morning dew;
> Crook-knee'd, and dew-lapp'd like Thessalian bulls;
> Slow in pursuit but match'd in mouth like bells,
> Each under each. A cry more tuneable

Was never holloa'd to nor cheer'd with horn
In Crete, in Sparta, nor in Thessaly.
IV, i, 122-129

And thus we have one aspect of Theseus. He is a man
who is willing to take his hounds a little slow in pursuit
so be their voices are matched like a peal of bells, each
under each. Such a one is not altogether hunter; he is
in part a romantic, and might be expected to think
charitably of the arts, even poetry. But it is not entirely
so. A little later (V, i), we come upon them again.
Hippolyta is all agog with talk about the strange stories,
afloat just now, of the wondrous experiences of the four
young Athenian lovers:

> *Hip.* 'Tis strange, my Theseus, that these lovers speak of.
> V, i, 1

to which Theseus replies with broad manly skepticism:

> More strange than true. I never may believe
> These antique fables nor these fairy toys.
> Lovers and madmen have such seething brains,
> Such shaping fantasies, that apprehend
> More than cool reason ever comprehends.
> The lunatic, the lover, and the poet
> Are of imagination all compact.
> One sees more devils than vast hell can hold:
> That is the madman. The lover, all as frantic,
> Sees Helen's beauty in a brow of Egypt.
> The poet's eye, in a fine frenzy rolling,
> Doth glance from heaven to earth, from earth to heaven;
> And as imagination bodies forth
> The forms of things unknown, the poet's pen
> Turns them to shapes, and gives to airy nothing
> A local habitation and a name.
> Such tricks hath strong imagination
> That, if it would but apprehend some joy,
> It comprehends some bringer of that joy;

Or in the night, imagining some fear,
How easy is a bush suppos'd a bear!

                                        V, i, 2-22

This speech has been so often lifted out of context
and taken as Shakspere's word that we do well to remember faithfully that it is rather the questioning and less
even than half-serious word of another of our men of
action. And so it stands that what in its mid-section is
a fine bit of rhetoric on the subject of the creative fancy,
is, in its totality, a thoroughgoing piece of skeptical appraisal, bracketing the poet with lovers and madmen in
one moon-struck crew, a crew capable of thinking a
kitchen wench a Helen and any thick cluster of bracken
a bear.

Theseus is not quite the colorful swash-buckler that
Falconbridge is, but he, too, is a man of vigorous and
heroic action, and so, in their way, are Mercutio and
Hotspur, who are yet to be dealt with as anti-poets. It
is clear, of course, that Shakspere is not speaking his own
mind in what they say. Rather may it not be that he is
letting them speak for a large company of stout, virile,
honest-spoken fellows, who think it a bit unmanly to
praise beauty in its more delicate forms—to show care
for a flower or delight in a bird's song or to hearken to
poetry with an ear of pleasure?

Mercutio is not a simple figure. In one great passage
he is definitely among the poets, but in other passages,
much more typical, he is an anti-poet. In the large, he
belongs with Falconbridge and Hotspur and Hamlet,
who despise cant and are disgusted by affectation and
pretense. He is critical of Romeo's fantastical behavior
so long as the young lover follows the artificial courtly
process in wooing Rosaline. He detests the affected
speech of the foppish young blades of Verona:

> The pox of such antic, lisping, affecting fantasticoes—these
> new tuners of accent.
>
> *Romeo*, II, iv, 29-30

He questions their strange hair-splitting points of decorum in quarreling and fighting:

> Thou! why thou wilt quarrel with a man that hath a hair
> more or a hair less in his beard than thou hast. Thou
> wilt quarrel with a man for cracking nuts, having no
> other reason but because thou hast hazel eyes.
>
> III, i, 18-22

He is skeptical about the new Italianate fashion of sword
play with its thrust and parry:

> He fights as you sing pricksong—keeps time, distance, and
> proportion; rests me his minim rest, one, two, and the
> third in your bosom! the very butcher of a silk button,
> a duellist, a duellist! a gentleman of the very first house,
> of the first and second cause. Ah, the immortal passado!
> the punto reverso! the hay!
>
> **II, iv, 21-27**

But, to come to our point, he is put out of patience by
the fantastic qualities of verse, especially as it is connected
with the contrivings of lovers.

As Act II begins, it is not yet known abroad that Romeo
has in quick exchange forgotten Rosaline and taken up
Juliet, and that the promptings of the heart rather than
the formulae of the courtly convention are governing the
conduct of his love. Still under the impression that he
is as he has been, Romeo's friends go seeking him by
night. Benvolio calls him and urges Mercutio, too, to
call. "Call, good Mercutio":

> *Mer.*   Nay, I'll conjure too,
> Romeo! humours! madman! passion! lovers!
> Appear thou in the likeness of a sigh;
> Speak but one rhyme, and I am satisfied!

Cry but 'Ay me!' pronounce but 'love' and 'dove';
Speak to my gossip Venus one fair word,
One nickname for her purblind son and heir,
Young Adam Cupid. . . .

II, i, 6-13

This, obviously, derives from the general idea that associates love with riming and with conceits about Venus and Cupid. It echoes in its first full line Theseus' bracketing of lunatics and lovers in one category, and, with the fourth line, the missing member of the trio, the poet, is brought in. Also it anticipates Benedick's toiling with rimes which he cannot persuade himself to be pleased with.

Farther along in the act, Romeo comes in hailed by Benvolio in joyous iteration: "Here comes Romeo! here comes Romeo!" and Mercutio sees in him what he believes to be the signs of poetry:

> Now is he for the numbers that Petrarch flowed in. Laura, to his lady, was but a kitchen wench (marry, she had a better love to berhyme her), Dido a dowdy, Cleopatra a gipsy, Helen and Hero hildings and harlots, Thisbe a gray eye or so, but not to the purpose. Signior Romeo, bon jour!
>
> II, iv, 40-46

This, too, is a thrust at the conceits of the sonnets with their comparisons of Stella and Delia and Fidessa and many another to all the beauties of yesteryear to the great detriment of yesteryear's beauties, and it echoes, also, Theseus'

> Sees Helen's beauty in a brow of Egypt.

But its most delightful note is the flat appraisal of Romeo as being not quite up to Petrarch on the poetical side. This is a little in the fashion in which we thought we caught Rosalind sighing because the Arden Forest crop of poesy was running a little below top quality.

So Mercutio and Theseus go together as hearty and not-too-serious skeptics about poetry especially in the service of love. Falconbridge is more serious than the other two, for, in his mind, the slipping in of poetic conceits where the cue is action, is a violation of principle. The emptiness of patterned and fantastic talk in a situation that calls for deeds makes him bitter. With Theseus and Mercutio taste only is in question, and over that sort of matter a gentleman does not become angry.

The declamations of Hotspur against verse are much like Benedick's earlier estimations of women, when he asks:

> Do you question me . . . for my simple true judgment?
> Or would you have me speak after my custom, as being a
> professed tyrant to their sex?
>
> *Much*, I, i, 167-170

Most of what Hotspur has to say about verse is in the scene in Wales (*I H IV*, III, i) when he and Mortimer and Glendower seek to set up their coalition against the King. Hotspur is not going to ally easily with Glendower. The Welshman, he thinks, is affected, self-opinionated, pretentious. He challenges Glendower's claim to a miracle-attended birth, to power over spirits, especially the spirit of evil. A map is shown dividing England into three parts for the three conspirators. He defies natural boundaries—to please him the course of a river must be turned. He is being a very uncomfortable friend. Mortimer cautions him not to cross their Welsh comrade too far, but Hotspur persists in perversity. In the midst of the quarrel he cries out:

> *Hot.*   Who shall say me nay?
> *Glend.* Why, that will I.

Hot.   Let me not understand you then; speak it in Welsh.
Glend.   I can speak English, lord, as well as you;
For I was train'd up in the English court,
Where, being but young, I framed to the harp
Many an English ditty lovely well,
And gave the tongue a helpful ornament—
A virtue that was never seen in you.
Hot.   Marry,
And I am glad of it with all my heart!
I had rather be a kitten and cry mew
Than one of these same metre ballet-mongers.
I had rather hear a brazen canstick turn'd
Or a dry wheel grate on the axletree,
And that would set my teeth nothing on edge,
Nothing so much as mincing poetry.
'Tis like the forc'd gait of a shuffling nag.

III, i, 117-135

When this is all said, Glendower remarks quietly, "Come, you shall have Trent turn'd" (136), whereas, when the speech began he was loudly declaring, "I will not have it alt'red" (116). There can be scarcely more than one meaning to this, viz., that while Hotspur was declaiming, Glendower had a calm moment in which to appraise his testy ally and to see that he is not really so difficult. He has been speaking very much like this ever since he arrived in Bangor, not in simple true judgment, but as being a professed tyrant to pretense and conceit. So Trent will be altered because Glendower has caught sight of the true measure of his stormy friend and is himself altered.

In a quieter moment, later, Lady Percy seeks to calm her restless lord:

Lie still, ye thief, and hear the lady sing in Welsh.
Hot.   I had rather hear Lady, my brach, howl in Irish.

237-238

But he lapses into quietness; indeed, he takes it upon

him to ask for quiet: "Peace! she sings" (246), he enjoins, and then with husbandly pride he demands: "Come, Kate, I'll have your song too" (248).

How does Hotspur regard verse and song? Perhaps not too harshly, although it would be surprising to discover that he loved it. He, of all Shakspere's strong men, is most extravagant and uncontrolled in speech and act. The interpreter who called him Shakspere's realization of the national type; ("Hotspur is an Englishman"; the master type of manliness,[4]) is wrong. He is not even typically English. If he were my leader, I think I would love him and shout for him and, perhaps, follow him, but I would not trust his judgment or his discretion. What does he think of poetry? Well, at this moment, here in Wales, he will deprecate it, because a man whose behavior irks him professes to like it. At another moment he might take pleasure in it—at least, we must remember, he begs Kate to sing her song.

We have glanced already at Berowne and Benedick and Jaques, who are in slight degree anti-poets too. Berowne's renunciation of "taffeta phrases" we have sufficiently observed. Benedick, we know, finds riming difficult, and we also discover that it is part of his professed custom to dispraise song. In II, iii, Benedick, at one side, looks on as Don Pedro and Claudio and Leonato come in calling on Balthazar to sing. Balthazar, like Amiens, goes through a routine of demurring, but when the music begins to sound, he sets himself to come in at his singer's cue. Perhaps he is screwing up his face and adjusting his eyes to the mood of the song, for Benedick is amused:

> Now divine air! Now is his soul ravish'd! Is it not strange that sheep's guts should hale souls out of men's bodies?

[4] George Brandes, *William Shakespeare*, 192.

Well, a horn for my money, when all's done.

Much, II, iii, 60-63

Then comes the song—not a bad song, but there are better—and the Prince and Claudio applaud, but from behind his covert Benedick still protests:

An he had been a dog that should have howl'd thus, they would have hang'd him; . . . I had as live have heard the night raven, come what plague could have come after it.

81-85

Jaques asks Amiens to sing:

I can suck melancholy out of a song as a weasel sucks eggs. More, I prithee, more!

A.Y.L., II, v, 12-13

Amiens, of the long lineage of sore-throated singers, protests:

My throat is ragged. I know I cannot please you.
Jaq. I do not desire you to please me; I do desire you to sing.

14-17

That, of course, is pretty obvious and unkind, but Jaques is not exactly in the service of kindness, and he, too, has a custom of speech.

So these anti-poets—Berowne, Falconbridge, Theseus, Mercutio, Hotspur, Benedick, Jaques—stand, a fine array of brave, hearty, even brilliant chaps, alike in many respects but each a sharp, well-defined individual, each, in one way or another, skeptical about poetry. If there is a common aspect to this skepticism, it is clearest as a sort of sense that a really red-blooded fellow had better not appear too enthusiastic about such business as verse; as a matter of fact, he might do service to his reputation for being a manly fellow if he deprecates it a little. With a few of our friends this has led to a sort of assumed guise of deprecation from which it becomes, at times, a little difficult to retreat. Perhaps only Falconbridge, of the lot, is really serious in his objection.

But these are not bad fellows; indeed, they are very fine fellows and capable of being lifted by really good matter. Look at their situations candidly and you must admit that a good deal of what they have treated disparagingly is really pretty poor stuff. I would take a chance, I think, of having them all at my mercy for an hour while I read to them Chaucer's "Franklin's Tale" or Coleridge's "Rime of the Ancient Mariner" or Keats's "Isabella." Not a one of them but would rouse and stir at the greatness of a wonderfully told tale.

III. Bad Poets

Julius Caesar does not, at first thought, seem a likely play in which to meet poets, but be that as it may, there are in the play two persons designated as poets, and unless I am mistaken, they are the only persons in all Shakspere to be definitely and directly styled *poet*. Moreover, neither is called *poet* in the source. The designation and whatever of color it gives to the situation is Shakspere's responsibility. Following Antony's rabble-rousing oration over dead Caesar, the mob starts away in all directions, burning houses and laying hands on anyone remotely suspected of being among those who murdered Caesar. Along the way they come upon a certain Cinna, friend of Caesar, who is hurrying to be at the funeral. A mobster inquires his name and he says "Cinna." This is repeated to others of the mob until one, remembering that there was a Cinna among the conspirators, cries out that this fellow is one of the murderers. No protests

of his avail, and they beat him to death in the street. So
Plutarch tells it.[5] From the point of the mobster asking
the man's name, Shakspere's version is different. Shakspere's focus of interest is on the mob and not on Cinna,
so he has the mob fire a veritable volley of questions at
the poor frightened poet. Cinna takes a chance at a
humorous reply and tries to answer them in their own
tumbling terms, but they are truculent and in no mood
to be amused or answered. Once again a mobster asks
his name. "Cinna," he says, and another plebian shouts:

> Tear him to pieces! He's a conspirator.
> *Cin.* I am Cinna the poet! I am Cinna the poet!
> 4. *Pleb.* Tear him for his bad verses! Tear him for his
> bad verses!

III, iii, 31-35

They are not appeased, but go out shouting: "Tear him,
tear him!" (40). So they are off on their way to burn
more houses—Casca's and Cassius' and Brutus'—pushing
Cinna before them to tear him yet more.

As has been suggested, this is a mob scene. The additional color which Shakspere gives to Plutarch's already
sufficiently dramatic incident is the making of the man
into a poet and making bad verses the reason for tearing
him. Even that is a demonstration of the mob's senseless
reactions. But while that is the strongest purpose served
by this strange bit, it may well have in it also some suggestion of that innate quick distrust of poetry and the
broad uncritical appraisal of it as *bad* which is so generally found among rough practical men. And, like all
mob reactions, it is made louder by the fact of their being in a crowd.

In IV, iii, occurs the great scene of the bitter quarrel

---

[5] North's tr. of Plutarch's *Lives*, ed. 1595.

which almost separated Cassius and Brutus. It is also
the scene in which word comes of the death of Portia,
and it is the scene in which the Ghost of Julius appears
to Brutus in his tent. Sandwiched in among these highly
dramatic elements is a strange interlude of fifteen lines
in which a poet forces his way into the tent to speak to
the generals. Plutarch says it was "one Marcus Phaonius,
that had bene a frend and a follower of Cato while he
lived, and took upon him to counterfeate a Philosopher,
not with wisdome & discretion, but with a certaine bed-
lem and franticke motion." Plutarch goes on to describe
his fantastic conduct and his utter disdain of control and
tells how he broke in upon the generals despite efforts
to keep him out, and how he struck an attitude and recited
two lines from the *Iliad*, a speech of Nestor. The biographer says, "Cassius fell a laughing at him: but Brutus
thrust him out of the chamber, and called him dog, and
counterfeate Cynicke."[6]

This, like the Cinna story, is as well handled by the
ancient biographer as by our playwright. Everything
is essentially the same except for two details. (1) Mainly
by means of stage direction, (Enter a *Poet* [followed by
Lucillius, Titinius, and *Lucius*]), Shakspere makes him a
poet, but that designation is also glanced at in Cassius'
remark, "How vilely doth this cynic rhyme!" and Brutus'
query:

> What should the wars do with these jigging fools? Com-
> panion, hence!
>
> 137-138

(2) Shakspere's man does not quote Homer except in
echoic suggestion. That may be a device for making
it more proper to criticize his rimes.

---

[6] North's tr. of Plutarch's *Lives,* ed. 1595, "Life of Brutus," from
Variorum Shakespeare, "Julius Caesar," 310.

The touch of having tough old Cassius laugh at him while humorless Brutus is only irritated by his ineptness is made fine use of by both Plutarch and Shakspere for purposes of character emphasis.

So these poets in *Julius Caesar* contribute nothing toward the forming of a body of Shaksperean ideas about poetry. In the one instance, a poet is used to point up a mob's savagery and senselessness. In the other, a crack-brained poet ineptly but successfully breaks up a quarrel and is the means of underscoring an essential difference in personalities. Both of these services might have been done just as well by men of another profession. It *was* so done in Plutarch. Shakspere chose to make them both poets. Why? The question haunts me. All that comes to me that even hints at an answer is that both instances carry the idea of the quick and unreasoned distrust that men of the world and especially men of the street have for poetry.

IV.   Connoisseurs of Poetry and Song

Before I come to the one principal example in this category of the connoisseur I pause to remark briefly on young Lorenzo, who stole the Jew's daughter, and later did such a thoroughly comfortable job as interim keeper of the great house and grounds at Belmont.

It is a lovely night on the thick-turfed bank as Act V opens. The properties are moonlight, a sweet wind, and lovely little Jessica. The program is a delightful honeymooners' game of matching nights famous for love against each other, seeking the while for a parallel to this night of theirs. They ransack antiquity as they proceed. I give only the bare skeleton of the interchange:

> In such a night:
> *Lor.* Troilus . . .

Jes.   Thisbe . . .
Lor.   Dido . . .
Jes.   Medea . . .
Lor.   [To make it more contemporary and sweeter]
Jessica . . .
Jes.   [To fall in with this more intimate pattern] Lor-
enzo . . .

Merch., V, i, 1-19

and then there are footsteps and the contest of the matching of nights is broken up. Stephano comes with word
of Portia's present arrival; Launcelot, in such a night,
halloaing and capering most indecorously, comes with
news of Bassanio's present arrival. Surely we must go
in and attend to the last ordering of the house, but not
this Lorenzo, this master of perfect organization. He is
just too lazily happy with the night and Jessica for that,
for he says:

Sweet soul, let's in, and there expect their coming.
And yet no matter. Why should we go in?

V, i, 49-50

So he asks Stephano to send out music, and lapses again
into contemplation of the moonlight—and Jessica. Then
he shifts to a discussion of the music of the spheres, and
calls at length for a hymn to Diana.

"I am never merry when I hear sweet music," says
Jessica. For that our amateur esthetician has an explanation: *Young spirits are innately gay, but like animals,
they naturally respond to and fall quiet beneath the effects of music.* And now, finally, comes his splendid negative deliverance on the concord between love of music
and character:

The man that hath no music in himself,
Nor is not mov'd with concord of sweet sounds,
Is fit for treasons, stratagems, and spoils;

> The motions of his spirit are dull as night,
> And his affections dark as Erebus.
> Let no such man be trusted.
>
> 83-88

It is true that poetry is not specifically mentioned in the Lorenzo-Jessica episode, but this boy, who can so expansively draw on his reading for instances and who is so susceptible to moonlight, night breezes, a lady with dark eyes, and sweet music, would greatly surprise us did he turn an unfriendly ear to poetry. He speaks most masterfully of the heavenly spheres and of music—earthly and celestial.

But the real forthright connoisseur of verse and song in Shakspere's plays is Orsino, Duke of Illyria. *Twelfth Night* opens with his call for music:

> If music be the food of love, play on,
> Give me excess of it, that, surfeiting,
> The appetite may sicken, and so die.
> That strain again! It had a dying fall;
> O, it came o'er my ear like the sweet sound
> That breathes upon a bank of violets,
> Stealing and giving odour!
>
> I, i, 1-7

So he speaks of music, poetry's sister—and in good, fresh, critical language.

When the play begins, Orsino's affair with the Lady Olivia has reached the point where he does not go wooing himself but sends his emissaries of love. Valentine served for a time, but he is now superseded by the new page boy, Cesario. But although Orsino sends these messengers, he, it must be, writes their messages. When Viola-Cesario has brushed aside all obstacles, and gains admission to the Lady Olivia's presence, it is to pronounce a speech. All the ladies have let fall their veils, and the inexperienced messenger is at a loss toward whom to direct his speech. A voice from behind a veil calls upon him to speak to her, and he begins:

> Most radiant, exquisite, and unmatchable beauty—
>
> I, v, 181

but he gets no farther. Something untoward has happened; there is a wave of women's suppressed laughter, and poor Cesario is embarrassed as one is who does not know what he can have done to set off such a reaction.

Once more he asks, which is the lady of the house?

> I would be loath to cast away my speech; for, besides that it is excellently well penn'd, I have taken great pains to con it.
>
> 183-185

There are some routine questions from behind the veil, which the messenger declines to answer as being "out of my part; I can say little more than I have studied" (190-191). Then, at last, he asks to be permitted to be allowed to go "on with my speech in your praise and then show you the heart of my message" (202-203). But he is bidden to omit the praise and come to the important part. "Alas," he says, "I took great pains to study it, and 'tis poetical" (206). And that is all we shall ever know about Orsino's love messages. They may not have been any better than Berowne's or Orlando's or Hamlet's. (Personally, I believe they were). This fair messenger thought well of them, but, as a judge, she is disqualified, for she is already many fathoms deep in love with the writer. Such a message from the same hand, had it been for her, would have warmed the very middle of her heart.

For the purpose we have in hand the most effective scene is II, iv. It is evening in the Duke's music room.

He calls, as before, for music, and for a specific piece which had been part of the program of the night before. It is an old and antique song, and he pauses to praise the old songs as having more value, especially for the heavy heart:

> Give me some music . . .
> . . . that piece of song,
> That old and antique song we heard last night.
> Methought it did relieve my passion much,
> More than light airs and recollected terms
> Of these most brisk and giddy-paced times.
>
> II, iv, 1-6

But Orsino is too young (how old is he?) to be one of those perennial middle-aged people who have closed their minds to new things and think nothing good but what was in vogue when they were young. Orsino has genuine esthetic bases for his liking for this song. When they find Feste, the singer who should sing it, Orsino gives us quickly his personal program notes:

> O, fellow, come, the song we had last night.
> Mark it, Cesario; it is old and plain.
> The spinsters and the knitters in the sun,
> And the free maids that weave their thread with bones,
> Do use to chant it. It is silly sooth,
> And dallies with the innocence of love,
> Like the old age.
>
> 43-49

The Fool has been waiting with elfish attention to this prelude. "Are you ready, sir?" And the Duke says, "Ay; prithee sing." The song that follows is one of the loveliest of the songs in the plays, "Come away, come away, death." It is a haunting piece, and at its ending, Feste, Shakspere's beggar without peer, is so far rapt out of himself as to fail to snatch at a gratuity (68-70). This is our peep into Orsino's music room and into the artistic temper of his mind. He is not an unmanly man, and yet with the amateurish Lorenzo for his sole companion, he stands otherwise alone among Shakspere's people as a real connoisseur of art. In his case the special field is folk song.

Cassio's passion for a strawberry design on a handkerchief, and Imogen's midnight reading of Ovid, and the statuary, and the tapestry depicting the Alexandrian water pageantry in her bed chamber are most interesting in their suggestion of artistic tastes, but they are too slight to detain us here.

V.   Persons who Draw Unfavorable Comment for Poetizing

There are four persons among Shakspere's people who make poetry more or less by habit and who draw derisive comment because of it. The first instance is Mercutio, who, so far as his whole attitude goes, is much more of an anti-poet than a poet. On the one occasion of the Queen Mab speech, he really delivered himself of a considerable poetic cargo. It has seemed to some readers to be quite likely a scrap of fairy stuff left out of or left over from the fairy business in *A Midsumer Night's Dream*. This Mab, Queen of Fairies, is not of the loftier and more consequential type of fairy. She is more fit to be a queen for a nation of Robin Goodfellows than to be a consort for Oberon. Moreover, two fairy queens are one too many for the *Dream*. But this Mab speech is a good speech, full of zest and packed with every sort of mischief—too bad to waste it, so when a niche for it appears in *Romeo and Juliet*, here it is.

The cueing in of this speech is ingenious. Romeo says,

"I dreamt a dream tonight." "And so did I," says Mercutio.

> Rom. Well, what was yours?
> Mer.   That dreamers often lie.
> Rom. In bed asleep, while they do dream things true.
> Mer. O, then I see Queen Mab hath been with you.
>
>   I, iv, 49-53

and he is off for forty-six lines of delightful puckish fancy. Indeed, he does not conclude, for he is running on:

> This is she—
>
>   94

when Romeo breaks in:

>   Peace, peace, Mercutio, peace!
> Thou talk'st of nothing.
> Mer.   True, I talk of dreams;
> Which are the children of an idle brain,
> Begot of nothing but vain fantasy.
>
>   95-98

But the real point is in Romeo's "Thou talk'st of nothing," for it has become apparent that Mercutio's discourse on Mab, delightful though it is in itself, is to no good purpose, and someone must stop it.

The same general pattern, with better dramatic joinery, appears in the next two situations. The first is in *Richard II* in the scene (III, ii) in which Richard returns to a divided England from his foolish and fruitless Irish war. The intention of Shakspere in the depiction of Richard's character has already had attention as the subject of another chapter in this book, and so we shall attend only to one detail here. As has been pointed out, it has become a truism of Shakspere interpretation that Richard is a poet, and this scene is one of the prime manifestations of that quality. He weeps for joy to be back in his king-

dom and, in whatever posture or with whatever gesture
you will have it, he salutes this dear earth with his hand,
doing it, in his phrase, "favours with my royal hands."
Next he proceeds to conjure the earth to do despite to
his enemies, calling for various items to make up an aggregate of harm to come upon them from the earth:

> . . . [L]et thy spiders that suck up thy venom,
> And heavy-gaited toads, lie in their way,
> Doing annoyance to the treacherous feet
> Which with usurping steps do trample thee.
> Yield stinging nettles to mine enemies;
> And when they from thy bosom pluck a flower,
> Guard it, I pray thee, with a lurking adder
> Whose double tongue may with a mortal touch
> Throw death upon thy sovereign's enemies.
> Mock not my senseless conjuration, lords.
> This earth shall have a feeling, and these stones
> Prove armed soldiers ere her native king
> Shall falter under proud rebellion's arms.
>
> III, ii, 14-26

This is a highly fanciful succession of concepts, the
treatment poetical and the rhetoric impeccable, but the
good of it for practical purposes, sadly to seek. A kingdom is to be brought back to obedience and to be unified,
and the King prates in idle tropes on the shore. *We* see
that. So, also, do his attendants, for it is clear that as he
drove on through this passage, he caught out of the corner
of his eye a shrug or the flutter of an eyelid or the quick
down-turn of the corners of a mouth:

> Mock not my senseless conjuration, lords.
>
> 23

He says this because someone was mocking. And once
again we are on familiar ground in this discussion of
Shakspere's poets. They get short shrift from a world of

practical-minded men, whose habits of mind are active
but unimaginative.

The next instance is in some respects the most interesting of the four. It is the scene in *Hamlet* (II, ii) in which
Rosencrantz and Guildenstern, set on to it by the King,
are seeking to plumb the depths of Hamlet's mind to discover the cause of his sore distraction. The passage which
furnishes our illustration fits in a bit strangely into a discussion of verse, for it is a passage of prose, but when all
is said and done, it is one of the finest pieces of stylized
prose of the English Renaissance, and though it is not
verse its qualities are definitely poetic, and so I think it
comes properly within the compass of our study.

We should note also that this piece is not unconscious
or subconscious poetizing. It is, in contrast to the Richard
II and Macbeth speeches which we are dealing with,
the conscious effort of its creator. It is, indeed, produced and employed as a part of his whole tremendous
act of confusing the court with his strange behavior. Just
before he launches into it, he has browbeaten the King's
spies into an awkward admission of having been sent
for. They whisper together, and Hamlet urges, "Nay
then, I have an eye of you. If you love me hold not off."
And after a moment's further parleying, Guildenstern
gulps, "My lord, we were sent for." It is from that point
that the Prince plunges into his memorable speech:

> I will tell you why, so shall my anticipation prevent
> your discovery, and your secrecy to the King and Queen
> moult no feather. I have of late, but wherefore I know
> not, lost all my mirth, foregone all custom of exercises:
> and indeed it goes so heavily with my disposition, that
> this goodly frame the earth, seems to me a sterile pro-
> montory, this most excellent canopie the air, look you,
> this brave o'erhanging firmament, this majestical roof
> fretted with golden fire, why it appeareth nothing to

me but a foul and pestilent congregation of vapours. . . .
What a piece of work is a man, how noble in reason, how
infinite in faculties, in form and moving, how express
and admirable in action, how like an angel in apprehension,
how like a God: the beauty of the world; the paragon of
animals; and yet to me, what is this quintessence of dust?
man delights not me, no, nor woman neither, though by
your smiling you seem to say so.

II, ii, 304-324 [7]

And just as surely as Richard's attendants mocked, so
surely Rosencrantz and his companion smiled. They do
not deny that they smiled. Rosencrantz merely says that
that is not why they smiled:

Ros. My lord, there was no such stuff in my thoughts.
Ham. Why did you laugh then, when I said 'Man delights
not me'?
Ros. To think, my lord, if you delight not in man, what
lenten entertainment the players shall receive from you.

324-329

This hurried and clumsy answer is, of course, not a true
answer. They catch crazily at the imminence of the
players' coming and make that their explanation.

Why did they smile? Let me suggest that it was because, as they listened to Hamlet and caught the lift and
music of his words, they were recalled to other scenes
here at court or down in the beer halls at Wittenberg
when he had let his fancy soar, and they smile knowing-
ly at each other. *Listen,* their smiling says, *he's just as
he always was; there's not much wrong—at least not with
his speech; he can still make the rafters ring.* But there

[7] In citing this speech, I have departed from my practice of holding to the Kittredge text and have followed instead the punctua-
tion and spelling of the second (1604) quarto. I have no good
reason for this except that it gives some most stimulating turns to
meaning, and I like it.

may have been more than mere recognition of the old Hamlet whom they had known; there was possibly also derision of the sort that prosy fellows indulge in, in sheer defensiveness, in the presence of the poetic.

Hamlet's quick interpolation, "No, nor woman neither," is, of course, no part of the poetic display. It is a swift flick across the path of their search of the red herring of love-madness. Love-madness is now the settled opinion of the High Priest of Brevity and perhaps also of the Queen, as to the cause of Hamlet's distemper. So, in view of all this, what shall the spies report of him? That his mind is in fine creative fettle? That he has bad dreams (which are indeed ambition)? That there is a girl involved? Or that he is only mad north-north-west?

The remaining character who is chidden for running off into poetry is Macbeth. Macbeth's poetic bent is the sole subject of the next chapter, so it will draw but brief notice here. The specific passage for attention is the well-known speech about sleep. It comes as a result of his experiences as he came down stairs from having killed the King. Macbeth takes up the thread of his sudden realization and slips into the pattern of the speech:

> Sleep that knits up the ravell'd sleave of care,
> The death of each day's life, sore labour's bath,
> Balm of hurt minds, great nature's second course,
> Chief nourisher in life's feast.
>
> II, ii, 36-39

And the Lady says, "What do you mean?" with more strength of feeling but in the same general vein as Richard's mockers and Hamlet's smilers and even as Romeo, who says to Mercutio's poetic effusion, "Thou talk'st of nothing."

But Macbeth is in full cry and so goes on:

> Still it cried 'Sleep no more!' to all the house;
> 'Glamis hath murther'd sleep, and therefore Cawdor
> Shall sleep no more! Macbeth shall sleep no more!'

And Lady Macbeth stops him:

> Who was it that thus cried?
>
> 41-44

which means, *Nobody cried. Let us leave poetry and such and be practical.* This full stop given to the poet's flight has the same bearing on the active practical person's question as to the value of poetry, although, in contrast to the others, it is more serious and bitter in its tone.

VI.   Persons who Draw Favorable Comment for Poetizing

There are in the entire gallery of Shakspere characters just two who draw favorable comment because of their poetic faculties. They are anonymous and come late in the cycle of the plays, one of them appearing in *Coriolanus* (1608), and the other in the *Winter's Tale* (1610). They are slightly drawn but most interesting persons, and their assumption of the poetic function is frank and open and in no sense self-critical or skeptical.[8]

---

[8] I am mindful, of course, of the speech of the exiled Duke (*A.Y.L.*, II, i, 1-18), "Sweet are the uses of adversity. . . ." which Amiens commends:

> Happy is your Grace
> What can translate the stubbornness of fortune
> Into so quiet and so sweet a style.
>
> 18-20

All generations of Shakspere readers have admired, likewise, the speech which Amiens is praising, but I am disposed to think Amiens' praise is for the philosophical slant of the speech and not for its stylistic attributes. That, at any rate, is why most of the generations of admirers have praised it.

The first of these is the person who goes under the designation of *Second Citizen* in the first act of *Coriolanus*. In the scene with which this play opens the citizens are led by two who have speaking roles, being styled simply *First* and *Second Citizen*. It is the Second Citizen, who, as the scene unfolds, takes the front of the stage and attains almost, if not quite, to individuality. These two and their followers remind us of the artisans in the street scene at the beginning of *Julius Caesar*. They are the stuff out of which mobs are made. But after they have discussed a little the impending political crisis, there enters to them the old tried man of the world, Menenius Agrippa, whom the citizens hail with a mixture of conscious and unconscious irony as "one that hath always lov'd the people." After a few brief passages we understand why they think so of him, for we see a fine demonstration by a practiced politician of all of the arts of hand-shaking and back-slapping and of the rough give-and-take of the work-a-day political world. Even his insults please them. In the process of his setting forth of his political ideas, Menenius takes up his elaborate fable of the rebellion of the parts of the body against the insatiable and do-nothing belly.

From the beginning of this narration it is the Second Citizen who shows the liveliest interest in the story. "Well, sir," he says, "What answer made the belly?" "Sir," says the old patrician, "I shall tell you," and so he does, warming to his tale and playfully adding fantasy to fantasy:

> Sir, I shall tell you. With a kind of smile,
> Which ne'er came from the lungs, but even thus—
> For look you, I may make the belly smile
> As well as speak—it tauntingly replied
> To th' discontented members, the mutinous parts

> That envied his receipt; even most fitly
> As you malign our senators for that
> They are not such as you.
>
>   I, i, 111-117

And at this point the Second Citizen once more calls for the delayed answer of the belly:

>   Your belly's answer? What?
>
>   118

and he then moves quickly into his own full tide of aroused creativity:

> 2 Cit.   Your belly's answer? What?
> The kingly crowned head, the vigilant eye,
> The counsellor heart, the arm our soldier,
> Our steed the leg, the tongue our trumpeter,
> With other muniments and petty helps
> In this our fabric, if that they . . . .
>
>   118-123

Through all this old Menenius' jaw has fallen slack and he is agape with astonishment. Indeed, it has become his turn to be questioner:

> Men.   What then?
> Fore me, this fellow speaks! What then? What then?
>
>   124-125

So we and Menenius together have noted the swift unfolding of this Second Citizen into the full bloom of a poet. From him there is more but not much more. In the succeeding speeches, Menenius quickly resumes the leading role (I hope it is not too fanciful to say, becoming himself a better poet for having encountered a rival). So he sweeps on to the end of his fable:

> Men.   Note me this, good friend:
> Your most grave belly was deliberate.
>
>   131-132

devising a fabric of story and metaphor most whimsical
and delightful, and comes to the application:

> The senators of Rome are this good belly.
> And you the mutinous members . . . .
>
> * * *
>
> What do you think,
> You, the great toe of this assembly?
> 2 Cit. I the great toe? Why the great toe?
> Men. For that, being one o' th' lowest, basest, poorest
> Of this most wise rebellion, thou goest foremost.
>
> 152-162

At this moment Caius Marcius enters and with characteristic tactlessness flings out in his customary contempt at the rabble:

> What's the matter, you dissentious rogues
> That, rubbing the poor itch of your opinion,
> Make yourselves scabs?
>
> 168-170

And our friend, the Second Citizen, still not completely
deflated, still enough a poet for one parting irony, says:

> We have ever your good word.
>
> 170

The servant in the *Winter's Tale* is rather clearly to be
thought of as a court poet, one who has been in Leontes'
court at least since the time twenty-odd years before
when Hermione of Russia was a young and lovely creature inspiring his laureate muse. Now, after all these
years, this servant announces the arrival of

> One that gives out himself Prince Florizel,
> Son of Polixines, with his princess (she
> The fairest I have yet beheld) . . . .
>
> * * *
>
> Ay, the most peerless piece of earth, I think,
> That e'er the sun shone bright on.
>
> *W. T.*, V, i, 85-96

This hyperbole disturbes Paulina—Paulina, who for sixteen years, has been having something of a task in keeping this court, and especially the men of this court, loyal
to the memory of Hermione. So she berates this servant
poet:

                    O Hermione,
        As every present time doth boast itself
        Above a better, gone, so must thy grave
        Give way to what's seen now! Sir, you yourself
        Have said and writ so, but your writing now
        Is colder than that theme: 'She had not been
        Nor was not to be equall'd.' Thus your verse
        Flow'd with her beauty once. 'Tis shrewdly ebb'd
        To say you have seen a better.
        Serv.   Pardon, madam.
        The one I have almost forgot—your pardon.
        The other, when she has obtain'd your eye
        Will have your tongue too. This is a creature,
        Would she begin a sect, might quench the zeal
        Of all professors else, make proselytes
        Of who she but bid follow.
        Paul. [Skeptical, but interested in spite of herself].[9]
                        How? Not women?
        Serv. Women will love her that she is a woman
        More worth than any man; men, that she is
        The rarest of all women.
                                    95-112

    This is not the custom of old poets, for this poet must,
on a normal computation, be an old man. It would be
more in the order of things, if he had become like Paulina,
fixed in loyalty to the old days. But he is credible. If
there is less of life in him, there is still a great deal of the
love of life. One has only to remember Browning writing "Summum Bonum" and "Muckle-Mouth Meg" at
seventy-seven. And, moreover, this Perdita is a pretty

    [9] The stage direction is mine.

tremendous little piece of inspiration for a poet of any age.

If one were called on to give a reason why we must wait till the very end of Shakspere's career to find him presenting poets who are treated favorably for their poetic abilities, with no touch at all of the skepticism and derisive spirit which prevailed in the other plays, it would be found, perhaps, somewhat in the slightness of their roles and in their anonymity. Moreover, Shakspere is never through producing something new in the form of plot or character. Imogen, Autolycus, and Caliban are fire-new from the mint of his invention. But chiefly, these poets are, like all his other characters, servants of the plots in which they function, and their creator is making a play and not propounding an esthetic.

Conclusion

The business of defending poetry is the special occupation of the critic, not the poet, and perhaps least of all the dramatic poet. Sidney, Dryden, Wordsworth, Shelley, Eliot—all poets—did not fill their poetry with defenses and essays of poetry. They did that in other media.

One should not expect an esthetic from Shakspere—of him, the most objective of poets—least of all. And we get none. Two small segments of this chapter have shown Shakspere treating the poet favorably, the one about the connoisseurs and the one about the two anonymous poets, who surprise their hearers with the unexpected vigor of their expression. In all the other situations the reception of poetry is questioning, sardonic, or definitely unfavorable. This, of course, does not mean that Shakspere was unfavorable to poetry. It probably means that in every instance one of three things, or a combination of them, was true.

(1) Poets and poetry are used especially in love plots to create embarrassing situations for the lovers and hilariously amusing situations for unsympathetic readers or hearers among their fellow actors. There is not a single instance in which a love poem really, to use Cloten's word, *penetrates*. It is not permitted to. There is no instance where in her private chamber a lovely lady is alone with her lover's spiritual ecstasy, in sonnet form, spread out for her eye alone. It is too much fun to have the poem missent, or come upon by an unsympathetic eye, or misread by a bad reader.

(2) Moreover, Shakspere sees no reason for avoiding this comic and skeptical treatment of his own art. It is possible even that an innate defensiveness led him to the opposite extreme of assuming a derisive attitude. For, after all, it is almost as old as the world for the lawyer to derogate the fairness of justice, and the doctor to question the validity of diagnosis and the equity of doctor's fees. So may not the poet take a similar attitude in clapping together into one mad category the lunatic, the lover, and the poet, or, catching a chap running loose in the streets of Rome claiming not to be a murderer but a poet, to have him torn to bits for his bad verses? Shakspere thought too highly of poetry to have thought of its needing defenders, and he is just the sort of humorous man who does not mind having the jest come up occasionally against himself and his kind.

(3) Finally, much of what we have found in the way of deprecation of poetry comes from men who live hard, tough lives, and who either think it unmanly to be caught admiring or employing poetry or who wish to have it believed that they think so. Berowne, Falconbridge, Theseus, Mercutio, Hotspur, Benedick, Jaques: a fine array of vigorous colorful persons, who, for one reason

or another, disparage poetry because the time is not right for it, or it is their humor to appear contemptuous of it, or who genuinely feel that it is not manly stuff. The heirs of American pioneer stock should be quick to understand this. The viewpoint still lingers, perhaps especially in hard-boiled masculine circles.

The clearest alternative to Shakspere's treatment of poets and poetry as characters and plot material would have been a resort to a romantic and idealized method in which the laurel-crowned poet is knelt to and the measures of sweet poesy are listened to with reverence and bated breath. Such a world he knew in *Arcadia* and other pastoral romances, but such a treatment of verse and the verse maker would not march with his total realization of truth and humanity in the plays.

The very suggestion of such an idyllic and romanticized treatment points up as well as it can be done the cool, rational common sense of Shakspere's world. This world of Shakspere is inhabited by people and occupied by situations which are like the people and the situations of every day, and in such a world one has reticences about his finer tastes and his more intimate enjoyments. Such people do not air their esthetic joys nor wear their poetic hearts upon their sleeves.

So we have no definitive word from Shakspere as to what he thought of poetry as conveyed and convoyed by the poets in his plays. He made better shift for the defense of poetry than that. He wrote it.

CHAPTER VI

MACBETH THE POET

In the chronology of the plays, *Macbeth* comes near the point in Shakspere's workmanship when the most exciting poetry appears. Just a little later in *Antony and Cleopatra*, *Coriolanus*, and the *Tempest* the quick thrusts and flashes of poetry come most surprisingly, but *Macbeth* is full of breath-taking poetic experience:

> Thy letters have transported me beyond
> This ignorant present, and I feel now
> The future in the instant.
>> I, v, 57-59
>> The bell invites me.
>>> II, i, 62
> We are yet but young in deed.
>> III, iv, 144
> Thou hast harp'd my fear aright.
>> IV, i, 74
> I would not have such a heart in my bosom for
> the dignity of the whole body.
>> V, i, 61-62
> Canst thou not minister to a mind diseas'd,
> Pluck from the memory a rooted sorrow,
> Raze out the written troubles of the brain,
> And with some sweet oblivious antidote
> Cleanse the stuff'd bosom of that perilous stuff
> Which weighs upon the heart?
>> V, iii, 40-45

These are a random few. The play is rich with many more, but, in this chapter it is not my intention to dwell on the poetic richness of the play, but rather to seek

to show that Macbeth himself is endowed by the playwright with the poetic faculty in a respect different from
any other of the great tragic figures. He is himself a
poet, and in strange and often inappropriate moments we
find him leaving the practical point that is uppermost
and running off into a poetic construction of things
which, so far as the actualities of the play are concerned,
is of no profit.

The usual conception of Macbeth's nature—fierce,
ruthless, cruel, "brave Macbeth" (I, ii, 16), "his bran-
dished steel which smok'd with bloody execution" (17-
18), "Bellona's bridegroom" (54), "devilish Macbeth"
(IV, iii, 117), "this dead butcher" (V, viii, 69)—is well
marked in the play. What our imagination bodies forth
for him is a burly figure, powerful in movement, fierce
and ruthless in countenance. This is, no doubt, part of
Shakspere's conception too. But Macbeth is not left as
simple as that. All this fierceness and dauntlessness is
crossed with a strange admixture of tenderness. His address to his wife is to

> . . . my dearest partner of greatness.
>
> I, v, 11-12

And his regret at the end of the play is deep because his
course of life has cancelled out friendship and honor:

> My way of life
> Is fall'n into the sere, the yellow leaf;
> And that which should accompany old age,
> As honour, love, obedience, troops of friends,
> I must not look to have.
>
> V, iii, 22-26

Stranger still, this man's nature is not without a strain
of the poetic. It will be our business in this chapter to

examine seven passages in which this vein of poetry manifests itself.[1]

I

In the famous dagger scene (II, i), Macbeth sets the
stage for the sounding of the signal bell that is to send
him out to his first dreadful deed.

> Go bid thy mistress when my drink is ready;
> She strike upon the bell. Get thee to bed.
>
> II, i, 31-32

And through a long silence we watch Macbeth by posture and management of face begin the registering of a
growing horror until utterance breaks through and he
is confronted by the gory dagger and the overwhelming
sense of "the bloody business which informs thus to
mine eyes" (48-49). Then there must come another
pause—a long pause—as prelude to a passage which is
almost pure poetry and is not an essential part of the play
just as surely as it is most revealing of the inner nature
of the hero.

Let us direct Macbeth's action for a moment at this

[1] The idea that Macbeth is a poet is not a new one. Professor
Bradley says he does not know who first stated it. His own statement is in keeping with his characteristically fine insight: "There is
in Macbeth one marked peculiarity, the true apprehension of which
is the key to Shakspere's conception. This bold ambitious man of
action has, within certain limits, the imagination of a poet,—an
imagination on the one hand extremely sensitive to impressions of
a certain kind, and on the other, productive of violent disturbance
both of mind and body. . . . Macbeth's better nature—to put the
matter for clearness' sake too broadly—instead of speaking to him
in the overt language of moral ideas, commands, and prohibitions,
incorporates itself in images which alarm and horrify. His imagination is thus the best of him, something usually deeper and higher
than his conscious thoughts; and if he had obeyed it he would have
been safe. But his wife quite misunderstands it, and he himself understands it only in part." *Shakespearean Tragedy*, 352.

point.   After he is through with the business of the dagger, having dealt with it at the center of the stage, he stops
as if waiting, and slowly moves to a window at the side
and looks out into the night, beginning slowly and almost lyrically in an altogether different tone from what
has gone before:

> Now o'er the one half-world
> Nature seems dead, and wicked dreams abuse
> The curtain'd sleep.   Now witchcraft celebrates
> Pale Hecate's offerings; and wither'd murther,
> Alarum'd by his sentinel, the wolf,
> Whose howl's his watch, thus with his stealthy pace,
> With Tarquin's ravishing strides, towards his design
> Moves like a ghost.
>
> II, i, 49-56

This is the way to do it, for what is this speech but
a poetic upthrust of an aspect of the man which, if he
were only Bellona's bridegroom and nothing more, he
would not possess?   It is, in a sense, a poetic aside in which
Macbeth indulges himself, for with the next words he is
back on the path of his deed:

> Thou sure and firm-set earth
> Hear not my steps which way they walk, . . .
> 56-57

Recall that it is also at night, and also just before the
enacting of another dreadful deed, that Brutus found time
to comment on the state of a man's mind in such an interim:

> Between the acting of a dreadful thing
> And the first motion, all the interim is
> Like a phantasma or a hideous dream.
> The genius and the mortal instruments
> Are then in council, and the state of man,
> Like to a little kingdom, suffers then
> The nature of an insurrection.
>
> *Caesar*, II, i, 63-69

It would be an interesting—perhaps a profitable study to observe other tragic heroes in similar moments, but, for the present it is pertinent to remark that Macbeth uses this interval for the making of poetry. The imagery of the passage is most provocative: "wither'd murther" (52), "the wolf, whose howl's his watch" (53), "with his stealthy pace" (54), "with Tarquin's ravishing strides" (55). Note especially the vicious concord to which the mind is driven in taking *stealthy* and *ravishing* as functioning in the same essential image. And there is one more great image: "towards his design, moves like a ghost" (56). Every feature of this image—grammatical inversion, slow open vowels, word suggestion—goes to the making of one of the most effective lines in any poetry. Just outside the passage—but would not the poetic generator still be capable of a spark or two?—"The bell invites me" (62). What a world of bitterest tragic irony in the verb! "*Invites* me."

II

When Macbeth comes down to his waiting wife, saying, "I have done the deed" (II, ii, 15), he encounters a fact of experience which is common in the psychology of criminals, especially of criminals who have sensitive natures. It is the realization that events following upon the acting of the deed come with strange unexpectedness and with an emphasis not foreseen.

There were the bloody hands: "This is a sorry sight" (II, ii, 21). And the strange noises: "Didst thou not hear a noise?" (15). Then there is the terrible sense of moral commitment as he reflects on his inability to pronounce *amen* to the wakened attendants' prayer. Then before we realize it Macbeth is off in pursuit of a poetic lure:

> Methought I heard a voice cry 'Sleep no more!' (35)

We shall take up the entire speech in just a moment, but before we come to it, observe that it is a cluster of conceits on sleep such as were rife in the lyric practice of the Renaissance.

From Sir Thomas Wyatt's lyric, based on Petrarch's *In vita,* cxcviii, an oxymoronic little exercise called "The Lover to his Bed," come phrases which have the same essential slant of meaning as some of Shakspere's (or Macbeth's).

The Lover to his Bed

> The restful place, renewer of my smart,
> The labor's salve, increasing my sorrow,
> *Sore labour's bath*[2]
> The body's ease, and troubler of my heart,
> Quieter of mind, mine unquiet foe,
> *Balm of hurt minds*
> Forgetter of pain, rememb'rer of my woe,
> The place of sleep wherein I do but wake,—
> Besprent with tears, my bed, I thee forsake.[3]

Also the famous passage of Sidney's Sonnet XXXIX of *Astrophel and Stella:*

> Come sleep! O sleep, the certain knot of peace,
> *Sleep that knits up the ravell'd sleave of care*
> The baiting place of wit, the balm of woe,
> *Chief nourisher in life's feast   balm of hurt minds*
> The poor man's wealth, the prisoner's release,
> Th' indifferent judge between the high and low.[4]

Again, from Barthlomew Griffin's *Fidessa:*

[2] The italicized phrases inserted between the lines of these passages are phrases from Macbeth's sleep poem which carry the same general image-making approach as the phrase just above it in the lyric.

[3] J. W. Hebel and H. H. Hudson, *Poetry of the English Renaissance, 1509-1660,* 17.

[4] Hebel and Hudson, 112.

Care-charmer sleep, sweet ease in restless misery,
The captive's liberty, and his freedom's song,
Balm of the bruised heart, man's chief felicity,
Balm of hurt minds
Brother of quiet death, when life is too, too long![5]

And Daniel's well-known lines from *Delia:*

Care-charmer sleep, son of the sable night,
Brother to death, in silent darkness born,
Relieve my languish and restore the light;
With dark forgetting of my care return.[6]

And there are more, including the lovely bit of slumber music in John Fletcher's song in *Valentinian* (1619), beginning also "Care-charming sleep."[7] Of course, it is not necessary to argue that Shakspere knew all of these or any of them or any specific others. It is only necessary to accept the viewpoint that he was alive and alert and acquisitive of all experience in the generation when conceits on sleep and a thousand other matters grew on every bush and not alone in Arden. So Macbeth, anticipating the renaissance practioners of the lyric and the sonnet, goes conceit gathering:

Methought I heard a voice cry 'Sleep no more!
Macbeth does murther sleep.'—the innocent sleep,
Sleep that knits up the ravell'd sleave of care,
The death of each day's life, sore nature's bath,
Balm of hurt minds, great nature's second course,
Chief nourisher in life's feast.
Lady.   What do you mean?
Mach. Still it cried 'Sleep no more!' to all the house;
'Glamis hath murther'd sleep, and therefore Cawdor
Shall sleep no more! Macbeth shall sleep no more!'
Lady. Who was it that thus cried? Why, worthy thane,
You do unbend your noble strength to think
So brainsickly of things.
                                        II, ii, 35-46

[5] Hebel and Hudson, 224.   [6] *Ibid.,* 246.   [7] *Ibid.,* 396.

In this remarkable speech there are two principal matters of note: (1) At two points, the other person on the
stage, the Lady, who is keyed to intense participation in
the deed but whose role just now calls on her to be literal,
practical, undaunted, says first, "What do you mean?"
and second, calls his behavior thinking "so brainsickly
of things." Both remarks, but particularly the first, show
that she identifies this for what it is: poetry, and, as such,
stuff which has no bearing, no good use—stuff calculated
only to divert and confuse the speaker and involve him
in a mesh of emotional musings from which no action
can come. She, we may be sure, is as disturbed as he,
but she is not going to let him know it, nor even just
now admit it to herself. He unloads a heap of conceits
on sleep most eloquently and emptily, and, "What do
you mean?" she says with a flatness of tone that is a challenge to an actress's understanding and elocution.

She also says that to talk so is to "think so brainsickly
of things." This means that she knows him of old and
fears his nature as "too full o' th' milk of human kindness." Indeed, months later, when at the Banquet the
sight of Banquo's ghost unnerves Macbeth and he becomes distraught, the Lady's explanatory, "My lord is
often thus, and hath been from his youth" (III, iv, 52-53),
and "Think of this, good peers, but as a thing of custom"
(97-98), is her quick building of a structure of explanation on what too often had seemed to her a habit of
thinking brainsickly of things, a habit which we are
taking the liberty of calling *poetizing*.

(2) The other point is a further exploring of her
question, which is also ours: what *does* he mean? *Did*
he hear a voice that cried, "Sleep no more"? There is
no doubt that he heard the drowsy attendants, one saying, "God bless us!" and the other, "Amen!" and there

is no doubt that in trying to say *amen* he experienced a
sense of spiritual frustration, but he really did not hear
any voice that said, "Sleep no more!" That is the first
projection of creative fancy. Having just experienced
the shock of finding himself shut off from an act of grace,
his associative process flashes on to the thought of the
guilty soul unable to sleep, and out of this association
the poet begins to build his fancy. Even if a voice did
say, "Sleep no more!" (which it did not, certainly not
to all the house), and even if it did not say the rest of
the beautiful but futile lines, that is the poet's own
creative projection of a sudden feeling of the effects of
guilt. When the Lady says, "What do you mean?" he
pays her no heed but plunges on full tide to develop
his fancy into a torrent of mounting climax:

> Still it cried, 'Sleep no more!' to all the house;
> 'Glamis hath murther'd sleep, and therefore Cawdor
> Shall sleep no more! Macbeth shall sleep no more!'

III

At the end of the same scene, Lady Macbeth is above
stairs returning the daggers to their place and gilding the
faces of the grooms with signs of guilt. A knocking begins at the South Entry, and Macbeth, bloody-handed
as he is, reacting with horror to the unforeseen necessity
of opening to the knockers, indulges another swift flight
of poetry. Again it is the passage from one set of ideas
to another by processes of association—from the idea of
a sense of guilt to that of a stain that will not wash away.
Bloody hands! And water: how much water?

> Will all great Neptune's ocean wash this blood
> Clean from my hand? No. This my hand will rather
> The multitudinous seas incarnadine,
> Making the green one red.

60-63

Amid all the monosyllables of the first, second, and fourth lines, the strong polysyllabic beat of line three:

The multitudinous seas incarnadine,

is like the very roll and surge of all great Neptune's ocean.

It is hyperbole to think of one's guilt in terms of such magnitude, but hyperbole is one of the devices of the poet and, moreover, this is a great guilt and there *is* much blood, now and to come.

IV

In the three passages we have dealt with, the poetic function shows itself as a part of the poet's nature. He is a poet, and so makes poetry naturally and, shall we say, unconsciously; that is without intending to. But, in the passage to which we now turn, it seems clear that Macbeth is consciously invoking this faculty to serve the purposes of deception. He has been told, "Only look up clear, to alter favour ever is to fear" (I, v, 73). His Lady counsels him:

> To beguile the time
> Look like the time; bear welcome in your eye,
> Your hand, your tongue; look like the innocent flower
> But be the serpent under 't.
>
> I, v, 64-67

Once, at least, he has caught this idea for himself and voices it:

> I am settled . . . .
> Away, and mock the time with fairest show;
> False face must hide what the false heart doth know.
>
> I, vii, 79-82

The passage to which we now come is a part of his attempt to put false face upon false heart. The knocking of the preceding scene led to the opening of the gate and to the entrance of men in service of the King; one asks:

> *Len.* Goes the King hence today?
> *Macb.*   He does; he did appoint so.
>
> II, iii, 58

and, after a moment, Macduff, who has gone up to the King's chamber, rushes down with the terrible news: "Our royal master's murther'd!" (92). After this there is dashing about and confusion, Macbeth and Lennox go up to see—Macbeth to see what half an hour before he had declared:

> I am afraid to think what I have done;
> Look on't again I dare not.
>
> II, ii, 51-52

But now he *must* see, and as he sees dead Duncan again, he finds he can make poetry upon him. So, coming down into the midst of the others who are talking practicalities, Macbeth launches into poetry:

> Had I but died an hour before this chance,
> I had liv'd a blessed time; for from this instant
> There's nothing serious in mortality;
> All is but toys; renown and grace is dead;
> The wine of life is drawn, and the mere lees
> Is left this vault to brag of.
>
> II, iii, 96-101

Then it develops that Macbeth, coming upon the drugged and sleeping grooms in Duncan's chamber, had killed them.

> *Macb.* O yet I do repent me of my fury
> That I did kill them.
> *Macd.*   Wherefore did you so?
> *Macb.* Who can be wise, amaz'd, temp'rate and furious,
> Loyal and neutral, in a moment? No man.

*   *   *

> Here lay Duncan,
> His silver skin lac'd with his golden blood,

And his gash'd stabs look'd like a breach in nature
For ruin's wasteful entrance; there, the murtherers,
Steep'd in the colours of their trade, their daggers
Unmannerly breech'd with gore. Who could refrain
That had a heart to love and in that heart
Courage to make 's love known?

111-124 [8]

It is at this juncture that Lady Macbeth swoons, whether to put a period to what might have become the too profuse strains of her husband's poetry or whether in genuine distress. At any rate the poetry is stopped, perhaps the more that we who read may see how patently Macbeth has been drawing, for purposes of deception, upon the springs of his creative power, now, at last, attempting some practical use for his poetic faculty.

V

The wise stricture about the odiousness of comparisons has been admired and unheeded for so long that one is perhaps pardoned for suggesting that *Macbeth*, III, ii is one of the rarer gems in the jewel box of Shaksperean scenes. It is tense, full of omen, full of poetry. And much of the poetry is Macbeth's, that is, of his own making. Note to begin with, the tremendous irony of:

Better be with the dead,
Whom we to gain our peace, have sent to peace,
Than on the torture of the mind to lie
In restless ecstasy.

III, ii, 19-22

And then this quiet somber music:

[8] This is Macbeth's poetic development of what he had held too terrible to think on; impossible to see.

Duncan is in his grave;
After life's fitful fever he sleeps well.
Treason has done his worst. Nor steel nor poison,
Malice domestic, foreign levy, nothing
Can touch him further.

                                                    22-26

But in pausing beside the foregoing passages we have
run dangerously near to doing for Macbeth what we
might equally well do for almost any of the great persons of Shakspere, *i. e.*, merely cite lines that are fine poetry, without asking whether it is Shakspere or whether
it comes out of the sort of faculty we are claiming for
Macbeth, that of having a poetic manner of thought and
expression. Yet Macbeth is so characteristically the poet
that perhaps we shall be pardoned for thinking that even
these passages belong, in a way, to him. At any rate, there
is material enough in the rest of the scene which is in
the beaten path of his habit of poetizing. It is strongest
in his veiled and riddling report of the deed that's to be
done. As in the passage following the dagger speech,
here again he looks out to see the aspects of nature, knowing that at this hour down a gloomy, lonely road Banquo
and Fleance come riding. Evening is coming on; darkness closes in:

Ere the bat hath flown
His cloister'd flight, ere to black Hecate's summons
The shard-borne beetle with his drowsy hums
Hath rung night's yawning peal, there shall be done
A deed of dreadful note.
Lady.   What's to be done?
Macb.   Be innocent of the knowledge, dearest chuck,
Till thou applaud the deed. Come, seeling night,
Scarf up the tender eye of pitiful day,
And with thy bloody and invisible hand
Cancel and tear to pieces that great bond

Which keeps me pale! Light thickens, and the crow
Makes wing to th' rooky wood.
Good things of day begin to droop and drowse,
Whiles night's black agents to their preys do rouse.

40-53

The entire passage is intensely poetical. It is a fabric
built first, perhaps, on the conceit that day is good: "The
tender eye of pitiful day," "good things of day"; and
that night is evil: "night . . . with thy bloody and invisible hand," "night's black agents." But there is also
preoccupation with the aural phenomena of twilight:
"the shard-borne beetle with his drowsy hums," and "the
crow makes wing to th' rooky wood," and with the ocu-
lar phenomena as well: "Light thickens." Consider this
aspect of description: *what was light is becoming less
light by the intermixture of darkness;* "light thickens."
In another poem which must rank somewhere near *Macbeth* among the great poems of our tradition, Chaucer's
Troilus and Criseyde, is a passage which treats the same
phenomenon with an equal keenness of poetic insight:

The sonne—
Gan westren faste, and downward for to wrye,
As he that hadde his dayes cours yronne;
And white thynges wexen dymme and donne
For lak of lyght.

II, 905-909 [9]

One poet has the impression of thickening light; the
other finds his attention caught by what twilight is doing
to the appearance of things which were white in daylight
but are now growing "dymme and donne." Both passages are far above the ordinary in their validity as poetry;
one is by Chaucer, the other by Macbeth, for this, like
other passages we have cited, is of the stuff of Macbeth's

[9] F. N. Robinson, *The Complete Works of Geoffrey Chaucer,* 480.

mind and of his strange poetic tendency. There is in his thought, as he looks out into the thickening twilight, the drawing on to its enactment of a deed of dreadful note—and it is a fast-descending night—and the fusion of the two in the poet's mind makes a drear and dreadful succession of images of darkness and evil. It is not of the plot of the play. It is atmospheric and, even then, more atmospheric of the King's mind and spirit than of anything else.

Professor Bradley has summed up the impression of darkness as the element that "broods over this tragedy," and that, as he demonstrates, is easily established. A statement from his pen which falls in with our present emphasis on Macbeth's poetic bent will serve as a conclusion to our dealing with this passage. "The blackness of night is to the hero a thing of fear, even of horror; and *that which he feels* becomes the spirit of the play" (Italics mine).[10]

VI

Shakspere makes tremendous dramatic capital out of Macbeth's state of mind as, with the play drawing inexorably to its conclusion, the forces of retribution and the legions of hate crowd in upon him. The ending of *Richard III* offers a most interesting parallel, for there is the same nervous, irritable response to trifles, the same unreasonable impatience with the messengers of ill news, the same fundamental dauntlessness, which leaves these two almost the only ones of Shakspere's great folk who, in the clutches of disaster, do not consider suicide. And both die fiercely with harness on their backs. But while Richard is given a fine share of highly poetic lines, they do not come from any poetic faculty in him, but from

[10] A. C. Bradley, *Shakesperean Tragedy*, 333.

Shakspere. Richard sends word to Stanley in a terribly ominous phrase:

> Bid him bring his power
> Before sunrising, lest his son George fall
> Into the blind cave of eternal night.
>
> R III, V, iii, 60-62

And his self-confession of the sense of crisis is in unforgettable language:

> Give me a bowl of wine.
> I have not that alacrity of spirit
> Nor cheer of mind that I was wont to have.
>
> 72-74

But Shakspere is the artist here, not Richard. Richard does not lapse habitually into poetry.

But Macbeth's utterances in a similar crisis reach deeper and come not only out of his sense of doom but come in the idiom of his life-long bent for the poetic. Messengers have reported to him the coming of the English forces, ten thousand of them, and he calls impatiently for his lieutenant: "Seyton! Seyton, I say!" and while he waits, these lines come seething up from the depths of his sensitive being, clothed in the vestments of the highest poetry:

> This push
> Will cheer me ever or disseat me now.
> I have liv'd long enough. My way of life
> Is fall'n into the sere, the yellow leaf;
> And that which should accompany old age,
> As honour, love, obedience, troops of friends,
> I must not look to have; but, in their stead,
> Curses not loud but deep, mouth-honour, breath,
> Which the poor heart would fain deny, and dare not.
>
> V, iii, 19-28

We are almost at the end of the play, but there is yet to come the great soliloquy on the emptiness of life, which, no doubt, most lovers of Shakspere's fine things set at the top of the poetic passages in this tragedy. It is a magnificent passage, but I have long felt that the passage just cited is the most poignantly tragic and deeply personal of Macbeth's utterances.

First there is the image of the sere and yellow leaf, which is pure imagery and makes comment futile. Then there is the terrible realization that beneath all the huzza's and long-live-the-King's there is no love. Age looks forward to the enjoyment of honor, obedience, troops of friends—these he will never have. There are not only none of these; underneath the fan-fare of acclaim, the giving out of mouth-honor, there are curses, curses not loud but deep. The great actors who I hear read these lines may be saving their lower register of voice for "signifying nothing" at the end of the next great speech, but I have not heard them give what I have thought adequate depth of tragic profundity to "not loud but deep." It is a great nuance of tone.

VII

The words that follow Seyton's announcement, "The Queen, my lord, is dead" (V, v, 16), are most difficult of construction. If Macbeth means by "She should have died hereafter," *What an inappropriate time to die! Why couldn't she have waited till a quieter time?* then the voice must rise to exasperation, and the transition to the rest of the speech is less easy. However, in all fairness, it must be said that exasperation with the messenger (iii, 11-19), with the Doctor (37-56), with the fit of his armor (47, 54, 58), should make us cautious of too quick a rejection of it as the keynote here, but if he meant, *There would have come, and soon, a time for her to die; precisely when*

does not matter; perhaps now is as good a time as any,
then it seems easier to move from such a disillusioned
cast of thought on into the terrible probing of the emptiness and meaninglessness of life which follows. This
seems the more likely construction.

This great poetic analysis of life's futility is a broken
association of five images—four principal images (1, 2, 4,
5), the third a sort of subsidiary of the second:

> *Macb.*   Wherefore was that cry?
> *Sey.* The Queen, my lord, is dead.
> *Macb.* She should have died hereafter;
> There would have been a time for such a word.
> 1 Tomorrow, and tomorrow, and tomorrow
>   Creeps in this petty pace from day to day
>   To the last syllable of recorded time;
> 2 And all our yesterdays have lighted fools
>   The way to dusty death.   3 Out, out, brief candle!
> 4 Life's but a walking shadow, a poor player,
>   That struts and frets his hour upon the stage
>   And then is heard no more.   5 It is a tale
>   Told by an idiot, full of sound and fury,
>   Signifying nothing.
>
>   V, v, 15-28

What we are expected to see in response to the first
image is vague. Indeed, it may well be intended to be
vague. The picture is of a procession of the days, seen so
that the main impression is of creeping, creeping, creeping to the last syllable of recorded time, one tomorrow
as like every other as can be. Two bits from the writings
of much later days come to my mind as of some help in
clarifying this image. One is R. W. Emerson's little poem
"Days," the first four lines of which suggest the pace of
Macbeth's figures:

> Daughters of Time, the hypocritic Days
> Muffled and dumb like barefoot dervishes,

And marching single in an endless file,
Bring diadems and fagots in their hands.

The other passage may seem more remote, but it helps
in that it is much more in accord with the vagueness of the
Macbeth image, which is without form except for the
one tangible suggestion in *creeps*. It is a passage in a stage
direction in Scene II of Eugene O'Neill's the *Emperor
Jones:*

> The Little Formless Fears creep out from the deeper black-
> ness of the forest. They are black, shapeless, only their
> glittering little eyes can be seen. If they have any de-
> scribable form at all it is that of a grubworm about the
> size of a creeping child. They move noiselessly, but with
> deliberate, painful effort, striving to raise themselves on
> end, failing and sinking prone again.

> From the formless creatures on the ground in front of
> him comes a tiny gale of low mocking laughter like a
> rustling of leaves. They squirm upward toward him in
> twisted attitudes.

All I have undertaken to do by bringing in Emerson's
classic Frieze of the Days and O'Neill's symbolic embodi-
ments of vague horrors is to indicate that these help me
to see what it is in Macbeth's image-making faculty that
so insistently and forever *creeps*. For he, who elsewhere
has so vividly realized poetic effects: "wither'd murther
. . . thus with his stealthy strides . . . towards his design
moves like a ghost," "the bell invites me," "Light thickens," "My way of life has fall'n into the sere, the yellow
leaf"—this man sees something, something as real as Emerson's precise ladies, something as vague as Brutus Jones's
little formless fears.

The second image is unmistakable. It is a suggestion
of the Days as torchbearers, each in turn lighting folk
into and down a passage way to a crypt and out of sight—

to be resolved to dust. Two words are particularly strong. The first is bitter: "All our yesterdays have lighted *fools*." That is a cry of complete disillusionment. It is Macbeth's outcry on all who trust the luring torches of life and destiny. It is Macbeth's word. When shall we be done calling this Shakspere's mind on the meaning of life, and take it for what it is, the mind of Macbeth in all the bitterness of retrospective view? "All our yesterdays have lighted *fools*." There is no exception made here nor any grading of the victims; all who expect anything satisfying from life are *fools*. That is a bitter word.[11] And their path leads them straight and sure to *dusty* death. That is the second word, and with all its evocation of associations it is one of the great poetic words of the play. Not *cold* death, nor *rotten* death, nor *worms*—but *dust*. *Dusty* death. Only George Meredith gets such poetic return from this word. As a matter of fact, he almost manages to get both of Macbeth's suggestions: *fools* and *dusty*, into the one word:

> Ah, what a dusty answer gets the soul
> When hot for certainties in this our life.[12]

The third image is a link of association with the fundamental element of light in the preceding one. What one sees in the second image is a torch, and from that the quick associative faculty, which has worked so creatively in other passages, glances on to the suggestion of how short is the period of life and how swiftly it burns to the socket, and in the process it is transmuted from a torch to a candle—a brief candle, so quickly burned out. "Out, out, brief candle!"

[11] Does it remind you of the psalmist's "I said in my haste, All men are liars"? Psa. 116:11.
[12] George Meredith, *Modern Love*, Sonnet L.

The fourth image catches for a moment on the idea in *shadow:*

Life's but a walking shadow—

but swiftly seizes on the essential image of an actor as a trafficker in shadows, and the focus settles on the actor. This image of the actor as a dealer in shadows is a favorite renaissance image. Shakspere's fullest exploitation of it is in the elaborate speech of the professional melancholic, Jaques (*A.Y.L.*, II, vii, 139-167). But passages that come closer to the image here of a strutting actor, fretting and strutting his hour upon the stage may well be Bully Bottom's yearning for a part "to tear a cat in, to make all split" (*Dream*, I, ii, 31-32), or still better the lines against the strutting and fretting of actors in Hamlet's advice to the players:

> O, it offends me to the soul to hear a robustious periwig-pated fellow tear a passion to tatters, to very rags. . . . I would have such a fellow whipp'd for o'erdoing Termagant. It out-herods Herod . . . . O, there be players . . . that, neither having the accent of Christians, nor the gait of Christian, pagan, nor man, have so strutted and bellowed that I have thought some of Nature's journeymen had made men, and not made them well, they imitated humanity so abominably.
>
> *Ham.*, III, ii, 9-39, *passim*

So actors behave. Hamlet says, "I have seen [them] play." But this figure in Macbeth's image is not merely *an* actor; he is Mankind, Everyman, any man who has essayed the stage of existence and made his bid for life's rewards. Viewed from the vantage point of this vast, bitter disillusionment, he appears, a poor petty player strutting and fretting his little hour upon the stage, and then—dusty death; out, out, brief candle—he is heard no more.

The fifth image may well be the bitterest of them all. The effect has been and still is crescendo. The creeping petty pace, the torches of all yesterdays leading the sure way to dusty death, the brief candle, the strutting shadow, and now, bitterest of all, life is a tale told by a gabbling idiot with no beginning, no sequence, no focus, signifying nothing. William Faulkner's terrifying success in transcribing the stream of consciousness of the idiot, Benjy, in *The Sound and the Fury* is an amazing realization of this dreadful image.

I had not intended to be so long upon this passage, but it has lent itself to many suggestions. It is not a passage of great wisdom; it is not beautiful except in the largest sense; but it is a full view of the stripped, barren hopelessness of the King's spirit and it is a powerful demonstration of the image-making faculty of a poet.[13]

As the speech closes, a messenger comes with word that Birnam Wood is in movement toward the castle. At once Macbeth leaps to action:

> Arm, arm, and out!

he shouts.

> If this which he avouches does appear,
> There is nor flying hence nor tarrying here.
> V, v, 46-48

And then suddenly in the midst of this fury of activity come two lines which are not of the tone of their context. They are again personal, private poetry, and of the deepest of somber coloring. They are Macbeth's in his accustomed fashion of the image maker:

[13] Take this passage merely as a cluster of images and set it beside the similarly constructed sleep-image cluster of II, ii, 36-39, and observe the distinction between the conceitfulness of the earlier passage and the desperate seriousness of this. Both are poetry, but of what vastly different power and texture.

I gin to be aweary of the sun,
And wish th' estate o' th' world were now undone.
                                49-50

But that is the last of such poetic brooding, for in an instant he is back in the full passion of desperate attempt:

Ring the alarum bell! Blow wind, come wrack,
At least we'll die with harness on our back!
                                51-52

As I have endeavored to make clear, the great persons of Shakspere's stage speak their minds with great force and with a strong creative use of language. There is poetry in many and many a line, but, in general, they are not poets in the sense that in the midst of the business of their lives they turn aside to let imagination ring its changes on their circumstances. The purpose of this chapter has been to show that in a distinctive and characteristic way Macbeth is the one among them who is a poet, possessed of a creative faculty which even in situations of stress and confusion turns aside to weave fabrics of fantasy and imaginative patterning which are quite apart from the immediate and the tangible. This, as we have said is all the more striking because Macbeth is preeminently a man of action—fierce, cruel, and full of dauntless purpose. To find poetry in such a man is not only strange; it is, from the creative artist's point of view, highly individualizing.

It may, at first, seem more difficult to tie the materials of this chapter to our presiding idea of Shakspere's common sense than has been true for other chapters. But the difficulty is overcome if one reflects that the revelation of Macbeth as a poet is a part of his characterization. Characterization, one must keep in mind, is one of the chief concerns of the dramatic poet. In the process is involved selection of details and the fitting of them into a coherent and vital structure of personality. If the creator of a tragic hero can weave in with other traits of a warrior and king a penchant for poetizing, to which he gives way at inopportune times, and can still keep him an integrated and convincing personality, then we can score a special kind of success for the playwright.

I think we can say the idea of the streak of poetry in Macbeth is solely Shakspere's. There is no faintest hint of such a quality in Holinshed's account. But the possibility of weaving this trait in among the hot, hard attributes which make up the tyrant is borne out by parallels in life. There is always Nero, who, by the best accounts, was a tyrant in the worst sense, but a great lover of the arts. And England in Shakspere's time must have been rife with racy stories of the great King Henry VIII— braggart, boor, graceless tyrant, but with a strange streak of music and poetry in him.

It is the poetry, added to their other traits, which is the definitive and characterizing element in Nero and Henry and Macbeth. It is a sort of uncommon common sense which sees it and takes it up and infuses a great character with it.

CHAPTER VII

SHAKSPERE'S ACTORS: PLAYS WITHIN PLAYS

This chapter and the two which follow deal with some of the Shaksperean passages and scenes in which the business of the stage takes for a time the form of play acting. There are also situations in which an actor is led to assume disguise or a pattern of dissimulation of such scope as to make the quality of his acting of this make-believe an essential point and chief object of attention to the reader or spectator. Three principal types of situation will be noted, the first in this chapter and the other two in the chapters which follow: (1) plays within plays, (2) extempore dramatic skits, and (3) impersonations.

Love's Labour's Lost, A Midsummer Night's Dream, the *Taming of the Shrew,* and *Hamlet* are notable for the presence in them of plays or parts of plays. Those in the *Shrew* and *Hamlet* are by professionals; the plays in the two comedies are done by amateurs.

The Play of the Nine Worthies

In *Love's Labour's Lost* the King and his three noble young companions are caught in the net of a silly vow not to woo ladies. At the same time they are caught ironically in a mesh of love for four noble ladies thrown unexpectedly in their way. They must find some device whereby they can woo the ladies and yet save face in the matter of their vow.

The laying of their plan comes after they have caught one another preparing love odes for their respective mistresses. There is some hearty horseplay particularly at the expense of Berowne, who having been the loudest protester against the compact, is so much the more loudly jeered at for having secretly broken it. Now that they are reconciled, the question of procedure comes:

> *Long.* Shall we resolve to woo these girls of France?
> *King.* And win them too! Therefore let us devise
> Some entertainment for them in their tents.
>
> *   *   *
>
> *Ber.*   In the afternoon
> We will with some strange pastime solace them,
> Such as the shortness of the time can shape,
> For revels, dances, masques, and merry hours
> Forerun fair Love, strewing her way with flowers.
>
> IV, iii, 370-380

Well, as we know, their decision to guise themselves as Russians suffered most ignominious disaster. The device is that Moth, who has proved such a capable and quick little chap both of word and wit, is set forward as nuncio and spokesman for the Russians. But he is completely cast down and discomfited by the merciless heckling of Boyet and by the unexpected rude behavior of the ladies in turning their pretty and expressive faces away from the speaker to show him only their pretty backs. But the discomfited Russians are not so easily put down. They have yet a string to their bow. They have bespoken another entertainment item. If we may take Don Armado's word for it, the King has asked him to devise some form of amusement. He is in converse with the pedant Holofernes:

> [T]he King would have me present the Princess (sweet chuck) with some delightful ostentation, or show, or pag-

eant, or antic, or firework. Now, understanding that
the curate and your sweet self are good at such eruptions
and sudden breaking-out of mirth, as it were, I have ac-
quainted you withal, to the end to crave your assistance.

V, i, 116-123

Holofernes is quickly ready with a proposal: "Sir, you
shall present before her the Nine Worthies" (124).

Obviously it is an offering most congenial to the refined classical tastes of the schoolmaster, who has just
shown himself so deep-stored in learning at the great
feast of languages, which, scraps and all, had so delighted
Moth's ironic sense (V, i, 39-40). Also this quick selection is testimony to the familiarity of the piece. The catalog of the Worthies was as well established as that of
the Seven Wonders of the Ancient World or of the
Seven Deadly Sins of the Medieval Church. Everyone
had seen the procession of the Worthies. The form of
the play which Holofernes has in mind is probably that
called a speech play of the sort reproduced by Joseph
Ritson in his *Remarks Critical and Illustrative* (1783)
from a text of the time of Edward IV. A partial citation
will serve to indicate the type:

Ector de Troy:	Thow achylles in bataly me slow
	Of my wurthynes men speken I now.
Alisander:	And in romaunces often am I leyt
	As conquerour gret thow I seyt.
Josue:	In holy Chyrche ze mowen here & rede
	Of my wurthynes and of my dede.
Charles:	With me dwellyd rouland olyvere
	In all my Conquest fer and nere.[1]

Very quickly the Pedant casts the play. Four of the
parts are assigned, although it is not definitely sure which
gentleman, Holofernes himself or Don Armado, will

[1] In Furness, *Variorum Shakespeare*, "Love's Labour's Lost," 283.

play Judas Maccabeus. When the question arises as to
who will do the other Worthies, Holofernes with characteristic modesty, says, "I will play three myself." Observe, therefore, that according to their first hasty casting, Sir Nathaniel will represent Joshua, Costard will
play Pompey, either Holofernes or Don Armado will
be Judas Maccabeus and the page, Moth, will be Hercules. Three other parts are all for Holofernes, but even
so, two parts are unaccounted for. When in V, ii, 535,
the procession of the Worthies appears to act before the
Princess, there seem to be five parts assigned: Costard
and Moth, as before, are to be Pompey and Hercules,
but now Don Armado is Hector, Sir Nathaniel (who was
to be Joshua), is now Alexander, and Holofernes has
settled on Judas Maccabeus for himself. Though here
are clearly five, the King and Berowne engage in a silly
sort of quibble about the number; Berowne counts five;
the King insists there are only four. But Berowne's list
of clipped names seems to confirm five as the number of
parts:

> The pedant, the braggart, the hedge-priest, the fool, and
> the boy.
>
> 546

As the King suggests, the plan apparently is for some
doubling of roles:

> And if these four Worthies in their first show thrive,
> These four will change habits and present the other five.
>
> 541-542

There are a number of points of interest about this
casting of the Worthies. First of all there are the interesting shifts between the first list and the second.
This probably means nothing more profound than that
there is many a slip between rehearsal and presentation.

The same sort of disparity appears in the play in *A Mid-summer Night's Dream.* Also there is the forthright way in which Shakspere and Holofernes take liberties with the catalog of the Worthies. Pompey and Hercules are not regular members of the fraternity. Caesar and David, fixtures in the standard list, are not mentioned, and none of the Medievals—Arthur, Charles, Geoffrey—is mentioned. Pompey may have been brought in so Costard can perpetrate his vulgarism:

> I Pompey am, Pompey surnam'd the Big.
>
> V, ii, 553

Poor Costard is, on the whole, satisfied with himself, but he has a little compunction for this mistake. The Princess calls to him:

> *Prin.* Great thanks, great Pompey.
> *Cost.* 'Tis not so much worth. But I hope I was perfect. I made a little fault in 'Great.'
>
> 560-562

The spectators are still playing riotously with this "little fault" many minutes later after he has done his part in the discomfiture of Don Armado. They shout their approbation:

> *Dum.* Most rare Pompey!
> *Boyet.* Renowned Pompey!
> *Ber.* Greater than Great! Great, great, great Pompey! Pompey the Huge!
>
> 688-692[2]

[2] This, of course, could have been done for Alexander with no disturbance to the established list, but Alexander is for another actor and there are limits even to Holofernes' decorum. Costard would never do for "the world's commander." The association of the epithet, "Great" with Alexander is not prominent in the romances of the Middle Ages. Most often he is "King Alexander" or just "Alexander" as in the Scottish *Alexander Buik.* But Shakspere will play on Alexander's title too in Fluellen's "Alexander the Pig." *H V,* IV, vii, 14-19.

The drawing in of Hercules to be a Worthy is another concession to the possibilities of comedy. Moth must be cast. Which Worthy can this microscopic imp be? And then comes the swift inspiration to make him Hercules—great, towering, muscle-bound Hercules—what a laugh! But stay; we have more here than irony. We are to be treated to a display of cleverness. Casting quickly, Holofernes races on to the end of his list:

> . . . the page, Hercules—
> *Arm.* Pardon, sir; error! He is not quantity enough for that Worthy's thumb; he is not so big as the end of his club.
> *Hol.* Shall I have audience? He shall present Hercules in minority. His enter and exit shall be strangling a snake . . . .
> *Moth.* An excellent device! So, if any of the audience hiss, you may cry, 'Well done, Hercules! Now thou crushest the snake!'
>
> V, i, 135-146

So we have, I think, adequate *raison d' etre* for Pompey (the Big) and for Hercules (minor). Although two of the great Worthies of the standard list must step aside to make room for these two, the exchange in terms of comedy values seems more than even. If this liberty taken with the long-established list seems wanton, and if these playful reasons for bringing in two brand-new worthies seem light, we shall have to make the best of it. One would expect Holofernes, the great classicist, to be offended, but he who stays long in the company of Shakspere will not expect *him* to be offended. Two good laughs are worth the slight damage that has been done to tradition.

As you would expect, the Worthies acquit themselves awkwardly as actors. They are easily befuddled by hecklers. They are raw amateurs and so are unable to shake

off the feeling of being close to the audience. Costard
(Pompey) asks the Princess to help him with his concluding effect:

> If your ladyship would say 'Thanks, Pompey,' I had done.
> ii, 559

In the midst of the heckling of Alexander (Sir Nathaniel), Berowne suddenly calls out for

> Pompey the Great!
> *Cost.* Your servant, and Costard,
> 574-575

the heavy dolt answers, never having been really anything but Costard even though trying hard to be also
Pompey.

Don Armado presents a considerable target to the
hecklers, and he is easily thrown off from his role. Claiming great virtues for himself as Hector, he plows on:

> *Arm.* I am that flower—
> *Dum.*   That mint.
> *Long.*   That columbine.
> 661-662

And that turns Hector aside:

> Sweet Lord Longaville, rein thy tongue.

When the Princess shows special interest in Hector and
his speech, he slips out of his script to smirk upon his
fair auditor:[3]

> *Arm.* Sweet royalty, bestow on me the sense of hearing.
> *Prin.* Speak, brave Hector. We are much delighted.
> *Arm.* I do adore thy sweet Grace's slipper.
> 670-672

---

[3] Only the silly smiling and grotesque posturing of Malvolio before
his mistress, after the letter picked up in the garden walk has made
a contemplative idiot of him, can match this in quality and surpass
it in quantity.

What a refreshing conception this Princess is and how gracious of the young playwright to give us a French Princess with her sweet gifts of tolerance and humorous sense. Hippolyta in *A Midsummer Night's Dream* is a very stick beside her.

What follows is out of our part in discussing the acting and actors in this interlude, but it is, for the total play, one of its most hilarious moments. Berowne has coached Costard to catch Don Armado at a peak point of rhetoric and great gesture and suddenly to confront him with our girl Jaquenetta, who has been done wrong by Great Hector. The moment comes and Costard—more eloquent than has been prepared for by any precedent conduct—breaks in, and the Play of the Nine Worthies is broken up. Armado's first stunned reaction calls forth one of his best lines, for it shows how completely his character is given over to bombast. He may augment his role of boaster and braggart by studied effort, but strip him down to his essential self and you still have a boaster and a braggart. Costard flings the accusation in his face, and he roars back, still keeping his braggart's style:

> Dost thou infamonize me among potentates?
>
> 685

Surely this is his best line!

The old unending war between the actors and the hecklers is another matter of note. One of the recourses of the playwright was to overcome the wit of the fops and groundlings by coming back at them with a better crack than any of theirs. Still another was to turn some crudity of theirs to good quick use for the purposes of the play. So it will be handled if anyone hisses; someone in the cast is to cry out:

> Well done, Hercules! Now thou crushest the snake!

That, Moth says, "is the way to make an offence gracious, though few have the grace to do it" (V, i, 144-148). My regret is that this is not allowed to come off in actual presentation. Would such high-ranking hecklers as Boyet and Berowne have been silenced thereby?

It is noticeable that in the heckling episodes in these plays, the hecklers almost always overwhelm the actors and drive them into panic. It is to be hoped that that happened oftener in these plays within plays than it did in the theater. As it is played, it is a demonstration of superior cleverness on the part of the stage audience, and the theater audience may take indirect credit to itself from that. Moreover, the actors in these interludes are the rawest of amateurs; tough practiced professionals will be better able to take care of themselves. One would think twice before undertaking to heckle Alleyn or Kemp.

No one, not even Holofernes ("Allons! we will employ thee" [V, i, 158]), thinks of casting Goodman Dull for a Worthy. But he offers himself as music maker for the show. His idea of the dance for the Worthies may not go quite well with decorum, but it is no worse than Bottom the Weaver's "tongs and bones" (*Dream*, IV, i, 31), and it is offered with the best of helpful intentions.

> I'll make one in a dance or so; or I will play
> On the tabor to the Worthies, and let them dance the hay.
> V, i, 160-161

The more I study *Love's Labour's Lost*, the more convinced I become of how thoroughly delightful and full of mirth it is. The fine spirit of gaiety that pervades the play comes from such sane and quick and deviceful persons as Berowne and Rosaline, Moth and Boyet, and the French Princess, but much also must be credited to

the earnest clumsiness and honest ineptitude of the Play
of the Nine Worthies, one of the most hilarious pieces
of horseplay in all the world.

The Most Lamentable Comedy and Most Cruel Death of Pyramus and Thisby

The play of the Nine Worthies is a command performance, but the Lamentable Comedy of Pyramus and Thisby in *A Midsummer Night's Dream* is offered by the
actors as an item on a list of available entertainment features being compiled in the notebook of Philostrate,
Master of the Revels in Duke Theseus' household. For
some days, the yokels, who are to do this play, have been
rehearsing it. On a day, by a strange, wry circumstance,
their leading actor has become unavailable. The report
is that he has undergone a mysterious transformation and
has disappeared. Without him they cannot go on, but
there is still a desperate hope that he will return, and in
his own proper person, and that their play may be preferred. Then Bottom reappears, and from some source
of information unknown to his fellows, he has the magic
word:

> . . . [O]ur play is preferr'd.
>
> IV, ii, 39

On Philostrate's list it is item number four. But Theseus
quickly rejects "The Battle of the Centaurs" as being
a story he has already told his lady. "The Riot of the
Bacchanals" is too old, and the "Thrice Three Muses
Mourning for the Death of Learning" is too critical and
satirical for the hymeneal mood. And that brings us to

> A tedious brief scene of young Pyramus
> And his love Thisby; very tragical mirth.
> V, i, 56-57

Theseus is reading from Philostrate's list of "how many sports are ripe," and his eye is caught by the oxymoron in the description:

> Merry and tragical? tedious and brief?
> That is hot ice and wondrous strange snow.
> How shall we find the concord of this discord?
>
> 58-60

So, mainly because of this strange contradiction in the title, our play is preferred. It is only fair to say that in preferring it, Theseus says a few of the most democratic words in Shakspere:

> I will hear that play;
> For never anything can be amiss
> When simpleness and duty tender it.
>
> 81-83

Hippolyta, lovely humorless Amazon, can see no point in choosing a play the very advance notices of which say it is not good. She protests:

> He says they can do nothing in this kind.
>
> 88

But Theseus overrides her objections, and already the Prologue is at the door.

But we are getting ahead of our story. The proper place to begin is at Peter Quince's house in Athens a few nights earlier. The whole community is agog with preparations for the great Duke's wedding. There will be revels, and many plans are afoot to provide items for the program at the Palace. Our attention is called to a group of craftsmen (all non-victualers, if the old medieval classification of tradesmen still means anything), who are together to prepare a play. Six make up the company. The titular head of the enterprise is Peter Quince, a carpenter, who can read and write. Perhaps all the others

can read; Snug, the joiner can. But likely only Quince
can write. But the dynamic personal force in the company is a weaver named Bottom, who has a fine conceit
of himself and of his wit and devicefulness. And his fellows defer to him and to his opinions: (Note: Bottom
is not present during the following exchange of speeches).

> *Quince.* Have you sent to Bottom's house? Is he come
> home yet?
> *Starv.* He cannot be heard of. Out of doubt he is trans-
> ported.
> *Flute.* If he come not, then is the play marr'd; it goes
> not forward, doth it?
> *Quince.* It is not possible. You have not a man in all
> Athens able to discharge Pyramus but he.
> *Flute.* No, he hath simply the best wit of any handicraft
> man in Athens.
> *Quince.* Yea, and the best person too, and he is a very
> paramour for a sweet voice.
>
> IV, ii, 1-12

So the sheep languish, and then, in an electric moment,
Bottom reappears and they are galvanized into joyous
activity. But we are being turned away from our study
of actors and acting. And such is our danger in this unfolding study, for Shakspere is developing so quickly
into a consummate creator of character, that the personality of Bottom becomes more interesting than the acting
skills of Bottom. An absorption in the vagaries of character which threatened us as we dealt with Costard and
Dull and Don Armado, unless we are aware, will overwhelm us here.

Peter Quince has already cast the play. The names of
the characters mean nothing to Bottom and the others,
for they do not know the play. But they do know the
character types. "What is Pyramus," Bottom inquires,
"a lover or a tyrant?" and Flute inquires, "What is

Thisby? A wandering knight?" Bottom regrets that
Pyramus is not a tryant, for that role suggests Terma-
gant and Herod:

> A part to tear a cat in, to make all split.
>
> I, ii, 32

But he also knows what belongs to a lover:

> That will ask some tears in the true performing of it.
> If I do it, let the audience look to their eyes! I will move
> storms; I will condole in some measure.
>
> 27-30

There is, also, the usual reference to the difficult task
—held difficult even by a generation which had no experience of any other way to do it—of casting a male for
a female role. Flute's incipient beard is a problem, but
a mask is the solution. The voice may have to be simulated if Flute's own proper voice be cracked already
within the ring. It can, in a case of need, be done in a
monstrous little voice: "Thisne, Thisne!" (54-55).

The perils of realistic presentation confront these
amateur producers. A lion—God shield us!—is a very
dreadful thing, especially with ladies. That will have to
be cared for. A prologue can be written to explain it.
The lion can speak out himself to say:

> 'Fair ladies, . . . I would entreat you—not to fear, not to
> tremble. My life for yours! If you think I come hither as
> a lion, it were pity of my life. No! I am no such thing.
> I am a man as other men are.' And there, indeed,

and he can go farther—if there be a farther—

> let him name his name and tell them plainly he is Snug
> the joiner.
>
> III, i, 41-48

The matter of the use of swords and the representation

of the act of killing will also call for a prologue in which
perfect orientation will be established between fact and
semblance, and perfect identity will be made:

> [L]et the prologue seem to say, we will do no harm
> with our swords, and that Pyramus is not kill'd indeed;
> and for the more better assurance, tell them that I Pyra-
> mus am not Pyramus, but Bottom the weaver. This will
> put them out of fear.
>
> 18-23

These prologues, in good fourteener verse (III, i, 25),
will do much to assuage the fears of an audience accustomed to a method in the presentation of horrors a
little more orthodoxly Senecan.

These actors are also in some perplexity about properties. Moonlight is a problem somewhat set at rest by the
Athenian Almanac,[4] but there is still a feeling that there
should be some bodily representation of the moon, who
will

> Come in with a bush of thorns and a lantern, and say he
> comes to disfigure, or to present, the person of Moonshine.
>
> III, i, 60-63

When Moon appears in the actual presentation, he has
added a dog to his properties, perhaps some flea-bitten
confrere of Launce's Crab.

Another problem for the properties department is that
of Wall. How to bring a wall into the Duke's palace.
Up from Bottom's bottomless mind comes the device.
When it comes to the playing, it goes forward as he
sketched it: Snout the tinker as Pyramus' father (I, ii, 65)
can be spared for another role. So he is also Wall, carry-

---

[4] When the play opens we are to wait four days for the new moon
(I, i, 1-3). Now we are at the other end of the four days and we
have a new moon, but a new moon will not be much help in the
great hall of the Palace an hour or two after sunset.

ing some loam and roughcast and stone as a concession
to realism, and holding two fingers a little apart to sim-
ulate the chink in the wall. He is a speaking wall, delivering altogether twelve pentameter lines in riming couplets.
If there is anything sillier than this, where and when
would you find it?

Costuming details need not occupy us long. There
is a brief colloquy as to what beard Pyramus is to wear.
There is such amplitude of choice in their wardrobe that
no choice is made at the moment. This company had,
apparently, a lion mask, and one member achieved, but
out of the larger wardrobe of Shakspere's company, an
Ass's mask. Sixteen years later there is in this larger
storeroom a Bear's mask for the actor, who, as a bear,
tore apart and ate poor old Antigonus on the Bohemian
shore. If the humane intent of the company is carried
through, the Lion mask will suffer some impairment, for
one side of it is to be cut away to show the honest face
of Snug and so to mollify the ladies' fears. But it will
be no serious matter, for, even so altered, your lion will
appear a most fearful wildfowl.

It seems a sort of condign irony that a company committed already to mispronunciation and malaprop use
should be troubled by mispronunciation in rehearsal, but
there is Thisby's

> I'll meet thee, Pyramus, at Ninny's tomb.
> III, i, 99

This Quince dutifully corrects although it is not time for
that line yet. And there is the double flavor of Pyramus'

> Thisby, the flowers of odious savours sweet,

which patient Quince corrects to *odorous* and Pyramus,
with great good will, and coming a little nearer, still mis-
reads: "*odours* savours sweet" (84-86).

The performance, when it comes, is full of interesting innovations not prepared for by the rehearsal. There is, first of all, the mispointed prologue, which was not only read by Peter Quince but was written by him also, so no one can be blamed here for misreading another's text. There seems to be no special need for explanation. If in a welter of so much absurdity one is to seek for the rational at all, it must be that we simply have a Quince educated far beyond his fellows but still not up to some of the finer—shall we say—*points* of rhetoric. Moreover, the prologue mispointed and misread is funny, and things that are funny need not pass too close muster in the court of credibility. Then, in a second prologue, presumably also the work of Peter Quince, but, this time, perfectly pointed, we are given the argument of the play up to the time of Pyramus' suicide. And the play begins.

Stylistic devices come in for burlesque. There are passages which poke fun at alliteration:

> Whereat, with blade, with bloody blameful blade,
> He bravely broach'd his boiling bloody breast.
> V, i, 147-148

> I thank thee, moon, for shining now so bright;
> For, by thy gracious, golden, glittering gleams. . . .
> 278-279

The ranting, bombastic style which must be almost what Bottom longed for in the tearing, splitting verbiage of a tyrant's vein is his in the role of Pyramus:

> O grim-look'd night! O night with hue so black!
> O night, which ever art when day is not!
> O night, O night, alack, alack, alack,
> I fear my Thisby's promise is forgot.
> 171-174[5]

[5] One cannot resist a cross reference to the Nurse's lament upon the day, in these same terms, when Lady Juliet is discovered dead:

There is, too, the matter of the mismatched sensory verb
and its object:

> *Pyr.*   I see a voice. Now will I to the chink
> To spy an I can hear my Thisby's face.
>
> 194-195

This occurs also in Bottom's first effort to regather his
wits upon being untranslated:

> I have had a dream. . . . The eye of man hath not heard,
> the ear of man hath not seen, man's hand is not able to
> taste, his tongue to conceive, nor his heart to report
> what my dream was.
>
> IV, i, 208-218

When Snug comes on to do the Lion's office, he is not
quite the Snug of the first scene. Then he feared the
Lion's part or any other that might be over-long, for,
he says: "I am slow of study" (I, ii, 69). Now he speaks
eight lines of pentameter, riming a b a b c c d d and does
it without the vice of a syllable. What transformation
has taken place in Snug? Or has our playwright forgotten his earlier sketch for the joiner?

Whoever presents Moonshine, Tom Snout or Robin
Starveling, is much more easily put down than is Snug.
At the first words of the Moon, the heckling mounts in
scale. Among other remarks comes Hippolyta's best line,
not a very good line, but one rejoices in any flicker of

> O woe! O woful, woful, woful day!
> Most lamentable day, most woful day
> That ever ever I did yet behold!
> O day! O day! O day! O hateful day!
> Never was seen so black a day as this.
> O woful day! O woful day!
>
> *Romeo,* IV, v, 49-54

Bear in mind that this is most likely intended to be laughed at, for
the audience knows that the girl is not dead and ere this they have
discovered the comic qualities of the Nurse.

pleasantness from some folk. "I am aweary of this moon,"
she says. "Would he would change" (256). The Moon
is urged to proceed, but he is bedaffed and put down.
His verse medium fails him entirely and so he folds his
verbal tent and gives all of his duty in a rush of good
simple prose:

> All I have to say is to tell you that the lanthorn is the
> moon; I, the man i' th' moon; this thornbush, my thorn-
> bush; and this dog, my dog.
>
> V, i, 261-263

Then the Lion roars "O!" and then the Lion tears
Thisby's mantle. How good old Snug has been drawn
out to say speeches and do deeds we nor he ever dreamed
were in him! Truly some folk have to have greatness
thrust upon 'em.

The passion of Pyramus and Thisby is couched in
short jiggling lines reminiscent of the poorer romances
of the Middle Ages, perhaps particularly reminiscent of
the parody of those poor romances in Chaucer's "Tho-
pas." Note the wild nothings in Pyramus' death speech
and the inappropriate epithets (so remindful of "Tho-
pas") in Thisby's lament:

> *Pyr.* Come, tears, confound!
> Out, sword, and wound
> The pap of Pyramus!
>   Ay that left pap
>   Where heart doth hop.
> Thus die I, thus, thus, thus.
>   Now I am dead,
>   Now I am fled:
> My soul is in the sky.
>   Tongue, lose thy light;
>   Moon, take thy flight,
> Now die, die, die, die, die!
>
> 300-310

This. O Pyramus, arise!
Speak, speak! quite dumb?
Dead, dead? A tomb
Must cover thy sweet eyes.
  These lily lips,
  This cherry nose,
These yellow cowslip cheeks,
  Are gone, are gone.
  Lovers, make moan!
His eyes are green as leeks.

333-342

Pyramus, of course, is all the while lying dead, but as the stage clears and the spectators begin to discuss the burial of the corpses, he (Bottom) raises himself on one elbow and denies being dead:

> No, I assure you; the wall is down that parted their fathers. Will it please you to see the Epilogue, or to hear a Bergomask dance between two of our company?

358-361

The epilogue is brushed aside, and the dance is brought on, and "The most Lamentable Comedy and most Cruel Death of Pyramus and Thisby" is over. If time served, we might point out in some detail how the serious tragic plot of *Romeo and Juliet* is essentially the same as that of the Pyramus and Thisby story. If we assume *A Midsummer Night's Dream* to be the earlier of these plays, and if we assume that Shakspere could hardly have been entirely indifferent to the similarity of the stories, then we have the rather unusual situation of a plot treated in the hilarious spirit of burlesque and later given a serious and poignantly tragic handling. The reverse process—serious treatment first and then burlesque—is more usual, but the process as we have assumed it is quite within Shakspere's compass. We have not only parody (if parody may come before what is being parodied) but we have enmeshed with it a delightful agglomeration of humorous characters, one of them one of the great comic creations of all literature. So, taken together—casting, rehearsal, loss and recovery of Bottom, presentation—this Pyramus and Thisby piece has taken on an integrity of its own quite apart from the burlesque intentions of the total plot.

Again, as in the presentation of the Nine Worthies, we have had mainly fun. Our playwright will break almost any pattern and defy almost any principle of decorum for the sake of a good laugh.

One final question suggests itself. Are we to suppose that dramatic presentation in Shakspere's time was ever as inept and naive as this or as that of the Nine Worthies? Why not? Have we not all seen some time or other an amateur performance, well-intentioned and most earnest, come to very much the same sorts of grief that happen to these plays? In most such cases the merciless heckling is absent, for likely it is a school play and our own little Nicky (Bottom) has the leading role and the off-spring of neighbor bellows-menders and tinkers and tailors are in the cast. But it is bad. Looked at objectively and with all personal feelings blocked out, it is bad.

One recalls the delightful anecdote Halliwell-Phillips tells of the old masker who announced himself:

> 'I am Hector of Troy'; on which, one of the people exclaimed,—'Thou Hector of Troy! why, thou'rt Jwon Thomson oth' Lwonin steed—what didst fancy I'd not know thee because thou art disguised?' The play proceeded, and it being necessary to the conduct of the piece that Hector should die, this son of the sack, having been previously instructed that it would not be quite natural to die instantaneously on his fall, not without two or three convulsive pangs, when he fell on the floor, as he had been directed, first fetched a deep groan, counting as

it were to himself the while, was heard to say, *ae pang;*
on fetching another groan he again said, *twae pangs;* and
in like manner, when a third groan was uttered, he said
faintly, *three pangs and now I's dead.*[6]

But the best of our parallels and the best recollections
from our own experience of bucolic plays do not quite
serve to account for the aggregate of success achieved
by Shakspere in these delightful travesties. Above all
else there is injected here the great reagent of character,
and our interest, however much it may be in what is
done and how, is increasingly in who does it.

As a maker of plays and as an actor, Shakspere is, of
course, coming close home in handling these matters that
have to do with preparing and producing of plays. In
the same spirit in which he let poetry be jostled about
in jest and takes it smilingly, because the jest is on himself,
he lets playing and play-making be burlesqued. Perhaps
no single situation of rehearsing and producing was ever
so crowded with the incongruous and inept as are these
two pieces, but that, too, is part of the spirit and practice
of burlesque. To have attempted to defend his art against
the clumsy efforts of rustic hands, to have sought to show
Costards and Bottoms, Don Armados and Snugs doing
anything smoothly or with sensitiveness would not be
common sense. The common-sense way—the delightful,
hearty, free way of creative ignorance and honest bum-
bling—that is Shakspere's way.

The Mouse Trap

As has already been suggested, the situation of the
players in Hamlet is completely different from that of
these amateur actors, for the Danish players are profes-

---

[6] Furness, *Variorum Shakespeare,* "Love's Labour's Lost," 284.

sionals, and they are in Elsinore in the exercise of their
craft to see if there is demand for a play.

There are questions as to how they come to be traveling, as to which players they are, and as to whether their
vogue is as great as it once was. All of these questions—
they are Hamlet's questions—Rosencrantz is prompt to
answer, and the answers are almost surely definite topical
references in terms of the current London theatrical situation. Much discussion of these points is available, and
the principal matters are reasonably in agreement. Then
there is talk about a company or companies of children,
boys:

> [A]n eyrie of children, little eyases, that cry out on the
> top of question and are most tyranically clapp'd for't.
> These are now the fashion.
>
>   II, ii, 354-357

This, too, is almost certainly a reference to the vogue
of companies of boy actors on the London stage in the
years when *Hamlet* was a new play.

These matters occupy us for the moments between the
announcement that the players are coming and their
arrival in the Prince's presence. But in this interval Hamlet checks over the list of stock roles: the king, the adventurous knight, the lover, the humorous man, the
clown, and the lady. When they enter, Hamlet greets
them all, for he knows them better than just passingly.
One of them he hails as "my old friend" with whom
he seems to have a close personal acquaintance. He is
the one called in the stage direction *First Player*, and
the one with whom the Prince confers about the choice
of play and the insertion of the mousetrap passage in it.
He is, if you will, the Dick Burbage of this traveling
company.

Two of the stock gibes about boys outgrowing their availability for female roles Hamlet lets fly at the lad, whom he hails:

> What, my young lady and mistress? By'r Lady, your ladyship is nearer to heaven than when I saw you last by the altitude of a chopine. Pray God your voice, like a piece of uncurrent gold, be not crack'd within the ring.
>
> II, ii, 444-449

This familiar mingling with the players, as we know, shows Hamlet in a situation and an atmosphere in which he is most thoroughly at home and at ease. He falls at once into critical chit-chat with the players. Talk arises about a speech from a play that never came to the stage, or if it did the play folded after the first performance. Hamlet says:

> [I]t . . . pleas'd not the million, 'twas caviary to the general.
>
> 458

Perhaps there is a certain minimum of critical snobbishness in that comment. But it is part of a constant experience on the part of those who are artistically concerned with the niceties of dramatic production. In it Hamlet puts himself (modestly) in the company of the critically elite, who judge plays and assess values more fastidiously than the million:

> But it was (as I receiv'd it, and others whose judgments in such matters cried in the top of mine) an excellent play, well digested in the scenes, set down with as much modesty as cunning.
>
> II, ii, 459-463

After a remarkable feat of memory wherein Hamlet, who had heard the speech only once and that some while ago, recites thirteen lines of it and tosses it to the First

Player as a cue for the rest, the First Player picks it up, declaiming it in the bold orotund style of Shakspere's stage. As the speech and scene build up, he comes to Hecuba, and his voice vibrates, his eyes fill with tears, and his countenance pales with the feeling he generates for this simulated passion. This impresses Polonius strangely and Hamlet also, for later, alone, he returns to it as a sort of text for self-castigation for his delay:

> Is it not monstrous that this player here,
> But in a fiction, in a dream of passion,
> Could force his soul so to his own conceit
> That, from her working, all his visage wann'd,
> Tears in his eyes, distraction in 's aspect,
> A broken voice, and his whole function suiting
> With forms to his conceit? And all for nothing!
> For Hecuba!
> What's Hecuba to him, or he to Hecuba,
> That he should weep for her? What would he do,
> Had he the motive and the cue for passion
> That I have? He would drown the stage with tears. . . .
>
> II, ii, 577-588

So Hamlet defers to the masters of illusion who in his day made the great tragic roles of Marlowe, Kyd, Dekker, and Jonson, and his own creator, Shakspere, into living beings. For the shallower capacities of Polonius this realistic depiction of passion was almost too much. "Look!" he cries:

> Whe'r he has not turn'd his colour, and has tears in 's
> eyes. Prithee no more!
>
> 542-543

This is the player to whom Hamlet commits the enacting of the *Mousetrap*. There is the question, "Can you play the 'Murther of Gonzago'?" and the quick answer, "Ay, my lord." Since the entire situation is fiction, this readiness to comply with what sounds like a random selection may not be quite so remarkable, and, in the circumstances of Shakspere's theater, it may not be remarkable at all. In the sixteenth century when a play, even a highly successful play, had run twelve or fourteen performances, it had fairly exhausted the theater-going public even of London. Thus it was necessary for every company to have an elaborate repertory—to be able to do almost anything on short notice.

With a suggestion to the actor that he restrain the natural actor's impulse to mimic Polonius, Hamlet dismisses him until the briefing session with the players before the play.

That great passage of advice to the players (III, ii, 1-50), is so well known as to require no full explication here. Hamlet, in his role as dramatic coach, asks for clear, clean enunciation, restrained gesture, modest depiction of passion, proper but not undue fervor, fidelity to nature, restraint on the part of the clowns against *ad libitum* bids for a laugh. He decries with special vehemence "inexplicable dumb shows" and actors

> that neither having the accent of Christians, nor the gait of Christian, pagan, nor man, have so strutted and bellowed that I have thought some of Nature's journeymen had made men, and not made them well, they imitated humanity so abominably.
>
> III, ii, 34-39

In all of this Polonius' comments are not to be ignored, for they reflect the taste of the million. It is an important part of the portrait of this exemplar of brevity that is being etched in in his statement about the versatility of these actors, but it is also veiled dramatic criticism. They are, he says,

> The best actors in the world, either for tragedy, comedy, history, pastoral, pastoral-comical, historical-pastoral, trag-

ical-historical, tragical-comical-historical-pastoral; scene
individable, or poem unlimited.

II, ii, 414-418

So it becomes a part of the perennial quandary of those
who insist on categories and classifications, and find themselves driven to make shifts and compounded improvisations with almost every new specimen. For example,
what sort of play *is* Marc Connelly's the *Green Pastures*?
Comical-tragical-historical-pastoral-psychological perhaps? Should *sociological* be wedged in somewhere?

Polonius' objection to the length of the Player's reci-
tation gives Hamlet a fair chance to describe him as of
the type who want their plays enlivened with jigs and
spiced with bawdy suggestion. It is a delightful turn
in which Hamlet catches at the word *mobled* in the
Player's line:

But who, O who, had seen the mobled queen—

525

Polonius is pleased with the word. "That's good," he
says. "'Mobled queen,' is good." Hamlet completely
drops the matter as if it is of no consequence, or as if
it is not worth the effort of an argument against the heavy
legions of Polonius' logic. As a problem of direction,
the expression on the Prince's face at this point would
be a precious matter.

All the glossaries are clear on what *mobled* means.
I wonder if it was as clear to Hamlet and Shakspere and
Shakspere's audience. As it stands, it appears that Hamlet
either does not like the word or is puzzled by it. The
fact that Polonius likes it is no indication either that it
is good, or bad, or that he understands it. If Hamlet is
puzzled by it, then Shakspere must have put it in intentionally for the very point that it was unfamiliar and

would puzzle the Prince. Hamlet's is the best mind there, and if his perception is at fault, then this is the only instance in the play where that is so.[7]

As the time for the play nears, Hamlet says:

> They are coming to the play. I must be idle.
>
> III, ii, 95

That is, *I must not seem to be more than ordinarily aware of what is going on;* also, perhaps it means, *I must lapse into my appearance of madness and so play idly with—whatever offers itself.* And in a moment he slumps down at Ophelia's feet and begins a line of suggestive (idle) reference and innuendo such as a gentleman does not address to a woman he respects. But for our purpose, this results in a most important diversion. Polonius and the Queen note this open choosing of the girl as his companion, and they draw Claudius into close and excited conference and into fixed observation of the pair. This, for Polonius, is most important, for, only a short two hours before, Hamlet's treatment of this girl in the lobby had given a body blow to his theory of love-madness, and the King had left the scene saying,

> Love? his affections do not that way tend.
>
> III, i, 170

Now this open behavior toward his daughter is reviving and confirming the old man's theory, and he wants the Queen and especially the King to see it.

Meanwhile the Dumb Show enters and enacts in pantomime the scene of the poisoning. This Hamlet sees and with complete consternation. He condemned "in-

---

[7] The use of *mobled* here is the first cited by the *OED*. It was intentionally obscure. Delius says, "That an unusual word was intended is plain, both from Hamlet's objection to it and Polonius' approval of it." *Var.* "Ham." I, 190.

explicable dumb shows" in his advice to the players and this is worse than that; this is a rather easily explicable dumb show. "What means this, my lord?" the girl asks, and Hamlet replies with complete disgust:

> Marry, this is miching malhecho; it means mischief.
>
> ii, 149

For he is not yet ready for the King's conscience to be caught; they have not yet got to Hamlet's inserted speech which is the real device of the trap. But, as we have shown above, the principal spectators do not see the Dumb Show or, if at all, only glancingly, for Polonius is busy focusing their attention on the Prince and the girl.[8] And if the King has any inclination to note the Dumb Show, it likely will not be very great, for is it not, most probably of the same sort as all the other dumb shows he has ever seen—inexplicable?[9] Moreover, as Joseph Hunter pointed out long ago, dumb shows in this period were not expository but were like the moralizing choruses of Greek tragedy,[10] and, as Creizenach has noted,[11] no other dumb show in the Elizabethan period

[8] Obviously, I am following Dover Wilson on this point. His interpretation of it has seemed to me well-supported and entirely clear. *What Happens in Hamlet*, 144-153.

[9] If this same reasoning were applied to Hamlet's reaction it might seem he, also, would not heed it. But Hamlet's attention for this whole matter is on edge. He will not miss anything. Is there not a mousetrap to be sprung; a mousetrap which he himself has devised?

[10] Furness, *Variorum Shakespeare*, "Hamlet," I, n. on III, ii, 121, p. 242.

[11] After listing a number of Elizabethan plays in which dumb shows appear serving various purposes, mainly symbolic [inexplicable?] Creizenach particularizes. "The most famous of all these pantomimic representations is that at the beginning of the play inset into *Hamlet*. This occupies a place apart, in that it is neither an essential part of the action, nor an allegorical presentment of what is to follow, but simply a silent performance of the same scenes which are afterwards acted over again in words." W. Creizenach, *The English Drama in the Age of Shakespeare*, 390.

was in the form of an argument for the play. But when Hamlet sees that the King is not seeing, or at least not heeding the Dumb Show, he draws a sigh of relief. But only for a moment, for he is to be startled anew by the appearance of a prologue, and his disgust springs to his lips:

> We shall know by this fellow. The players cannot keep counsel; they'll tell all.
>
> 151-152

But, once again, Hamlet's consternation is for naught. This is only a sort of salutatory prologue. There is no matter in the speech; it is not expository in the fashion of the profuse prologues of Holofernes and Peter Quince. It is only "the posy of a ring," like the worn, empty rimes of the autograph albums of the nineteenth century, or the trite tributes college students write in one another's Year Books. So Hamlet may draw another sigh of relief.

Now two players come on and enact the play, seventy-three lines in rimed couplets with two interjected comments from the Prince, and then, after a longer interruption by Hamlet and the Queen and King, a third actor comes on making hideous and fearful faces and gesticulating wildly. He is about to speak Hamlet's lines, and he is behaving just exactly as Hamlet had counselled him not to behave.

"Pox," says the Prince, "leave thy damnable faces, and begin! Come, the croaking raven doth bellow for revenge" (263-265).

So we have come in this brief passage of the play to see Hamlet experiencing three crises of disgust: the Dumb Show, the prologue, and the gesticulating actor, each of which was a peril to the purpose upon which he had staked so much. I should like to tarry a moment to ask

why these intelligent and practiced players who knew
their art so well as is demonstrated by the First Player's
effective reading of the Pyrrhus speech, and who apparently respected Hamlet not alone as Prince but as a
dramatic critic

> [I hope we have reform'd that indifferently with us, sir.
>
> III, ii, 41]

should flout decorum and go against his counsel in these
matters? Perhaps this is a question which Shakspere
scarcely allowed himself, for there is a great deal going
on. Moreover, these three moments which are bad for
Hamlet, are good for the effects of suspense and, therefore, have high dramatic value. But let me at least suggest that these players, like so many folk in all sorts
of situations, listened to good advice and thought it good,
but so far as application to their own practice was concerned, paid it no heed at all, for, as to their own practice, that, they were sure, was above criticism. Indeed,
they had reformed it altogether, long ago.

But the most important point is in the fact that, true
to his own inner nature, Hamlet experiences three very
bad minutes of suspense lest the King be caught before
the real trap is sprung. It is almost as if he didn't want
the King caught if he is not caught by Hamlet's own
special, private device. When the scene is over—broken
up by the King's panic—this is even more clear. For
the King is caught, and by Hamlet's lines, and the Prince
is as happy as a boy whose self-whittled whistle really
does make a noise—happy not because the King is caught
but because the trap is a good trap and he an approved
trap-maker.

> Would not this, sir, and a forest of feathers—if the rest
> of my fortunes turn Turk with me—with two Provincial

roses on my raz'd shoes, get me a fellowship in a cry of
players, sir?
Hor. Half a share.
Ham. A whole one I!

                                                286-291

And out in the long Danish twilight the players are
trudging down the highway to the haven, their purses
heavier by what weight in crowns the Prince's treasurer
gave them. Their inner man is satisfied with roast beef
and good Danish ale and a sense of a play well done, but
there is mild wonder in their minds as to what it was
happened to the King. *Why did he break up the play?*

A Private Showing for Sir Christopher Sly

In the *Taming of the Shrew* we have a still different
pattern of the use of players. Here there is an Induction
such as there was in the earlier *Taming of a Shrew* and as
there was considerably later in Beaumont and Fletcher's
the *Knight of the Burning Pestle*. In the *Taming of a
Shrew* and in the Beaumont and Fletcher play we have
a stage set up with a group of persons on it as spectators
for whose benefit the play is being given. In the *Knight
of the Burning Pestle* the involvement of this spectator
group with the development of the plot of the play is
very intimate and remains a major factor of interest. In
both of the non-Shaksperean plays the participation of
the spectator group is kept up throughout the play.

In Shakspere's play, the *Taming of the Shrew*, the initial situation is similar. A beggar named Christopher
Sly, kicked out of an ale house by a hostess whose patience has been worn thin by his failure to pay his score,
falls asleep in a gutter and becomes the object of the
whim of a passing nobleman. This nobleman conceives

the idea of doing a socio-psychological experiment by undertaking to transform this wretch outwardly by rich apparel, and to surround him with all the accompaniments of refined living, and to provide him with a young and lovely wife, and so, upon his waking, to seek to persuade him he is a gentleman. While Sly is sleeping, a company of traveling players present themselves, and one of the items of the experiment becomes the providing of a play for him to enjoy.

The relationship of these players to the surrounding situations is very similar to that of the tragedians of the city who come to Prince Hamlet's Elsinore and are quickly employed to play before the King.

The Nobleman recognizes one of the actors as one he had seen before in a play he cannot now recall by title. It was a role of a farmer's son who wooed a gentlewoman but whose name he cannot remember. The player thinks he must have in mind the role of one Soto. These details fit with Beaumont and Fletcher's *A Woman Pleased* except that that play is still some six years in the future, but there may have been an earlier dramatization of the same story.

So the players are employed to play. And from this point these players, who are the men of Shakspere's company, take over, and our initial pattern fades out. Everything is swallowed up in the main play. Particularly is Christopher Sly swallowed up, for after line 259 of the first scene, Shakspere forgets him. As the first scene ends, his sponsors ask him how he likes the play:

> *1. Man.* My lord, you nod, you do not mind the play.
> *Beg.* Yes, by Saint Anne, do I! A good matter, surely. Comes there any more of it?
> *Lady.* My lord, 'tis but begun.

Beg. 'Tis a very excellent piece of work, madam lady.
Would 'twere done!

Shrew, I, i, 254-259[12]

Sly seems to me to have been well on the way to be-coming one of Shakspere's fine comic characters. He is, in his situation, own brother to Bottom the Ass unex-pectedly elevated to greatness in Queen Titania's realm, and there is a sort of dumb kinship in spirit with Goodman Dull and with poor sodden Bardolph. For reasons which are most likely textual, we have no more of him, and that is to be regretted, but we do have a lively well-built comedy presented by the Lord Chamberlain's Men, who appear in the Induction as a company of traveling play-ers. But, once past the Induction, they level out into a competent company of professional actors exercising themselves in their craft.

The two companies of traveling players in *Hamlet* and the *Shrew* are most surely transcripts from Shakspere's experience of such companies either as member or ob-server. They are cut down for reasons of economy to a bare minimum of personnel. They are travel-worn but are up to anything—the *Murther of Gonzago* with a mousetrap concealed in it, or entertainment for Sir Christopher Sly. They come in good time to situations ripe for their admittance. In each instance they fall in with those who recall their performances of old.

The Elsinore players are most urgently briefed on the whole business of stage decorum. Since their mentor is a prince and a good friend of their craft, they listen most

---

[12] Sly's "Would 'twere done!" is in line with Polonius' feeling that the Pyrrhus speech is too long, but in view of Sly's once-thwarted show of interest in the Lady (Ind., ii, 118-126), may it not be that he is clumsily suggesting that he hopes the play will shortly be over and that he may be left at last alone with her?

respectfully. All the abuses he points to they have reformed in their practice—so they say. But in performance
they are as bad as the worst. But this badness and the
Prince's consternation thereat become part of the plot,
the details of which they do not realize, either now or
ever. The main point is that these players, as well as the
inept amateurs of the comedies, are from the familiar
Shakspere world of reality. They are good—indifferent
good. The sort of players one has, not the sort his fancy
might wish for, or a romantic dream provide. They are
the common-sense sort of player—not anyone's ideal.

CHAPTER VIII

SHAKSPERE'S ACTORS:
IMPROMPTU DRAMATICS

If Hamlet is the most theater-minded of Shakspere's people, surely a close second is Prince Henry, later King Henry V, and in Falstaff he finds a most versatile and willing collaborator.

Qualities of character interest Prince Henry and so do the language and illusion demanded by acting. He is quick to sense the dramatic possibilities of a situation and to cast it into dramatic form. I said Falstaff is his best collaborator, and that is true, but there is also Ned Poins, who is willing and most capable.[1]

I

Actually all the instances of this extempore play acting on the part of the Prince and his associates are in one scene, but it is the great fourth scene of Act II, *I Henry IV*, the greatest comedy scene in English drama, and, therefore, expansive enough to contain every sort of

---

[1] Some day someone must write a chapter about Ned Poins. He has been much neglected. I think his answer when the Prince confronts him with the gossip's report that he is saying around town that the Prince is to marry his sister is one of the best of all answers. By its terms everyone is saved in reputation and dignity:

> *Prince.* . . . But do you use me thus, Ned? Must I marry your sister?
> *Poins.* God send the wench no worse fortune! but I never said so.

II H IV, II, ii, 150-153

thing and to make anything seem representative even though limited to the one scene. As the action begins, Prince Henry enters doubled over with laughter at the memory of an encounter he has just had with a group of waiters in the fat room of the tavern. He wants Poins to help him with an extension of this encounter. There is a new French waiter named Francis, whose English is scanty and uncertain, and to the Prince, as to most of us, anyone's helpless struggles with our easy and sensible language are funny. Practically all Francis knows to say is "Anon, anon, sir." Moreover, Francis himself is amusing because he is so nervously eager to please. Poins, therefore, is to choose a table at one side of the room and Hal one at the other. Francis comes in discomposedly muttering, "Anon, anon, sir—" and the Prince calls him. As soon as he is engaged with Hal, Poins calls from the other side of the room, "Francis, Francis!" "Anon, anon, sir," says Francis, but the Prince continues to hold him in question. "Francis!" Poins calls. "Anon, anon, sir," says poor bewildered Francis, and as he reaches a point midway between them, they both call and, as the stage direction has it:

The drawer stands amazed, not knowing which way to go.
1 H IV, II, iv, 89

This completely extempore bit tickles Hal's fancy, and after it is over he still talks of it. But his talk strays and comes upon the mention of Hotspur. From that point all the rumored oddities he has heard about the redoubtable Percy come tumbling into his thought and almost before we know it, the idea for a second extempore playlet is born. The play is cast and will go on as soon as the second actor appears:

I am not yet of Percy's mind, the Hotspur of the North;

he that kills me some six or seven dozen of Scots at a
breakfast, washes his hands, and says to his wife, 'Fie upon
this quiet life! I want work.' 'O, my sweet Harry,' says
she, 'how many hast thou kill'd today?' 'Give my roan
horse a drench,' says he, and answers 'Some fourteen,'
an hour after, 'a trifle, a trifle.' I prithee call in Falstaff.
I'll play Percy, and that damn'd brawn shall play Dame
Mortimer his wife. 'Rivo!' says the drunkard. Call in
ribs, call in tallow.

114-125

But when Falstaff enters he is full of his heroic deeds at
Gadshill and there is such a confusion of lies and bombast
and swagger that the Prince's Play of Hotspur and his
Wife never comes to be.

In his wild boasting about all that he says took place
at Gadshill, Falstaff gets around to the point of why he
did not attack the Prince. Instinct prevented him:

Was it for me to kill the heir apparent? Should I turn
upon the true prince? Why, thou knowest I am as valiant as Hercules; but beware instinct. The lion will not
touch the true prince. Instinct is a great matter. I was
now a coward on instinct. I shall think the better of myself, and thee, during my life—I for a valiant lion, and
thou for a true prince. But, by the Lord, lads, I am glad
you have the money. Hostess, clap to the doors. Watch
tonight, pray tomorrow. Gallants, lads, boys, hearts of
gold, all the titles of good fellowship come to you! What,
shall we be merry? Shall we have a play extempore?
Prince. Content—and the argument shall be thy running away.

297-310

Once more, however, we are deprived of fulfillment.
There is an officer of the King at the door, and news of
rising war and a summons for the Prince to be in the
court tomorrow drive all thought of Falstaff's play extempore from their minds. But we are hard upon another

inspiration which is the fourth—all four from the Prince—
for, although the suggestion to have the third comes from
Falstaff, Hal supplies the argument, "thy running away,"
which makes it also his. On the point that Hal must
be at court tomorrow, Falstaff says:

> Well, thou wilt be horribly chid tomorrow when thou
> comest to thy father. If thou love me, practice an answer.
> *Prince.* Do thou stand for my father and examine me
> upon the particulars of my life.
>
> 410-414

What follows is fulfillment. It is the richest, cleverest,
raciest piece of extemporization that I know.[2] First there
is great scurrying about for stage properties. Falstaff,
elated at being cast in the part of the King, is very busy:

> This chair shall be my state, this dagger my sceptre, and
> this cushion my crown.
>
> 415-416

Further to temper illusion with a touch of reality:

> Give me a cup of sack to make my eyes look red, that
> it may be thought I have wept; for I must speak in pas-
> sion. . . .
>
> 422-424

Moreover, he constitutes the tavern riff-raff into his royal
retinue:

> Stand aside, nobility.
>
> 429

and the Hostess of the Tavern into his queen:

> Weep not, sweet queen, for trickling tears are vain.
>
> *   *   *
>
> For God's sake, lords, convey my tristful queen!
> For tears do stop the floodgates of her eyes.
>
> 431; 433-434

[2] One or two passages in Philip Barry's *Hotel Universe* compare
favorably.

Then, with a quick and almost ribald shift: "Peace, good pintpot. Peace, good tickle brain—" he glides out of this "King Cambyses' vein" into parody of the prose style of John Lyly:

> Harry, I do not only marvel where thou spendest thy time, but also how thou art accompanied. For though the camomile, the more it is trodden on, the faster it grows, yet youth, the more it is wasted, the sooner it wears. . . .
>
> 439-444

All the while that this preparation has been going forward the Hostess has been an admiring chorus:

> O Jesu, this is excellent sport, i' faith!
>
> 430
>
> O, the Father, how he holds his countenance.
>
> 432
>
> O Jesu, he doth it as like one of these harlotry players as ever I see.
>
> 436-437

There is in the Hostess a sort of proprietary pride in her beloved Sir John (He's an infinitive thing upon her score, but how can one keep remembering that when he is so wonderfully clever?). But the Hostess is also checking this quickly improvised skit against what she has seen from the pits of various London playhouses and is finding it wonderfully up to standard.[3]

---

[3] From the Hostess' comments we get unmistakable indications that Shakspere planned Falstaff's entire performance as dead-pan comedy. Elsewhere in the plays Falstaff's manner of countenance is referred to. The Chief Justice says to him:

> It is not a confident brow nor the throng of words that come with such more than impudent sauciness from you, can thrust me from a level consideration. *II H IV*, II, i, 121-123.

And Falstaff's own estimation:

> O, it is much that a lie with a slight oath, and a jest with a

The play itself *is* good almost beyond belief, that is, belief that so quickly, two men—even these two—could come through with anything so brilliant and full of clever device. Falstaff is a most kingly King. His language, a perfect parody, runs on to climax, a climax of praise for the goodly portly man and corpulent in whose company the Prince is said to have been seen: "Him keep with, the rest banish" (473). Then with a quick reversal of style, he comes down to his accustomed tavern prose:

> And tell me now, thou naughty varlet, tell me where hast thou been this month?
>
> 474-475

This is more than the Prince, not so much as Prince but as actor, can stand, so he breaks in and switches roles with the fat knight, thus introducing not only variety into the performance but, more important, the element of rivalry of skills. Falstaff perceives this instantly, and he emphasizes it for all it is worth:

> *If thou dost it half so gravely, so majestically, both in word and matter, hang me up by the heels for a rabbit-sucker or a poulter's hare.*
> Prince. Well, here I am set.
> Fal. And here I stand. *Judge, my masters.*

So the examination begins:

> sad brow will do with a fellow that never had the ache in his shoulders. V, i, 90-92.

The held countenance has been a mainstay of many schools of the comic. The rough, unrefined comedy of the late decades of the nineteenth century in America—Artemus Ward, Bill Nye, Petroleum V. Naseby, and Mark Twain—was dead-pan. Twain's narrator of the "Celebrated Jumping Frog," old Simon Wheeler, told his prodigious story without a flicker of facial expression. Modern radio comedians have not been able to make full use of this device. No doubt television will restore it.

> *Prince.* Now, Harry, whence come you?
> *Fal.* My noble lord, from Eastcheap.
> *Prince.* The complaints I hear of thee are grievous.
> *Fal.* 'Sblood, my lord, they are false! *Nay, I'll tickle*
> *ye for a young prince, i' faith.*
>
> 478-489

The italics (which are, of course, mine) point up the
lines in which Falstaff voices his sense of the exchange
of roles as an opportunity for comparison. So he throws
himself once more into the act and comes through at the
end with another eloquent defence of

> [S]weet Jack Falstaff, kind Jack Falstaff, true Jack Fal-
> staff, valiant Jack Falstaff, and therefore more valiant be-
> ing, as he is, old Jack Falstaff, banish not him thy Harry's
> company, banish not him thy Harry's company. Banish
> plump Jack, and banish all the world.
>
> 522-527

But now there is a knocking at the gate, and Bardolph
comes running in with a warning that the sheriff is at
the door. But, for the moment, the artist in Falstaff had
supervened the fugitive from the sheriff, and he brushes
Bardolph majestically aside:

> Out, ye rogue! Play out the play. I have much to say in
> behalf of that Falstaff.
>
> 531-532

But that is not to be; the play is at an end.

In later scenes there are quick and lively interchanges.
There is the scene of the Prince and Poins disguised as
drawers (*II H IV*, II, iv) which revives much of the spirit
of free give-and-take of the earlier play. Once, at least,
we hear Falstaff planning a skit (a monologue, no doubt)
on the idiosyncracies of Justice Shallow with which he
will regale the Prince upon his return to London (*II H*

IV, V, i, 87-94), but there are no more plays extempore partly because the two who make them are little together any more on the old carefree basis, and partly because we must forego frivolity and prepare ourselves for the apotheosis of Henry from a tavern playboy to be the very Grace of Kings. But while it lasted it was fun, some of the most riotous fun in all the world of fancy.[4]

II

One other example of extempore dramatics deserves our attention. It is the scene in *Twelfth Night* (IV, ii), in which in their merciless hazing of Malvolio, the lighter people of the play hit upon the plan of sending in a priest to conjure the devils from Malvolio's mad breast. It is a delicate situation, and there is no one present with a sense of delicacy. To tamper with a man's body is serious business, but to run a practical joke to the point of seeking to persuade a man that he is mad is more serious still. But once again, these custodians of Malvolio are not creatures of discretion.

Now it is obvious that no priest with any regard for his office will do this thing—not even Friar Lawrence, who would do and did do much, or Friar Francis of *Much Ado*.[5] But this deviceful company is not deterred by that difficulty; they will make a priest of their own out of Feste, the Clown. And a most convincing and remorseless priest he proves to be. There is, first, cos-

---

[4] If one needs more to constitute Prince Henry a dramatic producer extempore, he may invoke the scene of the trying on of his father's crown (*II H IV*, IV, v, 20-224), and the great scene of his incognito tour of the camp before dawn on the morning of Agincourt (*H V*, IV, i).

[5] The Duke of Vienna, disguised as a friar, in *Meas.*, also undertakes delicate matters, but he is no more a priest than is Feste.

tume: beard and gown which Maria has provided. Then
there must be disguising of voice to that of Sir Topas,
the Curate, whose voice and ways Malvolio knew as
well as they. So, for practice, Feste tries his ponderous
priestly style on Sir Toby:

> Bonos dies, Sir Toby; for as the old hermit of Prague,
> that never saw pen and ink, very wittily said to the niece
> of King Gorboduc, 'That that is is'; so I, being Master
> Parson, am Master Parson; for what is 'that' but that, and
> 'is' but is?
> *To.* To him, Sir Topas.
> *Clown.* What ho, I say. Peace in this prison!
> *To.* The knave counterfeits well; a good knave.
>
> IV, ii, 14-22

Twice or more as the scene develops Toby registers
approval of Feste's acting in much the same vein in which
Mrs. Quickly applauds Sir John. But the best proof of
the quality of the act is in the fact that Malvolio, who is
humorless but otherwise as sound as the foundations of
the earth, is completely taken in. Of course, he is quick
to catch hope out of the unexpected entrance of the
priest, for what he wants above all else is an ear to hear
his case. He does not seem ever to doubt that this is the
priest. So the dissimulator works his sad work on poor
abused Malvolio and then comes running off to join Toby
and Maria. Now it occurs to Toby for Feste to go back
in his own person to see how Malvolio is reacting to this
latest turn of the screw. So Feste goes back singing a
song the burden of which is "My lady is unkind, perdie!"
and Malvolio who was never an admirer of the Fool (I,
v, 89), nevertheless snatches at the straw of hope that the
Fool might help him and so pours out his latest woes to
his visitor:

> Fool, there was never a man so notoriously abus'd . . . .

> They have here propertied me; keep me in darkness,
> send ministers to me, asses, and do all they can to face
> me out of my wits.
>
> 94-101

And at the word *minister* the Clown has a quick flash of imagination and moves into the execution of another device (extempore):

> Advise you what you say. The minister is here.
>
> 102

So with no forethought or time for preparation he goes into his duologue as Priest and Clown. This calls for a high degree of cleverness and may necessitate some use of ventriloquism. I am rearranging the speeches here to indicate the shifts in role as managed by Feste in this brief but adroit display of duality:

> *Clown.* Advise you what you say. The minister is here.—
> *Priest.* Malvolio, Malvolio, thy wits the heavens restore!
> Endeavor thyself to sleep and leave thy vain bibble-babble.
> *Mal.* Sir Topas!
> *Priest.* (*To the Clown*) Maintain no words with him,
> good fellow.
> *Clown.* Who, I, sir? Not I, sir. God b' wi' you, good
> Sir Topas!
> *Priest.* Marry, amen.
> *Clown.* I will, sir, I will.
>
> 102-110

And all the while Malvolio is deceived. This is good fooling; it is also good acting.

When he sets in to read Malvolio's letter written with materials and by light which he provided him at the end of the Priest-Clown scene, he begins in a most horrendous burst of bombastic style:

> By the Lord, madam—
> *Oli.* How now? Are you mad?

> *Clown.* No, madam, I do but read madness. An your
> ladyship will have it as it ought to be, you must allow vox.
>
> V, i, 300-304

So another less dramatic reader must be found.

Finally, when Malvolio is brought in and the knots of
the tangled plot are almost all loosened at last, Feste takes
a parting shot at Malvolio. Perhaps most important of
all he lets Malvolio know that there never was any priest—
not a real priest, that is. He ties it all together into a fine
medley of bits from here and there in preceding passages
of the play:

> *Clown.* Why, 'some are born great, some achieve great-
> ness, and some have greatness thrown upon them.' I was
> one, sir, in this interlude—one Sir Topas, sir; but that's
> all one. 'By the Lord, fool, I am not mad!' But do you
> remember—'Madam, why laugh you at such a barren
> rascal? An you smile not, he's gagg'd'? And thus the
> whirligig of time brings in his revenges.
>
> V, i, 377-385 [6]

Other bits of extempore acting might well engage us,
but this Prince Henry-Falstaff team and Feste-Topas,
a team in himself, are the best and will serve to represent
the others.

III

We mentioned ventriloquism above. It seems clear
that both Robin Goodfellow (the Puck) and Ariel used

---

[6] At the risk of snapping up another unconsidered trifle, I note that
Feste was not present in the garden to hear Malvolio read the letter.
His knowledge of its wording had to come by hearsay unless Maria let
him see a copy. Quoting it, as he does now, he does not have the
words exactly. It was: "some have greatness *thrust upon 'em.*" He
says here, "*thrown upon them.*" So it would be if he was remembering hearsay. This (v. p. 302, *infra*), is a perfect example of the sort
of thing that comes out in the study and would not be noted one time
in a thousand in the theater.

it. These fairy chaps had a quick sense of the dramatic. Robin, coming upon the rustics at their rehearsal in the forest, is quick to scent the possibilities of impromptu mischief:

> What, a play toward? I'll be an auditor;
> An actor too perhaps, if I see cause.
>
> *Dream*, III, i, 81-82

And later as the plot is thickening, he states a major article of his philosophy in one couplet, a sweeping generalization that includes himself not only, but a whole world of other charming pixies:

> And those things do best please me
> That befall prepost'rously.
>
> III, ii, 120-121

Ariel, too, has a great gift for extemporizing. Prospero gives him a general sketch of whatever is forward, and he inks in the details. He loves his own devices, his ability to be invisible, his trick of being in more than one place at the same time:

> Sometime, I'ld divide
> And burn in many places; on the topmast,
> The yards, and boresprit would I flame distinctly,
> Then meet and join.
>
> *Temp.*, I, ii, 198-201

Then, for Prince Ferdinand's delectation, there is the lovely ceremonial pageant of the goddesses. It is Ariel's production. Prospero's order calling for it is most general:

> *Pros.*   For I must
> Bestow upon the eyes of this young couple
> Some vanity of mine art. It is my promise
> And they expect it from me.
>
> IV, i, 39-42

So it is to be "some vanity of mine art," but all the lovely detail is Ariel's devising. It goes forward lightly in the movements of a graceful dance in which some reapers engage the nymphs. Suddenly Prospero starts and breaks the spell, for his mind has fallen upon the ugly recollection of Caliban and his murderous intentions. Ariel says he thought of it too "When I presented Ceres" (167). I like to think that the use of *present* here is the same as that in *A Midsummer Night's Dream*:

> *Quince.* One must come in with a bush of thorns and a lantern, and say he comes to disfigure, or to *present* the person of Moonshine,

or

> *Bot.* Some man or other must *present* Wall.
> > *Dream*, III, i, 60-63; 68

Here, clearly, the word means *represent or take the part of*. There is a sense—a very full and real sense—in which Ariel did present the entire pageant, but may we not think, also, that he slipped himself into the choice role of Ceres and was chief actor as well as almost the only begetter of the entire performance?

No further comment could add clarification or emphasis to the effect of the instances of quick facile readiness to fall into a pattern of acting which calls for clever and careful attention to the details of the fiction and to the amosphere of illusion. There is enough of it to make it one of the rare delights of the reading of Shakspere.

Moreover, it is easy to believe that these scenes were a rare delight to their creator. Throughout their extent the artist demonstrates a high order of selectivity and yet a faithful adherence to the facts of human nature and common sense. Much matter of direct and indirect sort can be brought to support his interest in the mimetic instinct that is in so many people, but surely in greatest proportion among actors. Feste is the most delightful of his fools and Henry the most carefully wrought and fully realized of his kings. It is, of course, entirely accidental that these two are the two of all his characters most given to quick and brilliant mimicry. But his addiction to mimicry is, with each, a strong element in his charm. Mimicry is an especially effective social gift. It is not always kind but it is amusing to others and serves to fill up and color many an otherwise dull hour.

The peculiarly Shaksperean quality of this sort of impromptu dramatics is akin to his capitalization of Macbeth's bent for poetry. It lies in the recognition that there are persons who include in their stock of interesting and vivifying qualities a turn for quick improvisation and mimicry and that, while that quality might be omitted and they still be interesting and attractive persons, the inclusion of that quality and the provision of situations in which it may have play adds greatly to the tone of the total situation and to the charm of the characters.

CHAPTER IX

SHAKSPERE'S ACTORS: THE IMPERSONATORS

Two preëminent Shakspere characters are significant for their skill as impersonators. They are Hamlet, Prince of Denmark, and Edgar, eldest son of the Duke of Gloucester in *King Lear*.

I

The quality of Hamlet as an impersonator all heads up in his assuming and carrying through of what he calls an antic disposition. Practically all that seems to me worth saying about that is said in the two chapters which follow this one. Let us, therefore, state the matter as concisely as possible here and then go on to the discussion of Edgar and his role.

The idea of using the antic disposition came to Hamlet's mind through his observing of the whirling state of his thoughts after the revelations of the Ghost, both as he sensed it himself and as he saw its effect on his companions. When he began to employ it, a variety of uses for it occurred to him and he took them on, often making swift and baffling changes from one to another as his circumstances changed. Often as he mixed and blended the strains of this erratic behavior the situation became still more complex and bewildering. Always he lapsed from this into sane and sometimes almost happy intervals of balanced and companionable conduct in the company of his trusted friends or in situations which he enjoyed and which engaged his normal mind. But so pervasive and important had his management of the antic behavior become that he was, in a sense, always acting, for even upon a most sane moment old Polonius might enter, and then he must be at his act:

> O Jephthah, judge of Israel, what a treasure hadst thou!
>
> II, ii, 423

or

> Do you see yonder cloud that's almost in shape of a camel?
>
> III, ii, 392

There is with Hamlet not alone an obligation to act, but there is a pervading impression that, even though the mood is dark and there is a snarl beneath the whirl of words, there is also zest and gusto in the act, a sense of command, a sense of versatility and adequacy for the demands of the acting. There is nothing more repulsive, perhaps, than his disquisition to the King about the maggots in the dead body of Polonius and how a king may go a progress through the guts of a beggar, but it is done with the same philosophic zest for carrying a point to its utmost conclusion as is that perfectly sane discussion with Horatio in the churchyard on the dust of imperious Caesar and poor Yorick's skull.

The same Hamlet who almost hugged himself for having made so clever a mousetrap to catch the conscience of the King surely enjoyed just as heartily the management of his entire course of acting all the processes of the antic disposition. In this sense, he is Shakspere's greatest actor.

II

The whole impression of grandeur and of large-scale tragic forces which characterize *King Lear* so captures our attention that we accept without disturbance to our intelligence a good deal of rather insufficiently motivated plot material. The very lack of motivation of Cordelia's refusal to speak her love for her father in the first scene is best passed by with a minimum of question, for, when subjected to normal scrutiny, it does not enhance the credit of the young princess. Perhaps, even more, the deception of the Earl of Gloucester and of Edgar whereby they are persuaded each that the other is seeking his life, and the chain of devices employed by Edgar for his self-protection—and for other reasons—are matters too devious to be accounted for on rational grounds.

Our purpose in this chapter, however, is not to analyze motives but to study the acting abilities and skills of Edgar, to mark out the capital instances of it, the quality of it, and its variety. Edgar appears at the beginning and the end in his own proper person. But in between he assumes seven other guises. Moreover, most probably the actor who played Edgar was also the King of France in the first act. This suggests a very busy two hours and a half for a very versatile gentleman.

According to Professor Baldwin's listing of the actors in the plays at their earliest presentations, Henry Cundall (Condell) played Paris in *Romeo and Juliet*, Lysander in *A Midsummer Night's Dream*, Antonio in the *Merchant of Venice*, Don Pedro in *Much Ado about Nothing*, Oliver in *As You Like It*, Antony in *Julius Caesar*, Horatio in *Hamlet*, Cassio in *Othello*, Edgar in *King Lear*, Malcolm in *Macbeth*, and Octavius Caesar in *Antony and Cleopatra*.[1] There is much in common in all of these roles. Leaving aside, but only on the count of age, the Merchant Antonio, they are all young men of quick and active life, second to the great figures in their

[1] T. W. Baldwin, *Organization and Personnel of the Shakespearean Company*, 228.

plays but second to no one else, attractive, ambitious, generally admired and honored.

Each has, of course, his own singularities and is no mere duplicate of any other. So if Edgar's great singularity is his versatility as an impersonator of varied and highly different roles, that is a resource of Henry Cundall's art which he did not find it necessary to call upon in any other of these roles. If one could establish that the same actor played Robin Goodfellow, Feste, Hamlet, Edgar, and Ariel, then we might begin to assume the presence in the company of an especially gifted impersonator who enjoyed doing varied types of role and was valued for that ability. But no such theory can be even vaguely dreamed. So if we accept Cundall as Edgar, and if he was also the others in the Baldwin list, then Cundall, in this play, is undertaking a new sort of task for himself.

The villainous device by which Edmund, the Bastard, sets out to undermine his legitimate elder brother's standing with their father is itself a nice piece of acting, and once, at least, Edmund stands aside to view it in that light. The old Duke is easily persuaded of Edgar's perfidy and is quick to ascribe the wry state of the world to some recent eclipses. This arouses Edmund's cynical mind to assert with Cassius and Iago the sturdy self-determinism of the Stoics, pooh-poohing the eclipses and denying the validity of planetary influences:

> Fut! I should have been that I am, had the maidenliest star in the firmament twinkled on my bastardizing.
> I, ii, 143-145

At that moment he hears Edgar's footfall, and his move is to an assumed guise and a manner of speech into which he quickly falls:

Edgar—and pat! he comes, like the catastrophe of the
old comedy. My cue is villanous melancholy, with a sigh
like Tom o' Bedlam. O, these eclipses do portend these
divisions! Fa, sol, la, mi.

145-149

So Edmund proceeds completely to deceive both his
father and Edgar by the cleverness of his story but still
more by the convincingness of his acting.

Edgar is persuaded that his life is in deadly peril. He
must disguise himself, and the disguise he hits upon is
that of a Bedlam beggar. Its advantages are in its baseness:

> I will preserve myself; and am bethought
> To take the basest and most poorest shape
> That ever penury, in contempt of man,
> Brought near to beast.

II, iii, 6-9

The details of it are not spared:

> My face I'll grime with filth,
> Blanket my loins, elf all my hair in knots,
> And with presented nakedness outface
> The winds and persecutions of the sky.
> The country gives me proof and precedent
> Of Bedlam beggars, who . . . .
>
> *   *   *
>
> Sometime with lunatic bans, sometime with prayers,
> Enforce their charity. 'Poor Turlygod! Poor Tom!'
> That's something yet! Edgar I nothing am.

9-21

This role, with great variety and versatility Edgar
maintains until he is brought in by his father's friends
to lead the old blinded Duke to Dover (III, vii, 103-105).
In certain situations it seems clear he needs to keep his
identity hid. On one tense occasion (III, iv, 120-189),
Gloucester actually comes to the wretched hovel on the

tempest-blasted heath looking for the poor old King, and he stands with a lighted torch at the entrance questioning them—Tom o' Bedlam among them—as to their identities. There are other situations where it seems that Edgar's mad act is not only not necessary, but that it is being used ironically to hurt his friends. Perhaps there is no help for that. When the King, almost at the breaking point from tottering sanity to complete madness, comes to the hovel and sends the Fool in first, the Fool encounters the wild eyes and the hideous figure of the Bedlam and comes rushing out:

> Come not in here, nuncle, here's a spirit. Help me, help me!
>
> III, iv, 39-40

In a moment the Bedlam emerges, mumbling:

> Away! the foul fiend follows me! Through the sharp hawthorn blows the cold wind. Humh! go to thy cold bed, and warm thee.
>
> 46-48

And at this the King's wits break; from this point he is entirely mad.[2] That Edgar should thus be the unintentional means of giving the last impulse to the King's tottering mind is an irony that, like Cordelia's stubborn silence, may be but a part of the total irony of existence, and that may be an over-all theme for the entire play.

But our main point tarries. From the moment of the assumption of the Bedlam disguise until he doffs it somewhere on the journey to Dover, Edgar maintains this role and, horrifying and degraded as it often is, it is always most skillfully managed. Of course, we know that sometime not long before, Shakspere had been reading Richard

---

[2] A. C. Bradley in *Shakespearean Tragedy*, 287-288, settles on this as the moment of Lear's complete commitment to madness.

Harsnett's *A Declaration of Egregious Popish Impostures* (1603) and had fed his fancy on its lurid instances and its wild terminology. But, as always, this lore has been passed through the refining processes of his mind and what is useful for his purpose is now given into the possession of this fine loyal young chap, Edgar, for the purposes of a Bedlam impersonation. There are spectacular flashes of wit and whimsy and sometimes a sort of lurid grandeur in the mad maunderings of Tom: Lear says, "'Twas this flesh begot those pelican daughters," and Tom, quick as Hamlet, "Pillicock sat on Pillicock's Hill. 'Allow, allow, loo, loo'" (III, iv, 76-78). In his answer to Gloucester's question, "What are you there?" as he stands at the hovel entrance with his torch, Edgar describes himself and his filthy diet and ends:

> But mice and rats and such small deer,
> Have been Tom's food for seven long year.
> 144-145

When at the end of the scene, they hope they have the King asleep at last, Edgar with muted voice intones:

> Child Rowland to the dark tower came; His word was still
> Fie, foh, and fum!
> I smell the blood of a British man.
> 187-190

In speeches of which the following are examples, there is a sort of wild dissociated grandeur that haunts the memory:

> The prince of darkness is a gentleman! Modo he's call'd, and Mahu.
> 148-149
> Frateretto calls me, and tells me Nero is an angler in the lake of darkness.
> III, vi, 7-8

There is more, but this is enough to emphasize the keen wit and terrible resource with which Edgar maintains this acting. Of course, aside from the quality of it as acting, it has another use in filling up the roll of madmen at the great convocation of the mad in the hovel and later (III, vi), in the farmhouse. The Fool, not altogether fool but touched in his wits, who labors so loyally to outjest his master's heartstruck injuries; poor Lear himself, mad as the sea and wind; and Edgar, the fiend-ridden, demon-possessed Bedlam make up the convention. Kent, alone, is left sane to look on at this terrible congress of the mad. There is, obviously, one flaw in this picture as we have just drawn it. One of the madmen is not mad. But there come moments in the mad confusion when we forget that. Is it possible that there may be moments when even Edgar forgets or almost forgets it?

When Edgar is selected to lead his newly-blinded father, he starts in to maintain his Bedlam guise. The principal use for it is gone. The only value it can possibly have is for what it is worth as immunity from attack. But so struck is his heart with pity for the old Duke that he finds it bitterly hard to do. On the way he acquires a better costume and is now dressed like a common farmer or shepherd. Also he sloughs off the Bedlam talk although he persists in saying that he has not dropped it. Gloucester insists: "Methinks you are better spoken" (IV, vi, 10). But shortly they come to what Edgar avers is the very edge of Dover Cliff, and although he maintains that his speech is not altered, that only his garments are different, he delivers in beautifully modulated blank verse one of the greatest pieces of descriptive word painting ever spoken—the imagined appearance of the dizzying view from the cliff's verge (IV, vi, 11-24). He is preparing

to have the old man leap as if from the top. As a practical, well-informed man, he must have known the danger
in such a feat (42-48), but he says he does it to cure him
of his woes (34).

Whatever may have motivated Edgar the son or Edgar
the psychologist, Edgar the actor is at once very busy.
The old man leaps, and now there rushes to him Edgar,
who is now a man on the beach, onto which Gloucester
has presumably just "fallen." Into his expressions of wonder at the old man's fall and his proffers of help he interjects questions as to the creature which he says he saw
with the old man at the top just before he leaped:

> As I stood here below, methought his eyes
> Were two full moons; he had a thousand noses,
> Horns whelk'd and wav'd like the enridged sea.
> It was some fiend.
>
>   69-73

In this last flight of fancy regarding the creature, Edgar
etches in some rather terrifying final details as to its
appearance. It comes a bit like an old-fashioned signature
with an elaborate flourish of the pen to end it. Perhaps
this is Shakspere's and Edgar's way of being rid of Poor
Tom. At any rate we hear of him no more.

After their encounter in the fields with the mad King,
which comes next, Edgar once more offers to lead
Gloucester. As they move on they suddenly encounter
Oswald, Goneril's steward. Oswald is avid with the prospect of seizing Gloucester, a proclaimed prize, and he
is moving to take the old traitor back to his torturers when
the peasant, who is leading the blind Duke, swiftly inter-
poses to save him. But, by another of his quick changes,
he is now a peasant talking the conventional dialect of

"Chill not let go, zir, without further 'gacion."[3] This
is to shame the dandified man of the court for being
forced to defend himself against one so base, and Oswald
is properly shamed. "Out, dunghill!" he cries, and the
peasant thrusts him through saying, "Chill pick your
teeth, zir. Come! No matter vor your foins" (IV, vi,
250-251).

The letter which he takes from the slain steward's
pocket projects for Edgar a new set of disguises. Just
as the battle between the partisans of Lear and those of
Goneril-Regan is beginning, Edgar, now in disguise as
a commoner, rushes in to give the letter to the Duke of
Albany, saying:

> If you have victory, let the trumpet sound
> For him that brought it. Wretched though I seem
> I can produce a champion that will prove
> What is avouched there . . . .
>
> *   *   *
>
> When time shall serve, let but the herald cry,
> And I'll appear again.
>
> V, i, 41-48

The King's party loses the battle, and Albany, now in
effective charge of affairs, calls on the herald to sound
for the unknown challenger. Three blasts of the trumpet,
and Edgar enters armed this time but still with no marks
of identification. His fight with Edmund is fierce and

---

[3] This speech is used in Udall's (?) *Respublica* (1553) as speech of
the "people." It is called Cotswold speech in another interlude and is
used on the Elizabethan stage for country folk. Recall similar treatment of Northern speech in Chaucer's "Reeve's Tale," and Mak's
"southern tooth" in the Wakefield *Secunda Pastorum*. Kittredge
(*Sixteen Plays of Shaks.*, 1206, n. to *Lear*, IV, vi, 240 ff.), says of this
talk, "It accords well enough with the dialect of Somersetshire. Edgar
assumes the lingo that, from the Elizabethan time served as the stage
dialect of rusticity."

brief. Edmund is mortally hurt. Whereupon Edgar reveals himself as Edgar, after having been (1) Tom o' Bedlam, (2) a modified Bedlam leader of the blind, (3) a beachcomber who was at the foot of the cliff when Gloucester fell, (4) another beachcomber who became Gloucester's second leader, (5) a Somersetshire peasant, (6) an unknown bearer of a letter to Albany, (7) an unknown challenger of Edmund, supposed Earl of Gloucester—seven roles in quick succession, all convincingly borne.

In this rapid change and shift from one kind of impersonation to another there is a feeling of the extempore. Edgar is not following a carefully plotted sequence of roles any more than is Hamlet in the bewildering developments of the antic disposition. This is characteristic of a great deal that is interesting and stimulating in Shakspere—the feeling that characters are moving out adventurously, trying new devices, and exploring untried possibilities. One of the great exemplars of this sort of working is Iago, who more than once lets us know that, beyond the immediate moment, only in a general fashion does he know what he will do. The details he is leaving to the inspiration of their moment.

At the earliest inception of the idea of villainy, all he has is his stored-up hatred for the Moor and the will to do evil. The rest he will trust to work itself out in the instant of need:

> I have 't! It is engend'red! Hell and night
> Must bring this monstrous birth to the world's light.
> *Oth.*, I, iii, 409-410

Again, as the major lines of plot come to his mind—the plot to confound Cassio and to wreck the happiness of Desdemona and the Moor—that is all he has yet, but the details will come:

'Tis here but yet confus'd,
Knavery's plain face is never seen till us'd.

II, i, 320-321

Obviously the only kinship between Iago's technique and that of Edgar is in method. Edgar's sudden decision to use the "Cotswold speech" with Oswald was an inspiration of less than a moment. It is in this impression of inspired spontaneity that much of the sense of gusto and enjoyment of the act rests.

Let me remark also that the reluctance of many of these disguised persons to doff their masks is another mark of their enjoyment of their dangerous passages through the labyrinth of pretense. Portia and Nerissa are completely and entirely through with their disguises when the trial is over, but then comes the possibility of the hocus-pocus with their husbands' rings, and they go gleefully into it out of sheer bravado and the spirit of play. Rosalind went to the Forest of Arden specifically to place herself under her banished father's protection. Very soon she met him in the forest. Did she then throw herself into his arms, committing herself to his care? On the contrary, she held her disguise, bandied some clever words with him about being as well born as he, and stuck to her doublet and hose for purposes of some very trivial mischief which had fallen across her path.

So it is with the disguise of Kent, which surely might have been doffed, perhaps as early as the scene at dawn in Gloucester's castle yard as the King came upon him in the Duke of Cornwall's stocks. Certainly it could have been dispensed with after the storm. But he kept it and apparently kept it from everyone except Cordelia to the very end of the play. So Edgar did not need to hold onto the Bedlam role beyond the scenes of the storm, and, except for purposes of sheer suspense and display

of versatility, there was no compelling need for any of
his other guises. No use, that is, in the sense of rational
plot purpose. One is forced to admit that these changes
are interesting, and the appearance of the unknown challenger of Edmund (V, iii, 118), has the grandiose quality of the climactic passages in a Medieval Romance or
a Gothic novel.

This is all to say that Shakspere seems to have conceived for Edgar, as for Hamlet, a sort of self-realization
through his skill as an impersonator. *King Lear* without
all these varied presentations of Edgar would still be a
great and exciting play, but it would lose one of the most
pungent of its ingredients.

It is after Edgar's final doffing of his last simulated
role that there comes the strangest speech in the play,
and one of the strangest anywhere. It seems almost as if
it is to say that this Edgar, even though reduced to normal
and to his single self, is still strongly infused with whimsy
and is of such hair-trigger quality that only a little thing
would throw him again into some unexpected and erratic pattern of conduct. It is in the last scene—a crowded
and most gripping scene. Edgar is telling Albany of his
father's death and then of his unexpected discovery of
Kent's identity, when a gentleman of Goneril's household enters with a bloody knife, crying: "Help, help! O,
help!" and the strange question is Edgar's, "What kind of
help?" (V, iii, 222-223). I do not attempt either interpretation or analysis except to say that the very strange-
ness of the question is of the essence of Edgar, the great
impersonator.

It seems pertinent to repeat here what we said at the
end of the preceding chapter about the impromptu play
actors. The genius of Shakspere for character making
shows so often in the realization of a one-trait-more by

which he transmutes a strong and attractive character into something not only more attractive but more startlingly individual. The streak of coarseness in the fine-drawn personality of Mercutio, the poetic propensity of Macbeth, the mimetic instinct of Prince Henry—all these transform their total portraits. So it is with Edgar's persistent assumption of some role other than himself.

Remember, it is not because Condell the actor had shown proficiency at impersonation in preceding roles, and it is not even dramatically necessary that Edgar cloak over his real character beyond the mid-point of the play. But the dramatist's keen sense for fine shadings of portraiture has made him so and has left us at the end with a strange clue to the fact that the real Edgar, whom we have, in a sense, scarcely seen, is himself, an enigma. "What kind of help?" forsooth!

So we are, as before, the beneficiaries of a gifted observer of men and of a great application of a high order of common sense in the creation of character.

CHAPTER X

THE ANTIC DISPOSITION: WHENCE?

Hamlet's madness is a standard part of the story of the Prince of Denmark. It has its place in all the known versions of the tale. In Saxo Grammaticus' *Historia Danica* (1180), the story of the public murder of King Horwendil by his brother Fengo brings in Amleth, the son of the former and nephew of the latter. This Prince Amleth, to protect himself from his uncle's violence, feigns madness. This madness he maintains despite the suspicion of his associates that it is not genuine.

The use of madness as a means of protection is as old as the world. Notable instances in ancient story are of Odysseus seeking to evade Agamemnon's draft call by feigning insanity, plowing with his ill-sorted team on the sea shore and sowing salt in his field; of David frothing at the mouth in mad semblance to save himself from the Philistine king; and of Junius Brutus behaving like a dull thing to save himself from his vicious uncle, King Tarquin. It is based on a mystic connection between madness and divinity, and the belief that one so possessed is not to be dealt with but rather is to be left alone.

In F. de Belleforest's *Histoires Tragiques* (1570, but not in English translation until 1608) the story is essentially the same. So far as the madness goes, it *is* the same. The murder was a matter of public knowledge, and the Prince's madness was a means for self-preservation.

Between 1570 and 1600 or 1601—which last seems to fit best as a date for the first Shaksperean *Hamlet*—something of radical significance happened to the story. The reasoning I shall sketch briefly here follows a body of scholarly conjecture regarding a dramatic version of *Hamlet*, date about 1589, author possibly Thomas Kyd. This is what is called the *Ur-Hamlet*. Early in the next century this version seems to have been taken to Germany by a traveling company, who played it in Dresden in 1626. It is supposed that it was then adapted into a German version called *Der Bestrafte Brudermord*, which was printed in 1710. This German version exhibits some rather complete plot changes. In it the murder is no longer a matter of public knowledge. It is now an Italian Renaissance intrigue type of murder. No one knows it was murder. The murderer is most careful to cover up all clues. A court communique, much like that in Shakspere's version, was given out to establish a public understanding:

> 'Tis given out that, sleeping in my orchard,
> A serpent stung me.

Ham., I, v, 35-36

Since our major assumption is that both the German version and Shakspere's ultimate version took their cues from the *Ur-Hamlet*, it is most important to bear it in mind as the beginning point of change from the original story as it is found in Saxo and Belleforest. The madness carries over, as we have said, and appears in all versions, but we cannot know exactly how this *Ur-Hamlet*, in its changed plot, motivated the madness. For with the change in type of story, the motivating of the madness becomes a sort of plot-maker's *nonplus*. The original purpose of the madness was protection against a known violent man. In the changed plot no one knows it was murder, no one, that is, but Claudius and the King's Ghost and—most lately and secretly—Hamlet. Claudius does not know that a ghost is walking and, of course, does not know that Hamlet knows. So why does Hamlet assume the guise of madness? It is part of Shakspere's treatment not to say. And while Hamlet makes most amazing use of the madness and though he has much to say about it *per se*, he never even glancingly says what it is for.

In *Der Bestrafte Brudermord* it is explained twice. Each time Hamlet announces bluntly his intention of using it, and each time he says why. In both instances he is speaking to Horatio:

> From this moment I will begin a feigned madness, and thus feigning, so cunningly will I play my part that I shall find an opportunity to avenge my father's death.
> *Der Bes. Bruder.*, I, vi
> My worthy friend Horatio, through this assumed madness I hope to get the opportunity of revenging my father's death.
> II, v[1]

Let me propose two reasons why Shakspere elected to keep the madness in his plot. I do not mean to suggest that he thought long and deeply about omitting it. The idea probably did not occur to him, for there were these two strong reasons for keeping it. (1) It had become a fixed part of the Hamlet saga. It could no more be omitted, as Professor Parrott says,[2] than one could tell the story of Joan of Arc and leave out her "voices," or, we may add, than one could tell the story of Tom

---

[1] Translation from *Variorum Shakespeare*, "Hamlet," II, 121-142. These speeches to Horatio are paralleled in Shakspere's version by the unrecorded account of his father's death which Hamlet gave Horatio. III, ii, 81-82.

[2] T. M. Parrott, *Shakespeare, Twenty-three Plays and Sonnets*, 670.

Sawyer and omit the whitewashing of the fence, or the George Washington story and leave out the episode of the cherry tree. We can imagine the clamor in a London theater in 1600 at a *Hamlet* with no madness in it. (2) Madness real or feigned is a good dramatic element. The mad Hieronimo of Kyd's *Spanish Tragedy* and the mad Hamlet of the pre-Shaksperean play proved most effective. In the parlance of our day, it is good box-office. And feigned madness is better than real madness, for it adds the element of having the audience in on a secret which the people on the stage do not know. This sharpens interest. Such interest is clear in all cases of physical disguise; madness such as Hamlet's is disguise only of a subtler sort.

So it may be that Shakspere troubled himself not at all about this unmotivated madness. Many students of the play have not seemed aware of the question, and many spectators in the theater have not raised it at all. But even with all this, I am proceeding to suggest that it is motivated. It is my purpose in this chapter to seek to show not so much what it is for as whence the idea came. A consideration of what it is for will occupy the following chapter.

The processes of this discussion turn on the assumption that Shakspere's creative methods are fundamentally careful and conscious and of high integrity. He has, as all good artists do, moments of sheer inspiration, and frequently he falls short, as all artists do, of perfect coherence and validity. Especially he will sacrifice credibility for theatrical effectiveness as in the stopped marriage in *Much Ado*, the Dover Cliff business in *King Lear*, and the revivified statue in the *Winter's Tale*. But most of the time—more of the time, we believe, than is true of most artists—his genius is checked by observation and experience and his handling of situations, considered psychologically, is highly valid. We are much more likely to find him working so than otherwise.

The presiding thesis of this entire book is that Shakspere's genius is guided and implemented by common sense. All the varied materials that are included in it are oriented to that emphasis. It seems to me to be as clearly present in this matter of the motivation of the feigned insanity of Prince Hamlet as anywhere. The old practical motivation of self-protection has been invalidated by the change in the circumstances of the murder. But tradition and common acceptance have fixed insanity as a part of the plot and the audience will demand its use. Madness is good stuff dramatically considered, and not alone does the audience realize this; the playwright does too.

There are two alternatives (not three), the one is to go on and use the insanity for its dramatic value and leave it unmotivated. It will contribute much to dramatic effectiveness, and no one will note its lack of rational motive. The other alternative is to motivate it, if for no other reason, for Hamlet's sake. Hamlet is highly, sensitively intelligent and to shove off onto his shoulders a burden of conduct which will occupy him throughout much of the play with no motivation, is not creditable to his understanding. Accordingly Shakspere uses Hamlet's own realization of the strange working of his mind in the scene with the Ghost as a basis for his quick seizing upon the possible uses to be made of an antic disposition. This is, we are saying, for Hamlet's self-clarification, but it is also highly to the credit of Shakspere's basic appreciation of character and especially of the transcending fineness of this great character, who, if he does not precisely know what he is going to do with the antic disposition, at least knows now whence it came, and will be thereby more content. For what follows we shall be reaching to the very top shelf for our vindication of our author's integrity.

First let us state in concise form the progress of events and its conclusion. Our first observation of the Prince is in the State Council Scene (I, ii), in which we catch an impression of him as terribly distraught by his father's death but especially by his mother's infamy. In scenes iv and v he sees and talks with his father's spirit, which tells him that his death was murder and which enjoins upon him a solemn promise of revenge. At once, when the Ghost is gone, Hamlet finds his mind leaping from point to point of suggestion, behaving, indeed, most wildly and whirlingly. When his friends join him, he still finds strange mental associations coming in between himself and the sober level of thought, and he observes that this behavior is bewildering his friends. So, quickly, out of this the notion comes as if to say: *See what I am doing to bewilder and confuse these good fellows by my mind's strange antics which are unintentional. What may I not do to Heaven knows whom with such behavior as I may intentionally employ?* Thus is born the idea of the antic disposition. *What will be the use of it need not now be asked. Let us try it and see.*

It will now be our process to go back through the text with more care to observe the working out of this matter. It is understood that we are not at all concerned to explain the presence of the madness as a plot element in this play. That is long ago and ineradicably fixed by the Saxo history and its retellings by others. Nor are we dealing with Shakspere's reasons for retaining it. Those reasons we have stated and they are strong and clear. What we are seeking to show is that Shakspere's genius found a means for, shall we say, satisfying Hamlet himself with a motivation for it out of his shrewd observation of his own mind's behavior. This is a vastly different thing from the wooden process of the Hamlet of the German play, who announces with all the impersonality of Friar Bacon's Brazen Head: "from this moment I will begin a feigned madness."

Before we go farther with this, let us pause a moment to remark about the mind of Hamlet. It is well, also, to think now and again about the mind of Shakspere, but that is another matter. It is probably correct to say that for alertness, adroitness, inventiveness, for the contemplative quality, and for poetic fancy, Hamlet's mind represents the highest level of possibility. Many years ago, in recognition of the brilliant achievement and fine poetic gifts of Edwin Arlington Robinson, Hoyt Hudson of Princeton wrote a finely-conceived sonnet in which he celebrated the qualities of quickness, incisiveness, and clairvoyance which marked the New England poet's mind and concluded that this is the best mind among us since Prince Hamlet fell dying upon the palace pavement in Elsinore.[3] This is high praise for Robinson, for Hamlet, and perhaps especially for Shakspere, who, after all, made this Hamlet of the inimitable mind. It is this mind which now takes up this antic guise.

When the Ghost has made its full revelation and has provided Hamlet with his unforgettable watchword, "Adieu, adieu, adieu! Remember me" (I, v, 91), he vanishes with the shadows in retreat before the morning,

[3] *Literary Digest*, 107:24, Oct. 25, 1930.

and Hamlet is left alone with his *word*. So he proceeds to swear his oath of vengeance, swearing by heaven, by earth—even by hell—and as he swears, his hands go up to clasp his head, in which distracted globe his thoughts are seething. "Remember me!" that's the *word*. So he determines to erase all else from the tables of his memory—all else. Then by a quick side thrust his thought catches on the image of his mother, "O most pernicious woman!" and then on the villain King—smiling. And with the reference still close at hand to the metaphoric tables of his memory, he snatches from the folds of his doublet his commonplace book. "My tables! Meet it is I set it down that one may smile, and smile, and be a villain. At least I am sure it may be so in Denmark" (I, v, 107-109), speaking it slowly as with deepest intentness he makes his entry. "So," clapping to the book and pocketing it, "So, uncle, there you are." And he goes back to his *word*. The entire speech is its own best comment:

> *Ghost.* Adieu, adieu, adieu! Remember me.
> *Ham.* O all you host of heaven! O earth! What else?
> And shall I couple Hell? Hold, hold, my heart!
> And you, my sinews, grow not instant old,
> But bear me stiffly up. Remember thee?
> Ay, thou poor ghost, while memory holds a seat
> In this distracted globe. Remember thee?
> Yea, from the table of my memory
> I'll wipe away all trivial fond records,
> All saws of books, all forms, all pressures past
> That youth and observation copied there,
> And thy commandment all alone shall live
> Within the book and volume of my brain,
> Unmix'd with baser matter. Yes, by heaven!
> O most pernicious woman!
> O villain, villain, smiling damned villain!
> My tables! Meet it is I set it down
> That one may smile, and smile, and be a villain;

At least I am sure it may be so in Denmark.
Writes.
So, uncle, there you are.   Now to my word:
It is 'Adieu, adieu! Remember me.'
I have sworn 't.

I, v, 91-112

To recapitulate further would be tedious. It is chiefly necessary to observe here the operation of a powerful and most active mind in a situation of sore distraction. It is fixed upon a point and is driving swift and straight for that point, but, at the same time, it is working so strongly as to be generating an excess of power, throwing off sparks of suggestion and association beyond the need of the normal purposes of the machine. Those of you who have minds at all creative and active will catch the reality of the situation. All who work with ideas have repeatedly had the experience in the midst of concentrated effort of finding the mind or the fringe of the mind running out of bounds to the most irrelevant side issues. There could scarcely be a better illustration of this than the business of the quick entry in the commonplace book. What the admirers of Hamlet would not give for a peep into that book! What does he think he'll ever do with this entry? But back to our word. Hamlet's mind is at full speed.[4]

Just at the moment when he closes the notebook and completes his oath, Marcellus and Horatio call from the other side of the stage through what must be understood to be darkness. Marcellus calls, "Illo, ho, ho, my lord" (115), and the call, as he gives it, is so like the call that

[4] Other Shakspere characters show this same propensity for the mixing of intensity of attention with irrelevancies. Juliet, Cleopatra, and Imogen are persons with a capacity for high seriousness and at the same time for whimsicality and inadvertence. Philip Falconbridge and Mercutio exhibit it in a lesser degree.

one hunter gives to his companion, hid from him in the
thick cover of the field, that Hamlet, by another quick
association, matches it with the familiar return, "Hillo,
ho, ho, boy! Come, bird, come" (116). And now they
rejoin him and are all agog to hear his story:

> *Hor.*   What news, my lord?
> *Ham.* O, wonderful!
> *Hor.* Good my lord, tell it.
> *Ham.*   No, you will reveal it.
> *Hor.* Not I, my lord, by heaven!
> *Mar.*   Nor I, my lord.
> *Ham.* How say you then? Would heart of man once
> think it?
> But you'll be secret?
> *Both.*   Ay, by heaven, my lord.
> *Ham.* There's ne'er a villain dwelling in all Denmark
> But he's an arrant knave.
>
> 118-123

Mr. Dover Wilson's point that for some reason Hamlet suspects the purposes of Marcellus and is therefore
secretive here may be taken as you will.[5] It is not carried
through to any use in the further developing of the plot.
It is true, of course, that very soon after this, Hamlet
does seek out Horatio alone and tells him "the circumstance . . . of my father's death" (III, ii, 81-82). But for
whatever reason, he is not telling it just now. This is a
scene of strangely mixed values. But among its elements
this wildly unstable condition of the Prince's mind is a
major one. Note the scene once more: *Hor.* What news?
Ham. O, wonderful! *Hor.* Tell it. *Ham.* No, you'll
reveal it. *Hor.* and *Mar.* O, no, no! *Ham.* Very well.
So he draws them into a close huddle:

> There's ne'er a villain living in all Denmark
> But he's an arrant knave.
>
> 122-123

[5] *What Happens in Hamlet*, 80.

And they are dumbfounded, and Hamlet steps back, almost as a craftsman steps back to view his work from a better angle, to watch their faces and take note of the effect of this complete blank of revelation. The next speech shows how this erratic conduct strikes his fellows. Horatio says:

> There needs no ghost, my lord, come from the grave
> To tell us this.
> *Ham.*   Why, right! You are in the right!
> And so, without more circumstance at all,
> I hold it fit that we shake hands and part;
> You, as your business and desire shall point you,
> For every man hath business and desire,
> Such as it is; and for my own poor part,
> Look you, I'll go pray.
>
>   124-132

What could be more disturbing to a rational exchange than such a speech as this? The quick drawing together to hear the "wonderful" news, the flat blank of nothing coming from the revealer, Horatio's almost stupid literality in reply, and now the solemn procession of the Prince's words toward conclusion—possibly relevation—and then the sudden drop to the cryptic

>   . . . and for my own poor part,
>   Look you, I'll go pray.

Our verdict is the same as Horatio's:

> These are but wild and whirling words, my lord.
>   133

So it is clear that Hamlet's mental erraticism, which made its entrance first when he stood alone on the threshold of distraction after the Ghost's departure and which continued when his friends rejoined him—a behavior marked by irrelevancies, by capricious leaps from one crag of

232   SHAKSPERE AND COMMON SENSE

association to another unseen before—has now become a
subject for observation and comment by those who share
these events with him. It is possible—I think it likely—
that beginning with the burst bubble of expectancy as
they huddled to hear Hamlet's news, he has been consciously trying this trick on his friends.

Now he says:

> I am sorry they offend you, heartily;
> Yes, faith, heartily.
> *Hor.*   There's no offence, my lord.
> *Ham.* Yes, by Saint Patrick, but there is, Horatio.[6]
>
> 134-136

Then there is Hamlet's quick (and serious) word about
the authenticity of the Ghost and he turns to the matter
of securing an oath from these friends.

The terms of the oath are simple enough and the reason for requiring it clear enough and natural enough.
It is merely to enjoin them to swear not to tell what they
have seen tonight. It is to be a solemn oath sworn upon
the cross-like hilt of the Prince's sword. But just as they
prepare to swear there comes the strange business of the
voice beneath the platform which is, at its best construction, an intrusion on the solemnity of the oath taking;

[6] The Folio reading of this line is:
  Yes, by Saint Patrick, but there is, my lord.
Textually, this reading seems to lack authority, but what a beautiful
added example it would be, were it proved valid, of the ironic and
whimsical play of Hamlet's mind in this "wild and whirling" scene.
  Compare with this reading a whimsical parallel from another play:
  Mess. Where is my lady?
  Por.   Here. What would my lord?
                        Merch., II, ix, 85.
And another:
  Groom. Hail, royal prince!
  Rich.   Thanks, noble peer.
                        R. II, V, v, 67.

at its worst, it may portend the coming in of a diabolic agency. Again they prepare to swear, and the sepulchral voice intrudes. They shift ground to be away from its blasting influence and once more prepare to swear. Again the voice has burrowed its way through earth to be once more beneath them. So a fourth time they prepare to take the oath—but this time the terms of the oath have changed, changed completely. It is no longer to swear not to tell what they have seen and heard. It is really not an oath about tonight at all but about days and nights to come:

> But come!
> Here, as before, never, so help you mercy,
> How strange or odd soe'er I bear myself
> (As I perchance hereafter shall think meet
> To put an antic disposition on),
> That you, at such times seeing me, never shall,
> With arms encumb'red thus, or this headshake,
> Or by pronouncing of some doubtful phrase,
> As 'Well, well, we know,' or 'We could, an if we would,'
> Or 'If we list to speak,' or 'There be, an if they might,'
> Or such ambiguous giving out, to note
> That you know aught of me—this not to do,
> So grace and mercy at your most need help you,
> Swear.
>
> I, v, 168-181

Thus does Hamlet's antic disposition come to be. Now it lies a more or less unproved weapon in the arsenal of his devices. Being new and sharp and already proved a little in brief trial upon his friends, it is far more than likely that he will use it, but just now it is

> As I perchance hereafter shall think meet.
>
> 171

Perhaps as much as two months elapse between this

closing scene of Act I and the beginning of Act II. In those two months much takes place, and when Act II opens, the antic disposition has been for some time in full wear.

CHAPTER XI

THE ANTIC DISPOSITION: WHY?

I am by no means the first to point out that Hamlet found the suggestion that led him to assume the antic disposition in the erratic behavior of his mind, first alone and later with his friends, after the departure of the Ghost.

In his *Shakespere—His Mind and Art*, Professor Dowden says:

> It is now, in a sudden inspiration of excited feeling, that Hamlet conceives the possibility of his assuming an antic disposition. What is Hamlet's purpose in this? He finds that he is involuntarily conducting himself in a wild and unintelligible fashion. He has escaped "from his own feelings of the overwhelming and supernatural by a wild transition to the ludicrous—a sort of cunning bravado, bordering on the flights of delirium." His mind struggles "to resume its accustomed course, and effect a dominion over the awful shapes and sounds that have usurped its sovereignty." He assumes madness as a means of concealing his actual disturbance of mind. His over-excitability may betray him; but if it be a received opinion that his mind is unhinged, such an access of over-excitement will pass unobserved and unstudied.[1]

Professor Dover Wilson's statement is also of extreme interest:

> In short, this passage of a hundred lines [I, v, 92-191] exhibits Hamlet in a state of extreme emotional instability,

[1] 127-128. Dowden credits the two quoted passages to S. T. Coleridge and Hartley Coleridge, respectively.

and with an intellect tottering on its seat. Furthermore the "antic disposition" has manifested itself on three separate occasions before Hamlet ever refers to it at all: in the "table-book" speech, at Horatio and Marcellus's entry, and in conjuring the "worthy pioneer" underground. The second of these is as typical an example of its use as may be found anywhere else in the play; and like the other two it is clearly partly deliberate and partly involuntary; that is to say, the mood comes unsought but is welcomed as affording relief when it does come, and is accordingly purposely elaborated and prolonged. In a word, Shakespeare wishes us to feel that Hamlet assumes madness because he cannot help it. The tragic burden has done its work, and he is conscious that he no longer retains perfect control over himself. What more natural than that he should conceal his nervous breakdown behind a mask which would enable him to let himself go when the fit is upon him? [2]

Between my statement in the foregoing chapter and these two statements just cited the primary difference is in my belief that the assuming of the madness was conscious and voluntary, and the opinion of these gentlemen that it is involuntary. Dowden: "His mind struggles to resume its accustomed course, . . . He assumes madness as a means of concealing his actual disturbance of mind." And Wilson: "Hamlet assumes madness because he cannot help it. . . . [H]e no longer retains perfect control over himself."

This view that the madness or the idea of the madness was forced upon him seems to me untenable in view of all that follows. In favorable situations, *i.e.*, when alone with Horatio or when the players come, Hamlet is delightfully and stimulatingly sane. There is no faintest suggestion of him as one in the grip of uncontrollable tendencies toward unbalance. Moreover, in the solilo-

[2] *What Happens in Hamlet*, 91-92.

quies, although in two of them (I and III) he discusses
suicide, and although in two of them (II and V) he is
most severe with himself for his inaction, he is never inco-
herent, never erratic, but always logical and relevant in
his processes of thought. As to the mad behavior, it comes
at call; it changes to suit the person involved; it is put
off as quickly as it is assumed. On this subject Hamlet
himself has the clearest words. To Rosencrantz and
Guildenstern:

> I am but mad north-north-west. When the wind is south-
> erly I know a hawk from a handsaw.
>
> II, ii, 396-397

And to his mother:

> My pulse as yours doth temperately keep time
> And makes as healthful music. It is not madness
> That I have utt'red.
>
> III, iv, 139-142

> . . . I essentially am not in madness,
> But mad in craft.
>
> 187-188

There is also in the plot the genuine, involuntary, uncontrolled, and uncontrollable madness of Ophelia, a
clear and serviceable device, if we need one, to show
how different that is from the antic disposition. But we
are not primarily concerned to discuss whether the madness is real or feigned. We are engaged only in an attempt to show that it is not thrust upon Hamlet nor is it
something behind which he hides to cover the near unbalance of his mind.

It springs out of the excess of his mind's activity. It
strikes him as he snatches his notebook to make his ironic
entry; it strikes him as he shouts back the lost hunter's
answering cry; and it strikes him as he sets up the situation of seeming about to tell his news only to let the

revelation terminate in a prolix nothing. At this point
he begins to see his friends' bewilderment at his strange
words, so he definitely prepares the next episode, com-
mending them to their respective businesses and desires,
ending with the strange erratic words:

> . . . and for my own poor part,
> Look you, I'll go pray.
>
> I, v, 131-132

and then standing aside to watch them as their puzzled
reaction comes:

> *Hor.* These are but wild and whirling words, my lord.
>
> 134

Professor Adams says, "Possibly the stratagem of pre-
tended insanity was suggested to Hamlet by his antic behavior toward his friends, and the remarkable effect it
produced upon them."[3] With that I quite agree except
that I go further to omit "possibly." It seems to me to be
clearer than that.

We shall come shortly to some conjecture as to the
purpose of the madness, but before that let us linger a
little over the matter of the bulk it has in relation to the
whole play. The one theme or plot element which might
challenge it for first interest is the suspense created
by the slowness of Hamlet's program of vengeance—
the much-discussed problem of delay.

In the line numbering of the Kittredge text, *Hamlet*
contains 4062 lines. There are 1200 lines which have to
do in one way or another with the madness. The passage
having to do with the inception of the idea in I, v, consists of 53 lines; actual displays of the madness in all its
varieties occupy 618 lines. Of this there are twelve separate instances: 130 lines with Ophelia, 83 lines with

[3] J. Q. Adams, *Hamlet*, 218.

Polonius, 98 with the King, 282 with Rosencrantz and Guildenstern, and 15 lines with the entire court present. There are 333 lines devoted to talk about the madness by others; 28 lines are given to a use of it as explanation of an action; and 178 lines are taken for the presentation of the genuine madness of Ophelia.

Except for his public speeches from the throne and his bitter hour alone with his conscience after the play is broken up, Claudius talks of little else. It is also much a subject of Gertrude's thought. Polonius buzzes with accounts of it and theory about it. It is a major element.

Varieties of Madness: With Ophelia

This mad behavior has its varieties governed by the person with whom Hamlet is in converse. In his encounters with Ophelia it is often of a terrifying and intimidating sort such as the scene in the sewing closet and the "Get thee to a nunnery" speech in the lobby. With her in the Palace before the play begins, it is not pretty behavior, for it runs to the suggestive and salacious. The terrifying type of speech is surely not for its effect on her, but for the indirect effect the report of it will have when she tells her father and, more particularly, when he tells the King. In the lobby (III, i) Hamlet knows who is behind the arras, and his speech is mainly not for the poor terrified girl but for the eavesdroppers:

> Where's your father?
> 134

> I say, we will have no more marriages. Those that are married already—all but one—shall live; the rest shall keep as they are.
> 156-157

The indecent and off-color nuances in his talk with

the girl in the lobby scene and in the Hall of the Palace
are warranted, in part, by his belief that she is of tainted
character. How can a girl be otherwise who is so much
in the rotten atmosphere of this court and so much in
the society of this King? "Let her not walk i' th' sun"
(II, ii, 185). And what sort of girl is it that goes open-
eyed into the business of letting herself be used as the
decoy in a sanity trap? "I'll loose my daughter to him"
(162). And who can accept as innocence her gilding
of the ugly action with a prayer book and a show of
devotion? "Ha, ha! Are you honest?" (III, i, 104). The
whole purpose, therefore, of both the terrifying passages
and the obscene is to feed the Polonius theory ("Mad
for thy love?") and then by his rude indifference to her
in the lobby to confuse that theory. Says Claudius after
watching Hamlet's rough indifference and violent outcry:

> Love? his affections do not that way tend.
>
>   170

Varieties of Madness: With Polonius

For his mad exchanges with Polonius the pattern is
derision and mockery with, from time to time, an infusion
of the sort of thing that will feed the love-madness
theory. The first scene of the antic behavior that we actually see is II, ii, 168-221. Through this exchange Hamlet's wit lashes out at the old man:

> You are a fishmonger.
>
>   174

and a few lines later:

> Have you a daughter?
>
>   183

Then there is the recital of the symptoms of age—checked

against the present specimen, and the quizzing of Polonius about his career as an actor at the university. But most delicious of all:

> Do you see yonder cloud that's almost in shape of a camel?
>
> III, ii, 392

Shakspere must have conceived of something in Polonius that he feels will be almost irresistible to the mimetic instinct of an actor, for, as he sends the First Player away to be cared for by Polonius, the Prince says:

> Follow that lord—and look you mock him not.[4]
>
> II, ii, 570

Varieties of Madness:
With Rosencrantz and Guildenstern

Hamlet's mad behavior with Rosencrantz and Guildenstern is of a mixed sort. He tantalizes them with refences to Denmark as a prison, to his bad dreams, and to his loss of delight in the world and in man—and in woman. His quick intelligence tells him they are in the King's employ and have been sent for to spy upon him. He browbeats them into an admission of this. Then in the deserted Palace Hall after the play is broken off, he finds their clumsy efforts to plumb his secret increasingly irritating, and he loses his temper as he spins his mad devices for them:

> *Guil.*   If it shall please you to
> make me a wholesome answer . . . .
> *Ham.* Sir, I cannot.
> *Guil.* What, my lord?
> *Ham.* Make you a wholesome answer; my wit's diseas'd.

---

[4] Professor Alwin Thaler has noted this reference in his *Shakespeare and Democracy*, "The Original Malvolio," 135, as a possible sidelight on Shakspere's own early experience with Lord Strange's steward, William Ffarington.

Ros.   My lord, you once did love me.
Ham.   And do still, by these pickers and stealers!
Ros.   Good my lord, what is your cause of distemper? . . .
Ham.   Sir, I lack advancement.

                                 III, ii, 327-334; 347-354

And then with a sudden shift of tempo and mood he
takes a recorder from a passing musician and begins to
urge Guildenstern to play upon it. Guildenstern demurs,
but Hamlet explains the governance of it carefully and
in literal detail, only to fly from that into his bitter application:

> Why, look you now, how unworthy a thing you make
> of me! You would play upon me; you would seem to
> know my stops; you would pluck out the heart of my
> mystery; you would sound me from my lowest note to
> the top of my compass; and there is much music, excel-
> lent voice, in this little organ, yet cannot you make it
> speak. 'Sblood, do you think I am easier to be play'd on
> than a pipe? Call me what instrument you will, though
> you can fret me, you cannot play upon me.
>
>   379-389

In the remaining passages involving Rosencrantz and
Guildenstern, as their close dealings with treachery become more and more clear, Hamlet's simulated madness
becomes so confused with genuine rage that it is difficult to know which is which. It has been the very essence of this hero's tragic experience to find persons
whom he had trusted turning out to be in reality false
and unworthy. His mother, whom he had idolized, is
fickle, shallow, incestuous, evil. Little Ophelia, who had
caught his fancy by her beauty and air of innocence, is
a willing tool of his enemies. And now, these old schoolfellows are easily and shamefully branded as disloyal
to him and creatures of the wicked King. And at their

treachery Hamlet's anger rises to great heat. When he knows that they are to accompany him to England, he leaps to a quick and ominous conclusion:

> There's letters seal'd; and my two schoolfellows,
> Whom I will trust as I will adders fang'd,
> They bear the mandate; they must sweep my way
> And marshal me to knavery. Let it work;
> For 'tis the sport to have the enginer
> Hoist with his own petar; and 't shall go hard
> But I will delve one yard below their mines
> And blow them to the moon. O, 'tis most sweet,
> When in one line two crafts directly meet.[5]
>
> III, iv, 202-210

Except for the briefest moment when they undertake to quiz him as he is lugging the guts into the neighbor room, that is the last we see of the old schoolfellows—the last we see but not the last we know. In Hamlet's breathtaking account of the night on shipboard when he rifled his companions' dispatch cases and got unsealed the commission for his instant execution, he comes to speak of the part borne in it all by Rosencrantz and Guildenstern. We assume he realized that they did not know the precise contents of their packet. In a sense they are simply feed servants doing their duty, but that he brushes aside. They know for whom they are working and, as we have suggested, Hamlet's whole recent experience seems to be more and more one of

> Being . . . benetted round with villanies.
>
> V, ii, 29

[5] This is the metaphor of Hamlet, the Navy man, the Sailor Prince, the one who led a boarding party onto a pirate ship, got left alone on her, and talked himself most adroitly out of a pirate's quick noose (IV, vi). The figure of the two crafts meeting in one line is clearly taken from the methods and maneuvers of naval fighting in Shakspere's time.

So he shows them not only no mercy; he goes out of his way to show them unmercy. For he changes their commission; erases his own name not only, but writes in theirs, adjuring the English King:

> *Ham.* That, on the view and knowing of these contents,
> Without debatement further, more or less,
> He should the bearers put to sudden death,
> Not shriving time allow'd.
>
>   *   *   *
>
> *Hor.* So Guildenstern and Rosencrantz go to 't.
> *Ham.* Why, man, they did make love to this employment!
> They are not near my conscience.
>
>   V, ii, 44-58

Varieties of Madness: With King Claudius

The other principal variety of madness which Hamlet manifests is that shown in the presence of the King. It, too, is mixed with genuine rage, and the two strains mingle in a fashion which adds to the color of the situation, but makes separation most difficult.

As we have suggested, not all of the mad rage of the lobby scene with Ophelia is for the poor terrified girl's benefit. Some of its bitterest speech is for the King, who is behind the curtain as we and Hamlet know.[6]

At the play, as the court assembles, Hamlet parries

---

[6] I am satisfied to go along with Dover Wilson's idea (*What Happens in Hamlet*, 106-108) that at II, ii, 160 the audience sees Hamlet about to enter. Line 160, "You know sometimes he walks four hours together/Here in the lobby" is an unwitting gesture of Polonius, which however unwitting, serves to direct the eye of the spectators to the Prince, who stops, waits, and patiently hears all the plot of the loosing of Ophelia to him. So when he comes down the lobby in III, i, and finds her there, he recalls that part of the plan and that the King and Polonius are to be present as "lawful espials" and he recognizes the situation and knows who is behind the curtain.

briefly with Claudius. His speech is riddling and broken. His rapier thrusts become swifter as he explains the play to the King. This talk, as Claudius himself said of a less important passage:

> though it lack'd form a little
> Was not like madness.
>
> III, i, 171-172

As Hamlet and his mother talk together in this scene, the King breaks in:

> *King.* Have you heard the argument? Is there no offense in 't?
> *Ham.* No, no! They do but jest, poison in jest; no offense i' the world.
> *King.* What do you call the play?
> *Ham.* 'The Mousetrap.' Marry, how? Tropically . . . . 'Tis a knavish piece of work; but what o' that? Your Majesty, and we that have free souls, it touches us not. Let the gall'd jade winch; our withers are unwrung.
>
> III, ii, 242-253

To us, knowing what we know, this is trenchant speech, terrible in its irony; but the court knows that Hamlet is mad, so those who hear him—all but one—take it as madness.

Hamlet's colloquy with the King about the dead body of Polonius is one of the unsavoriest passages in any book. It is mad speech of a madness concocted out of disdain for its subject and contempt for the hearer:

> *King.* Now, Hamlet, where's Polonius?
> *Ham.* At supper.
> *King.* At supper? Where?
> *Ham.* Not where he eats, but where he is eaten. A certain convocation of politic worms are e'en at him. Your worm is your only emperor for diet. We fat all creatures else to fat us, and we fat ourselves for maggots. Your fat King and your lean beggar is but variable service—

two dishes, but to one table. That's the end.
King. Alas, alas!⁷
Ham. A man may fish with the worm that hath eat of
a King, and eat of the fish that hath fed of that worm.
King. What dost thou mean by this?
Ham. Nothing but to show you how a King may go a
progress through the guts of a beggar.

IV, iii, 17-33

And then in the flattest and most vulgar descent of wit in
the whole play:

King. Where is Polonius?
Ham. In heaven. Send thither to see. If your messenger
find him not there, seek him i' th' other place yourself.

34-37

One more bit remains for note before we leave the subject of Hamlet's madness in the presence of the King. It
is an odd bit, for it is not spoken but written. It is the
note which Hamlet sends the King to tell him he is still in
life and back in Denmark. It is terse, impudent, threat-
ening. At least one of its adjectives is fiercely ironic:

High and Mighty,—You shall know I am set naked on
your kingdom. Tomorrow shall I beg leave to see your
kingly eyes; when I shall (first asking your pardon there-
unto) recount the occasion of my sudden and more
strange return.

Hamlet.
IV, vii, 43-48

Thus, in quick survey, we have seen the four varieties
of madness which Hamlet devises for use with these different persons. The fact that he varies it as he does

⁷ One would like to know whether the King's exclamation, "Alas,
alas!" is from his troubled conscience as these crude images of mor-
tality are brought in, or merely the conventional compassion of those
who speak pityingly of the mad and other unfortunates. This King,
we know e'er now, is a good dissimulator.

is only one more proof of his complete control of it, and
is also suggestive of its various purposes.

His high rage with his mother in her chamber, in the
course of which he sets up a mirror for her soul and reads
her a vehement lecture on her relations with two kings—
a rage punctuated by a quick thrust at a rat behind the
arras, and later by the entrance of the Ghost—is not madness. Note it carefully; it is coherent and full of desperate
earnestness even though its tempo rises and the tone of it
becomes shrill. It is not madness, but Gertrude thinks it
is; especially is she quick to label as "ecstasy" his terrified
reaction to the Ghost which she cannot see (III, iv,137).
And in the next scene the terms she uses in describing to
the King Hamlet's condition are:

> Mad as the sea and wind.
>
> IV, i, 6

and

> . . . this brainish apprehension.
>
> 11

But that is quite understandable. This story of the
Prince's madness is a big story and anyone about the
court at Elsinore not knowing how otherwise to characterize the Prince's conduct will catch up and use some
such epithets as these of Gertrude. If, as we believe, Gertrude is now, as a result of Hamlet's exhortations, more
firmly his partisan, and convinced that he is not mad, she
not only will not betray him to the King, but she will
use the very terms of the madness to protect him.

We may seem to have been over-long occupied in describing the varieties of Hamlet's madness, but perhaps
not unprofitably, for, as we have hinted, the variety of
it suggests, at least to a degree, the purposes it was designed to serve. Or if the word *designed* assumes too

much in the way of foresight and cool planning, then let us speak of the purpose it *was made to serve*.

The Uses of the Antic Disposition
1. As a License to Speak Truth

One use which Hamlet made of the antic disposition, and perhaps the least serious, is the use of it as a privilege to speak and act things which are not allowed to balanced adult persons. Children and fools and madmen have a privilege. Pert, shrewd little chaps such as little Richard of York in *Richard III* and little Macduff and little Caius Marcius may say things that are too sharp and bare in their truth and insight to be permitted to mature persons. Launce and Touchstone and Lear's Fool and others of that ilk speak home truths under their license as fools. And so a madman may infuse his speech with truths of a bare and daring sort.

This use of his madness is clearest in Hamlet's interchanges with Polonius and the King. As a child and youth about his father's court he had plumbed the shallows of this Polonius. He had writhed under his prolix utterance and sickened listening to his platitudes. Long since, he had marked him for a "glass-gazing, superserviceable, finical rogue," and had most likely yearned for a means of meeting him and dealing with him in plain terms of contempt and so leaving him enmeshed in a jumble of words, the victim of dumb bewilderment.

With the King, Hamlet's processes are perforce different, for in spite of all he and we may feel toward Claudius, the King is not a fool; he is not prolix and bromidic; he is capable and resourceful, and—I think—kingly. His intellect and his personality are difficult of assault. But it is only fair to remark that in what I have just said, I have gone considerably farther than Hamlet would go. It is one of the deftest of Shakspere's characterizing strokes that he has made Hamlet so bitterly averse to his uncle. Before he knows him to be a murderer, he is severe in his judgment of him. He stigmatizes him then in one of his most ingenuous speeches—ingenuous principally for the delightful underestimation of himself which it includes:

> [W]hy she, even she . . . .

> *   *   *

>   . . . married with my uncle;
>   My father's brother, but no more like my father
>   Than I to Hercules.

> I, ii, 149-153

There is another association of contrast of his uncle and his father, who was

>   So excellent a king, that was to this
>   Hyperion to a satyr.

> 139-140

After the Ghost's revelation of murder and murderer, Hamlet's epithets are tremendous:

>   [E]re this
>   I should have fatted all the region kites,
>   With this slave's offal. Bloody, bawdy villain!
>   Remorseless, treacherous, lecherous, kindless villain!

> II, ii, 605-608

>   A murtherer and a villain!
>   A slave that is not twentieth part the tithe
>   Of your precedent lord; a vice of kings;
>   A cutpurse of the empire and the rule,
>   That from a shelf the precious diadem stole
>   And put it in his pocket!

>   *   *   *

>   A king of shreds and patches! —

> III, iv, 97-102

In the scene in his mother's chamber Hamlet comes
to his disquisition on the contrasted natures of the two
kings—no more like my father than I to Hercules; Hyperion to a satyr, and he makes it more striking by somehow
using two pictures:

> Look here upon this picture, and on this,
> The counterfeit presentment of two brothers.[8]

III, iv, 53-54

In this passage he most vehemently proclaims his distaste for his uncle. It is with similar violence of speech
and act that he kills him at last:

> Here, thou incestuous, murd'rous, damned Dane,
> Drink off this potion!

V, ii, 336-337

But all this aversion and distaste is not madness, nor

---

[8] Stage history records more ways than one of presenting this business of the pictures. There can be lockets: one of the dead King,
Hamlet wears; Gertrude wears one of Claudius. Or there is a portrait of Claudius on the wall of the chamber and Hamlet wears his
father's likeness in a locket. I would have two portraits in matching
frames on the wall, large enough for the audience to see with some
clearness of detail. You may put, if you wish, a bit of crepe on King
Hamlet's picture, for the Gertrude who displays both pictures, would
drape the one with mourning. It is a mark of her character.
With this arrangement the pictures are large enough for the audience
to see that Claudius is far more like his kingly brother than Hamlet's
aversion will allow. He is more like King Hamlet than is a satyr to
Hyperion. He is not a "mildew'd ear blasting his wholesome brother."
His hatefulness is in his vicious character and even that has been
blasted blacker than the facts in the fires of his nephew's terrible hate.
It is one of the strongest instances in literature of a bitter and un-
compromising aversion, strong beyond the warrant of actuality. Lear
and Kent and Edgar have the same unreasoning I-do-not-like-thee-
Doctor-Fell distaste for Oswald, but Claudius and Oswald are no
more like each other than I to Hercules, and an aversion to Claudius
may be allowed to be stronger by the degree that Claudius is the
stronger. Also this aversion may be less clear to others by the degree
that Hamlet is a strong and opinionated person of great fastidiousness
and of deep-rooted preferences.

need it be confused with the madness. It is only in a few speeches, but some of them most potent, that he takes the privilege of the madman in speech to Claudius. Take, as an instance, the bitter irony of

> 'Tis a knavish piece of work; but what o' that?
> Your Majesty, and we that have free souls, it touches us not.
>   III, ii, 251-253

or

> *Ham.* The body is with the King, but the King is not with the body. The King is a thing —
> *Guil.* A thing, My lord?
> *Ham.* Of nothing. Bring me to him.
>   IV, ii, 29-31

And I have already suggested that there is something really terrifying in the little scrap of paper Hamlet sent to the King:

> High and Mighty—
>   . . . Tomorrow shall I beg
> leave to see your kingly eyes.
>   IV, vii, 43-44

These are liberties of speech such as only a maimed wit is privileged to utter. But in the exchanges with Claudius, they cut deep.

This use of madness as a license to speak round unvarnished truth may not have occurred to Hamlet until the situation had developed. It seems extremely doubtful that he had in mind at all what serious purposes it might serve, when, at the end of those hectic post-midnight hours on the platform he enjoined upon his friends an oath not to reveal him if he should "think meet to put an antic disposition on." But if, as I think, the swift idea commended itself to him as he observed the confusion of his companions at his wild and whirling words,

then, most likely the first use which suggested itself is the
second one we are offering, viz., this very creation of
confusion.

2. To Confuse Others

In a way it was harder for Claudius to form a theory
as to the cause of Hamlet's strange conduct than for the
others. He is most firmly sure that Hamlet does not know
the real secret of his father's death. That is to say, Claudius does not, so far as we can see, entertain the theory
that vengeance is Hamlet's motive. His first thought
seems to be that Hamlet is disaffected because his succession to the throne has been pre-empted. This he anticipates in the early scene when Hamlet's behavior is
only the darkest melancholy. He says to the Prince:

> [L]et the world take note
> You are the most immediate to our throne . . . .
> I, ii, 108-109

And when Hamlet rouses himself to accord obedience
(to his mother), the King says:

> Why, 'tis a loving and a fair reply.
> Be as ourself in Denmark.
> 121-122

Rosencrantz and Guildenstern, who are "sponges"
soaking "up the King's countenance," have this in their
little kit of probing tools when they undertake to sound
Hamlet as to the cause of his transformation. Ambition
is the theme to which they try to fit their interview:

> *Ham.*   To me it [Denmark] is a prison.
> *Ros.* Why, then your ambition makes it one. 'Tis too
> narrow for your mind.
> *Ham.* O God, I could be bounded in a nutshell and count

myself a king of infinite space, were it not that I have
bad dreams.
Guil. Which dreams indeed are ambition; for the very
substance of the ambitious is merely the shadow of a
dream.
Ham. A dream itself is but a shadow.
Ros. Truly, and I hold ambition of so airy and light a
quality that it is but a shadow's shadow.

II, ii, 257-268

After the play is broken up, they are bolder:

Ros. Good my lord, what is your cause of distemper? . . .
Ham. Sir, I lack advancement.
Ros. How can that be, when you have the voice of
the King himself for your succession in Denmark?
Ham. Ay, sir, but 'while the grass grows'—the proverb
is something musty.

III, ii, 350-359

In direct converse with Claudius, just a little while before
this, Hamlet is at work upon this theme:

King. How fares our cousin Hamlet?
Ham. Excellent, i' faith; of the chameleon's dish.
I eat the air, promise-cramm'd. You cannot feed capons so.

III, ii, 96-100

Thus Hamlet lets this theory be built up and at the
same time he does what he can to confuse it. Concurrent-
ly he furnishes fuel for Polonius' theory that it is love-
madness and that Ophelia is the object. There is first the
wordless sequence in the sewing closet, in which he presents himself to the affrighted maid, distraught in mien
and disheveled enough to send her packing straight to
her father. Hamlet has known for years that once to get
an idea rooted in Polonius' mind is to have it grow there
stout as an oak forever. Once this idea is implanted in
the old Busybody's mind, he goes about to persuade the
Queen that this is it. Almost, if not quite, they persuade

the King. In the meantime, in the midst of the build-up of the thwarted ambition theory with Rosencrantz and Guildenstern, Hamlet, in a great flight of rhetoric, suddenly flicks from "man delights not me" to "no, nor woman neither," and they, too, are confused.

The loosing of Ophelia to Hamlet in the lobby was to be a final counter-check on Polonius' theory of love-madness. But Hamlet, by a happy accident, was ready for this and chose to thwart it. It failed completely, and Claudius turned away from it firmly convinced that love was not the cause: "Love? his affections do not that way tend" (III, i, 170). But an hour later, as they are settling themselves into their places in the Great Hall to see the play, Gertrude calls to her son to sit beside her. He answers: "No, good mother. Here's metal more attractive" (III, ii, 116). And as Hamlet establishes himself at Ophelia's feet, Polonius notes it and cries out, calling on the King to witness it: "O, ho! do you mark that?" (117). So everyone is confused. For Claudius this confusion is an ever-increasing torment of spirit. What he felt in this hour must have been very like what he expresses later:

> . . . [L]ike the hectic in my blood he rages,
> And thou must cure me. Till I know 'tis done,
> Howe'er my haps, my joys were ne'er begun.
>   IV, iii, 68-70

Hamlet stops short at the thought that to kill the King at prayer might be to send him to heaven. That will not do. There will be a more auspicious hour. And, in the meantime, by the confusing use of the antic disposition, he manages to give his uncle a fairly uncomfortable sort of hell here.

3.   Outlet for his Love of Acting

There is a third use for the antic disposition, which

like the first, the privilege of madness to speak truth, is
not to be taken so seriously as the use we have just dealt
with, the use for the confusing of the minds of his antagonists. It is that in the development and carrying
through of his mad conduct, Hamlet found outlet for
his well-demonstrated interest in acting. Apparently
the King is the only one who seriously doubts the reality
of his insane state, although Polonius once or twice
touches the point. But he never admits him to be sane.
He remarks, "Though this be madness, yet there is
method in 't" (II, ii, 207), and again, "How pregnant
sometimes his replies are" (212). But he hastens to account for this as

> [A] happiness that often madness hits on, which reason
> and sanity could not so prosperously be delivered of.
> 213-215

The entire court is convinced of his madness. There
are various names for it: antic disposition, sore distraction,
ecstasy, transformation. Ophelia's estimate of it is, no
doubt, representative:

> O, what a noble mind is here o'erthrown!
>
> *   *   *
>
> Now see that noble and most sovereign reason,
> Like sweet bells jangled, out of tune and harsh;
> That unmatch'd form and feature of blown youth
> Blasted with ecstasy.
> III, i, 158; 165-168

All this he has done by his unaided ability as an actor.
And there seems to be no contingency of plot or circumstance to which he cannot successfully apply it. Some
of the episodes are rather clearly planned and prepared
for, such as the Ophelia Sewing Closet scene, parts, at
least, of the lobby scene ("Get thee to a nunnery"), and,

perhaps, the account to the King of the cycle of existence
illustrated by the Polonius-worms supper party. Other
episodes are just as obviously extempore and on instant
inspiration. Examples are the demand that Guildenstern
play the recorder, the surprising twist in the declamation
to Rosencrantz and Guildenstern on "What a piece of
work is a man" which ends "Man delights not me—no,
nor woman neither." The brilliant stroke when the King
asks, "What do you call the play?" in Hamlet's inspired
reply, "The Mousetrap," and the taunting nuances in
"O Jephthah, judge of Israel, what a treasure had'st thou!"

I cannot prove out of his own mouth that he enjoyed
the developments of this antic act. He says nothing about
it from that viewpoint. But it seems relevant to recall
that the inspiration to use it came in a quick observation
of the effect of wild and whirling words. It seems, also,
pertinent to note his almost irresponsible delight in the
success of the *Mousetrap* not because it catches the King,
but because he has devised a trap that works. It is some
minutes before he comes around to the realization that
the serious object of the device has been accomplished.
There is zest, also, in his story of the encounter with the
pirates, and part of his gratification is in feeling that his
ready wit and tongue did him such yeoman service.
Finally there is the quickness and mercilessness of his
analysis of Young Osric and his cynical mocking of this
verbose waterfly. Osric, whose English (or Danish) is
fuller of ink-horn elements that the inkhorn itself, comes
to confer with the Prince:

> *Osr.* Sir, here is newly come to court Laertes; believe
> me, an absolute gentleman, full of most excellent differ-
> ences, of very soft society and great showing. Indeed, to
> speak feelingly of him, he is the card or calendar of
> gentry; for you shall find in him the continent of what
> part a gentleman would see.

Ham. Sir, his definement suffers no perdition in you; though, I know, to divide him inventorially would dozy th' arithmetic of memory, and yet but yaw neither in respect of his quick sail. But in the verity of extolment, I take him to be a soul of great article, and his infusion of such dearth and rareness as, to make true diction of him, his semblable is his mirror, and who else would trace him, his umbrage, nothing more.
V, ii, 110-125 ⁹

For this Horatio has much applause. All of these deft and humorous turns of speech and situation mark Hamlet's enjoyment of his abilities in the field of apt and facile expression. Add to this his attitude of competence in coaching the players, his modest but masterful feat of memory and declamation as he speaks a speech—thirteen lines of it—which he says, "I heard thee speak *once*," his enjoyment of the macabre setting of the churchyard and the morbid theme of his discussion with Horatio and the sexton. All of these he carried through with every show of delight and self approval. And if he enjoyed these exercises of his mind, surely he must in the same fashion have enjoyed the turns and whims and unexpected developments of the feigned madness.

We conclude this exploration of the uses of the madness by recalling the three we have suggested: (1) the use of the state of madness as a license for speaking plain truths; (2) the use of the madness to confuse and harass his antagonists; and (3) the auxiliary use of it as a further outlet for his abilities as an actor.

---

⁹ An enjoyable cross-reference is to Don Pedro's mockery of Dogberry's scrambled sequence:

First I ask thee what they have done; thirdly, I ask thee what's their offence; sixth and lastly, why they are committed; and to conclude, what you lay to their charge?
Much, V, i, 223-226

It remains to say a word about a use of the madness
which Hamlet pounced upon in a situation which is,
everything considered, the least favorable of all the situations of the play to our regard for him. When the funeral
cortege of Ophelia enters the churchyard, Hamlet finds
himself unexpectedly a spectator. Laertes is in a bad
mood with the priest, who is giving only "maimed rites"
to his sister. Her death, the priest says, "was doubtful."
Laertes loses his bitter protest with the priest and plunges
then into a course of lamentation for his sister, which, to
say the least, lacks dignity. He leaps into the grave to
take her in a last embrace and as he does so, calls for
curses to fall upon

> that cursed head
> Whose wicked deed thy most ingenious sense
> Depriv'd thee of.
>
> V, i, 270-272

In a moment across the churchyard Prince Hamlet comes
striding and makes his presence known. He leaps into
the grave, grappling with Laertes, shouting wild protests:

> I lov'd Ophelia. Forty thousand brothers
> Could not (with all their quantity of love)
> Make up my sum.
>
> 292-294

He calls for mountains of earth to be piled upon them
both. The court is shocked and in panic. The King
says, "O, he is mad, Laertes" (295), and the terrified
Queen, "This is mere madness" (307). The two men are
parted and Horatio, whose Danish holiday is becoming
much occupied in convoying the mad, leads Hamlet
away.

Even when taken at its best this is not a creditable

scene. But we are not the first to say this. Hamlet felt
it himself and spoke his regret to Horatio:

> But I am very sorry, good Horatio,
> That to Laertes I forgot myself;
> For by the image of my cause I see
> The portraiture of his. I'll court his favours.
> But sure the bravery of his grief did put me
> Into a tow'ring passion.
>
>   V, ii, 75-80

We have already acknowledged Laertes' grief and its
bravery to be an offence to good taste, a violation of
decorum. Hamlet is here saying that that is how he
saw it. It offended his taste. His cue at the graveside
was to render it ridiculous by trying to outdo it:

>   Nay, an thou'lt mouth,
>   I'll rant as well as thou.
>   V, i, 306-307

This is an explanation. If it does not satisfy you, it is
to be feared you may have to remain unsatisfied. But in
this explanation to Horatio there is no suggestion that he
was mad in Ophelia's grave. When he comes to meet
Laertes for the sword-play in the Great Hall of the
Palace, it is true he apologizes for his wild behavior by
invoking his madness as an explanation:

> . . . [Y]ou must needs have heard how I am punish'd
> With sore distraction. What I have done
> That might your nature, honour, and exception
> Roughly awake, I here proclaim was madness.
> Was 't Hamlet wrong'd Laertes? Never Hamlet.
>
>   *   *   *
>
> Who does it, then? His madness.
>   V, ii, 240-248

But this is only because it is the easiest explanation.

Indeed, it is already the current explanation. It was so at the grave; both King and Queen so labeled it, and all the buzz-buzz of the court gossips since has had it so. All about the court and down on the streets they are saying: *The Prince was mad at the Lady's grave.* And, for the situation, it is the kindest and politest explanation. It is not true, of course. But it is more considerate than the truth. However well it might or might not fit into the movement of good blank verse, it would not sound well to say, *Laertes, your vulgar display of unmanly grief at your sister's grave offended my taste and thoroughly disgusted me. That's why I lost my self control and acted as I did. Please forgive me.* It is, you see, much kinder to take the way of social amenity and evasion which Hamlet took.

The behavior itself seems still to be unjustified. But its real quality is of the nature of a genuine outburst of passionate indignation such as marked his conference with his mother. Now if one showing such uncontrolled rage is thought to be mad already, it will be most natural for such behavior as that in the grave to be taken as simply another manifestation of his madness. So there may come situations such as this at Ophelia's grave, when even the most skillful dissimulator of madness may be almost caught in his own net, almost hoist with his own petar.

The Ophelia madness is obviously set into the play to serve as contrast with the feigned madness of Hamlet. It is wild and uncontrolled, and it completely possesses her. After it takes her, there are no lucid and controlled intervals, and it does not shift and vary in the presence of different persons. In and of itself, and as a bit of dramatic management it is skillfully handled. It shows surprising understanding of various aspects of mental aberration

without becoming in the least technical. In this respect
it is like that fine piece of layman's psycho-therapy, the
scene in which the Doctor labors to restore King Lear
to a balanced mind.

But so far as its relation to the main *Hamlet* plot goes,
it is almost completely dissociated. Ophelia's madness is
because of her father's death:

> I cannot choose but weep to think they
> Would lay him i' th' cold ground.
>
> IV, v, 69-70

In the respect that Hamlet unwittingly was her father's
slayer, Hamlet is, of course, to blame, but she appears to
make no such association. Nor is there in her mad behavior the faintest suggestion that she is mad for love.
We must conclude, therefore, that her madness and her
tragic end are important to the total play only for contrast—to show to all who see and hear, the difference between real mental collapse and the putting on of an
antic disposition.

As we introduced the preceding chapter, which was
an inquiry as to the source or the essential motivation of
the antic disposition, we said that at the time of the inception of the idea of feigned madness, Hamlet did not
foresee all or even any of the uses he might make of it.
Now, at the end of a chapter on the purposes or uses of
the antic disposition, we look back over a pattern of
events in which the mad behavior was much of the time
active and was never far away. As a result of this retrospect we realize how extempore and unplanned were most
of its uses. There come to be certain channels of conduct
through which it runs. Different individuals evoke different manifestations of it. Happy, lucid intervals come
when it is not in use at all. Strange, tangled moments

come when it is so mixed with honest bitter anger and outrage that it is difficult for us to know which is which —difficult for many in the play, who are with him and observe all his changes to take it otherwise than as madness. Once at least we see such a situation in which he himself almost loses his way, for it is a perilous business.

Now, in retrospect, consider how valid a presentation this antic act of Hamlet's has been! It is not accompanied by any wooden structure of declared purpose as it was in the German version of the story. Indeed, Hamlet never explains it or justifies it. To Horatio, who was present when it was conceived and who must have watched it with a particular knowingness of appreciation, he never subsequently mentions it.

In life situations most people, though possessed and activated by balanced codes of philosophy and creed, are nevertheless given to trusting to the moment for the ordinary issues of decision and action. I think this to be especially true of great persons. It is part of their greatness that they can meet the rising moment quickly and fittingly; it is in such alert adaptiveness that much of their attractiveness lies.

Hamlet was such a person, and Shakspere's unerring sense of character has so made him as to give an impression of a sure creative readiness for whatever comes. Add to that the impression that Hamlet, all the while, is carrying this precarious role with enjoyment and an undercurrent sense of self-realization and you have the main elements of the formula out of which the dramatist has evolved him. It is a peak achievement of an artist whose perceptions are sharp and whose creative strokes are startling in their truth but who remains faithful to reality because his common sense is his sure guide.

CHAPTER XII

MANNER OF SPEECH AS AN ASPECT OF SHAKSPERE'S CHARACTERIZATION [1]

Shakspere's characters are his mouthpieces. He speaks only through them. Indeed this is so nearly the entire truth that many who have read his plays often and carefully come to the conclusion that perhaps we never really hear the poet speak at all. This is the measure of his objectivity as an artist. One errs, then, who says, "As Shakspere said, 'Who steals my purse, steals trash,' or 'We are such stuff as dreams are made on,' or 'A rose by any other name would smell as sweet,' or 'The man who has no music in himself is fit for treasons,' " for these are not Shakspere's words; they are Iago's, Prospero's, Juliet's, and Lorenzo's.

If they are, then, so truly the speeches of his characters, these speeches reward attention not alone for what they say, which reveals the minds of his creations, but for how it is said, for the *manner* of speech and for what this manner reveals of personality and of the dramatist's skill in marking personality.

I

We shall survey at first very briefly some of the more openly discernible devices of speech by which characters are marked.

[1] Reprinted with alterations from the *Sewanee Review*, XLVII, 406-423. The title in *S. R.* was "Shakspere's Mouthpieces. "

Dialect

Shakspere makes very little use of dialect. Only a few of his persons employ it. Among those who do are the group of provincial army captains in *Henry V*, the Welsh Fluellen, the Scotch Jamy, and MacMorris, the Irishman. These men have their respective varieties of broken English. There is also the delightful gibberish Welsh-English of Sir Hugh Evans of Windsor. Another most interesting use of dialect is the situation in which Edgar in *King Lear*, coming into conflict with the super-serviceable Oswald, breaks out into a rustic dialect, hoping, we may suppose, by its suggestions of his base origin to make more humiliating his defiance of the foppish steward (*Lear*, IV, vi, 235-252).

Foreign Speech

Only a very little use is made of awkward handling of foreign tongues. One of the most notable examples is the amusing attempt of Princess Katherine, who has a little English, to learn English from the old French gentlewoman, Alice, who has almost no English at all (*H V*, III, iv). But the wheel comes full circle when Henry makes his own laughing, stumbling effort at French (*H V*, V, ii, 224-232). There is also to be recalled the advance publicity given by Sir Toby Belch in *Twelfth Night* concerning the intellectual versatility of his dear knight, Sir Andrew Aguecheek, who, he says, "speaks three or four languages word for word without book" (I, iii, 27). If we assume what was surely the case, that a man of general learning in Western Europe in Shakspere's time knew his own language and at least French and Latin beside, these would be Toby's "three or four

languages." But very quickly Sir Andrew shows himself ignorant of each in turn. He comes upon Sir Toby
in the company of Maria, but he appears not to know
the girl, so, after saluting Sir Toby, he gives her an
awkward general greeting, "Bless you, fair shrew." But
Toby urges acquaintance:

> *To.* Accost, Sir Andrew, accost.
> *And.* What's that?
> *To.* My niece's chambermaid.
> *And.* Good Mistress Accost, I desire better acquaintance.
> *Mar.* My name is Mary, sir.
> *And.* Good Mistress Mary Accost—
> *To.* You mistake, knight; 'Accost' is front her, board
> her, woo her, assail her.
> *And.* By my troth, I would not undertake her in this
> company. Is that the meaning of 'accost'?
> I, iii, 51-62

So he has showed himself most shallowly rooted in the
vernacular, call it English or whatever Illyrian dialect
you will.

"I'll ride home tomorrow, Sir Toby," he announces.
"Pourquoi, my dear knight?" inquires Sir Toby. "What
is 'pourquoi,'" asks the linguist, "do or not do? I would
I had bestowed that time in the tongues that I have in
fencing, dancing, and bear-baiting" (I, iii, 94-98). So
much, then, for French, also![2]

Some two or three scenes later Toby greets Andrew:

> Approach, Sir Andrew. Not to be abed after midnight is
> to be up betimes; and 'diluculo surgere,' thou know'st—
> II, iii, 1-3

and Sir Andrew replies, "Nay, by my troth, I know not,"

---

[2] Days later, when Andrew meets Cesario in the street he greets the
page in French and *understands* the French reply (III, i, 76-82). This
is a point for which I have no explanation of my own and none from
anyone else which satisfies me.

thereby showing not only his ignorance of Latin, but what is even more indicative of his wholly lost condition, he is practically confessing to the possession of no formal learning at all, for the proverb Toby started and assumed Andrew knew well enough to complete from memory is to be found in William Lily's *Latin Grammar*, the indispensable elementary textbook of all schools of Shakspere's day, its exercises and examples a part of the memory of every competent school boy.

Ignorant Misuse

A great deal may be said regarding the assignment of ignorant, inappropriate, and misapplied word uses to certain persons as a mark of character. This is the sort of thing which two centuries after Shakspere, Sheridan took as the core of the characterization of Mrs. Malaprop. Shakspere uses this device of speech almost more freely than any other. A mention here of little more than the bare names of some of the most flagrant abusers of words will have to serve. Costard in *Love's Labour's Lost*, Bottom the Weaver in *A Midsummer Night's Dream*, Dogberry the Chief of the Watch in *Much Ado About Nothing*, his cousin Elbow in *Measure for Measure*, Juliet's Nurse, Mistress Quickly the Hostess of the Boar's Head Tavern, and a number of others are to a greater or less degree given to ignorant word use.

Drunken Speech

On a few occasions Shakspere represents the speech of drunken men. Notable instances are Sir Toby Belch in *Twelfth Night*, "A plague of these pickle-herring!" (I, v, 128), Cassio in *Othello*, the Alexandrian feast staged for the Romans by the much-traveled Antony and Enobarbus at which we have the silly gabbling of Lepidus after a cup or two, and the realization by great Caesar that his own speech was being rendered less and less sure, and, in the *Tempest*, the drunken talk of Trinculo and the speech of Caliban in his first surprised experience of Stephano's "celestial liquor."

Garrulity

A sort of speech which is more indicative of a type of mind and personality than those previously mentioned is garrulous, unplanned speech. Two examples of this come to mind: The first, Juliet's Nurse, the other, Falstaff's long-suffering hostess, Mrs. Quickly. It is, of course, only incidental that both are women, but be that as it may, the dramatist has given to each a number of speeches which are capital examples of garrulous talk. Recall the Nurse's effort to compute exactly Juliet's age, remembering that

> Susan and she (God rest all Christian souls!)
> Were of an age. Well, Susan is with God;
> She was too good for me. . . .
> > *Romeo*, I, iii, 18-20

and so on through rememberings of the homely happenings of many a year ago, with fond lingering on the recollection of her husband's salty pleasantry:

> (God be with his soul!
> 'A was a merry man)
> > 39-40

and so after many repetitions and digressions, at last to the conclusion, which is the identical major premise with which she started:

Come Lammas Eve at night shall she be fourteen.
16

Even better than this example from the Nurse is Dame
Quickly's narrative to the Chief Justice of how once
upon a time Sir John had as good as proposed marriage
to her. The speech is directed to Sir John but it is for
the Justice's ears:

> Thou didst swear to me upon a parcel-gilt goblet, sitting
> in my Dolphin chamber, at the round table by a seacoal
> fire, upon Wednesday in Wheeson week, when the Prince
> broke thy head for liking his father to a singing man of
> Windsor—thou didst swear to me then, as I was washing
> thy wound, to marry me and make me my lady thy wife.
> Canst thou deny it? Did not goodwife Keech, the butcher's
> wife, come in then and call me gossip Quickly? coming in
> to borrow a mess of vinegar, telling us she had a good
> dish of prawns, whereby thou didst desire to eat some,
> whereby I told thee they were ill for a green wound?
> And didst thou not, when she was gone down stairs, desire
> me to be no more so familiarity with such poor people,
> saying that ere long they should call me madam?
>
> -   *II H IV*, II, i, 92-110

There is also her sadly beautiful but rambling old-wivish
account of the last hours of Falstaff (*H V*, II, iii, 9-28).
If one could be brief about Polonius, he should have
mention here in this treatment of garrulity.

Fixed Habits of Speech

As a rule, the characters of Shakspere are not marked
as are those of Jonson and Dekker and Dickens, by stock
phrases, by means of which they may always be identified. Only a very few have any fixed habits of speech,
but there are a few. Ancient Pistol is always swaggering,
and his speech is couched generally in the ranting blank

verse of the tragedies of the foregoing generation. "King Cambyses' vein," Falstaff called it (*I H IV*, II, iv, 425). His compeer, Corporal Nym in *Henry V*, is even more definitely tagged by a habit of speech. "That's the humour of it," or "that's the rendevous of it" (*H V*, II, i, *passim*). In this connection may be noted, also, the sort of violently abusive and profane speech employed more or less seriously by Thersites in *Troilus and Cressida* (V, i, 51-72), and by the disguised Earl of Kent in *King Lear* (II, ii, 15-26). Perhaps it is in place here more than anywhere else to mention the type of disillusioned blunt truth-telling in which Hotspur in *I Henry IV*, the melancholy Jaques in *As You Like It*, Casca in *Julius Caesar*, Hamlet in some phases of his madness (*Ham.*, II, ii, 249-253; III, i, 147-157; III, ii, 243-253; IV, ii, 30-33), Kent in *King Lear*, Enobarbus in *Antony and Cleopatra*, and Menenius Agrippa in *Coriolanus* distinguish themselves. This habit of speech is very well described in the unfriendly terms of the Duke of Cornwall's characterization of Kent:

> This is some fellow
> Who, having been prais'd for bluntness, doth affect
> A saucy roughness.
>
> *Lear*, II, ii, 102-104

Prolixity

It is in point, also, to mention a habit of prolixity by which Shakspere has marked a few of his characters. Most outstanding in this particular are Richard II and Polonius. Neither of them can be brief. Richard seizes every occasion for a speech. One remembers his melodramatic speech on returning to England from his foolish Irish wars (III, ii), also his calling for a mirror in the abdication scene (IV, i, 264-291). The clearest instance of sheer prolixity, however, is in the scene in prison where Richard alone in his cell is working out a simile of his condition. We come upon him in his cell trying to compare it to the world, but it will not come right:

> . . . for because the world is populous
> And here is not a creature but myself,
> I cannot do it. Yet I'll hammer it out.
>
> V, v, 3-6

Polonius is, of course, the very type of prolixity. His immortal "brevity is the soul of wit," convoyed as it is by living proofs of his utter inability to be brief, is part of the stark comedy of *Hamlet*. His advice to Laertes (I, iii, 55-86), his unrecorded "prescripts" to Ophelia (II, ii, 142), his general wordiness on all occasions are an essential part of his personality. There is also more than a hint that Boyet (*L. L. L.*, V, ii, 460-481), and Monsieur Le Beau (*A. Y. L.*, I, ii, 97-101) are of this wordy brotherhood.

Speech Mannerisms

Just a few little tricks or mannerisms of speech deserve mention. First there is Touchstone's habit of frequent speaking of the name of the person to whom he is talking. He is speaking to Corin:

> Truly, shepherd, in respect of itself, it is a good life.

And after a few lines:

> Hast any philosophy in thee, shepherd?

And so on down the scene:

> Wast ever in court, shepherd?

and,

Mend the instance, shepherd
> *A. Y. L.*, III, ii, 12; 23; 34; 71

Hear him, also, addressing Audrey:

> Come apace, good Audrey. I will fetch up your goats, Audrey.
> And how, Audrey, am I the man yet?
> > III, iii, 1-3

and later,

> We will find a time, Audrey. Patience, gentle Audrey.
> > V, i, 1

There are two persons in *Hamlet* marked by habit or trick of speech. One is Horatio; the other is Hamlet. Horatio's trick is that of not replying directly. On the sentry's platform, as the watch is changing, Bernardo cries out, "What, is Horatio there?" "A piece of him," Horatio answers (I, i, 18-19). Again when Hamlet is planning the play to catch the conscience of the King, he asks Horatio to watch the King's face intently as the climax of the play comes on. "Give him heedful note," Hamlet enjoins him, and Horatio replies:

> Well, my lord,
> If he steal aught the whilst this play is playing,
> And scape detecting, I will pay the theft.
> > III, ii, 92-94

Hamlet's habit of speech is the repetition of a word or brief phrase almost as if absent-mindedly turning it on his tongue:

> I am sorry they offend you, heartily;
> Yes, faith, heartily.
> > I, v, 133-134

> Rest, rest, perturbed spirit. . . .
> > 182

Ophelia asks, "How does your honour?" and he answers,

"I humbly thank you, well, well, well" (III, i, 92). Polonius inquires, "What do you read, my lord?" "Words, words, words" is the reply (II, ii, 194). And at the play when the player queen speaks of murdering her first husband, Hamlet, looking intently in his mother's face for signs of guilt—for he still believes her an accomplice in his father's murder—turns aside to mutter:

> Wormwood, wormwood!
>
> III, ii, 191

and to Polonius, once more, when that worthy suggests that he will take his leave of Hamlet:

> You cannot, sir, take from me anything that I will more willingly part withal—except my life, except my life, except my life.
>
> II, ii, 219-221

Quality of Voice

There are in the plays many references to quality of voice; from among them these three typical ones will serve as examples. There is Falstaff's voice which he had lost

> . . . with halloaing, and singing of anthems.
>
> II H IV, I, ii, 212-213

Viola-Cesario's, which Orsino describes:

> [T]hy small pipe
> Is as the maiden's organ, shrill and sound.
> Twel., I, iv, 32-33

And Cordelia's, which her father says

> was ever soft
> Gentle and low—an excellent thing in woman.
> Lear, V, iii, 272-273

Stage Directions as to Voice

There are references, too, to the manner of speaking certain speeches. The manner of Iago's speaking of his crafty insinuations is suggested by Othello's comment:

> And, for I know thou'rt full of love and honesty
> And weigh'st thy words before thou giv'st them breath,
> Therefore these stops of thine fright me the more.
> > *Oth.*, III, iii, 118-120

Old Belarius identifies Cloten after long years of separation not alone by facial features but by

> > The snatches in his voice
> And burst of speaking.
> > *Cym.*, IV, ii, 105-106

Octavius Caesar feels the effects of Antony's wine and describes his own speech:

> > . . . mine own tongue
> Splits what it speaks. The wild disguise hath almost
> Antick'd us all.
> > *Antony*, II, vii, 130-132

Edmund, hearing Edgar approach and hastily composing himself to villainy, throws out a sort of stage direction for the manner of his succeeding speeches:

> Edgar—and pat! he comes like the catastrophe of the old comedy. My cue is villanous melancholy, with a sigh like Tom o' Bedlam.
> > *Lear*, I, ii, 145-148

The lightest and happiest of all these passages is Feste's clownish insistence that if a madman's letter is to be read properly, then it must be read with suitable accompaniments of madness. He has just produced Malvolio's letter and Olivia commands him, "Open 't and read it."

Clown.   Look then to be well edified, when the fool delivers the madman. [*Reads in a loud voice*] 'By the Lord, madam'—
Oli. How now? Art thou mad?
Clown. No, madam, I do but read madness. An your ladyship will have it as it ought to be, you must allow vox.

Twel., V, i, 297-304

II

Less tangible than these devices of speech for marking personalities is the matter to which this discussion is especially directed. It is the sort of thing which may appeal in differing degree to every imaginative reader of Shakspere, differing in that it may appeal to one reader most strongly in one character and to another most strongly in another. But it must, in some degree, impress every attentive and sympathetic student of the plays. The point is that there are certain speeches of certain characters of Shakspere which are distinctive and individual in tone, even to the extent of producing an effect comparable to tone or manner of voice in a living person, so that one feels not only that this is a speech of Portia, or Brutus, or Othello, but that this is the way Portia, or Brutus, or Othello talked, and even beyond that, that no one else has ever talked or will ever talk precisely so.

For a number of years I have been so sure of the existence of this sort of thing that I have hoped not merely to point to passages which illustrate it, but to go so far in the analysis of a few such passages as to show not alone that it exists but further to show, at least in part, of what it consists. This is the purpose of the succeeding pages. Our study will be of six characters who, in certain

passages, it has seemed to me, illustrate this phenomenon.
They are Portia in the *Merchant of Venice*, Brutus in
Julius Caesar, Viola in *Twelfth Night*, Othello, Imogen
in *Cymbeline*, and Perdita in the *Winter's Tale*.

The passage in which Portia's speech seems most dis-
tinctively her own is that in which, after Bassanio's song-
prompted guess at the contents of the caskets, she makes
her modest, maiden appraisal of herself and speaks her
commitment of herself to her lover. Following the
passage I shall present a brief analysis of the peculiar
qualities of the speech:

> You see me, Lord Bassanio, where I stand,
> Such as I am. Though for myself alone   150
> I would not be ambitious in my wish
> To wish myself much better, yet for you
> I would be trebled twenty times myself
> A thousand times more fair, ten thousand times more rich,
> That, only to stand high in your account,   155
> I might in virtues, beauties, livings, friends,
> Exceed account. But the full sum of me
> Is sum of nothing, which, to term in gross,
> Is an unlesson'd girl, unschool'd, unpractic'd;
> Happy in this, she is not yet so old   160
> But she may learn; happier than this,
> She is not bred so dull but she can learn;
> Happiest of all is that her gentle spirit
> Commits itself to yours to be directed,
> As from her lord, her governor, her king.   165
> Myself and what is mine to you and yours
> Is now converted. But now I was the lord
> Of this fair mansion, master of my servants,
> Queen o'er myself; and even now, but now,
> This house, these servants, and this same myself   170
> Are yours, my lord's. I give them with this ring.
>   III, ii, 149-171

Note first the outstanding qualities of this speech.
They are dignity, poise, self-possession, a seriousness not

heavy but appropriate, a quality of proportion and a
sense of fitness, the speech of a lady, who in giving herself away will never be less than mistress of herself.

It is a speech of twenty-three lines. In eight of these
lines (150, 152, 154, 157, 161, 167, 169, 171) there is a
marked pause within the line, more than the merely customary caesural pause. Three examples will illustrate it,
taking in each case the preceding line and going on to the
pause in the line being considered:

> You see me, Lord Bassanio, where I stand,
> Such as I am.   150

> Happy in this, she is not yet so old
> But she may learn.   161

> This house, these servants, and this same myself
> Are yours, my lord's.   171

Do not these speeches contribute to the measured, poised
impression of the entire passage?

Another factor is disclosed by an examination of the
division of the lines into breath groups. Of course, as is
generally true in English pentameter verse, there is at
least one caesural pause in each line, but in eight of the
lines in this passage there are two such pauses—making
three breath groups, and in one line there are three pauses
—making four groups. Line 149 is a notable example:

> You see me,—Lord Bassanio,—where I stand.

The measured tread of that line is enough to serve as
prologue to the qualities of the entire speech. Line 159

> Is an unlesson'd girl,—unschool'd,—unpractic'd.

illustrates the point again as do the last three lines (169-
171):

Queen o'er myself,—and even now,—but now,
This house,—these servants,—and this same myself
Are yours,—my lord's. I give them with this ring.

The line with the four breath groups is line 156:

I might in virtue,—beauties,—livings,—friends . . . .

This factor of heavy phrasing of line goes hand in hand
with the first factor of strong punctuational stop in producing an effect of quiet and deliberate dignity.

The speech also contains a surprising number of repeated or parallel constructions:

A *thousand times more* fair, ten *thousand times
More* rich

Is an *un*lesson'd girl, *un*school'd, *un*practic'd

Happy in this . . .
                                        happier than this,
Happiest of all . . .

Note, moreover, how the little words *now* and *myself*
recur:

Myself and what is mine to you and yours
Is *now* converted. But *now* I was the lord
Of this fair mansion, master of my servants,
Queen o'er *myself*; and even *now*, but *now*,
This house, these servants, and this same *myself*
Are yours, my lord's. I give them with this ring.

It is particularly in producing the effect of proportion
and delicately woven pattern of tone that these studied
repetitions and parallelisms are so effective.

This analysis cannot fail to leave untouched some of
the less tangible aspects of the beautiful appropriateness
of this speech to Portia, but it may serve to indicate that
there is basis here, in structural and tonal detail, for the
impression that meets even the uncritical ear, of individual quality and tone in these lovely lines.

Some of the other speeches of Portia show hints, at least, of the same factors. The speech at the beginning of III, ii:

> I pray you tarry; pause a day or two
> Before you hazard. . . .

is the second-best example. The famous "quality of mercy" speech is only remotely similar in tone, but we should perhaps scarcely expect a Portia capable of playing the part of the young Doctor so completely well in all other particulars to talk exactly like her proper feminine self from beneath his gown. Indeed, may she not be reading this great speech from notes furnished her by Dr. Bellario? (III, iv, 51).

Our next example is Marcus Brutus. It is his speech in answer to Cassius' earnest and practical plea for the assassination of Mark Antony as a part of the move against Caesarism. Brutus is unfavorable to this proposal:

> Our course will seem too bloody, Caius Cassius,
> To cut the head off and then hack the limbs
> Like wrath in death and envy afterwards;
> For Antony is but a limb of Caesar.
> Let us be sacrificers, but not butchers, Caius.
> We all stand up against the spirit of Caesar,
> And in the spirit of men there is no blood.
> O that we then could come by Caesar's spirit
> And not dismember Caesar! But, alas,
> Caesar must bleed for it! And, gentle friends,
> Let's kill him boldly, but not wrathfully;
> Let's carve him as a dish fit for the gods,
> Not hew him as a carcass fit for hounds.
> And let our hearts, as subtle masters do,
> Stir up their servants to an act of rage
> And after seem to chide 'em. This shall make
> Our purpose necessary, and not envious;
> Which so appearing to the common eyes,
> We shall be call'd purgers, not murderers.

And for Mark Antony, think not of him;
For he can do no more than Caesar's arm
When Caesar's head is off.
                        Caesar, II, i, 162-183

The effect of this speech is principally an effect of deliberation, of careful reasoning and persuasiveness. In contrast to the effect of dignity in Portia's speech, the impression here is heavy and, if not pompous, at least didactic and almost stiff.

Instead of undertaking a detailed analysis, a few of the more observable matters will be noted. The most obvious feature is the employment of feminine endings in five of the first eight lines:

Our course will seem too bloody, Caius Cas*sius*,
To cut the head off and then hack the limbs
Like wrath in death and envy afterwards;
For Antony is but a limb of Cae*sar*.
Let us be sacrificers, but not butchers, Cai*us*.
We all stand up against the spirit of Cae*sar*.
And in the spirit of men there is no blood.
O that we then could come by Caesar's spir*it* . . . !

This lingering over the end of the line contributes much to the impression of slow thoughtfulness.

The use of the name of his interlocutor is, also, a factor in producing the impression of didacticism—even of placating condescension which is in the speech:

Our course will seem too bloody, *Caius Cassius* . . . .
Let us be sacrificers, but not butchers, *Caius* . . . .
Caesar must bleed for it! And, *gentle friends,*
Let's kill him boldly . . . .

This same quality of heavy deliberateness is found elsewhere in the speeches of Brutus, most noticeably in his prose funeral oration—itself an elaborately woven fabric of euphuistic design—but no where else is it quite as characteristic as in this speech about including Antony in the program of the purge.

In presenting the other speakers, characteristic speeches rather than details of analysis will be taken, not only to save time and patience, but because already, I hope, the method has been fully enough suggested.

To represent Viola's speech I take the often-cited passage in which she, disguised, disguises the story of her heart under the fiction of her father's daughter. She is speaking to Orsino:

> *Via.* My father had a daughter lov'd a man
> As it might be perhaps, were I a woman,
> I should your lordship.
> *Duke.*   And what's her history?
> *Vio.* A blank, my lord. She never told her love,
> But let concealment, like a worm i' th' bud,
> Feed on her damask cheek. She pin'd in thought;
> And with a green and yellow melancholy,
> She sat like Patience on a monument,
> Smiling at grief. Was not this love indeed?
> We men may say more, swear more; but indeed
> Our shows are more than will; for still we prove
> Much in our vows but little in our love.
> *Duke.* But died your sister of her love, my boy?
> *Vio.* I am all the daughters of my father's house,
> And all the brothers too—and yet I know not.
>   *Twel.*, II, iv, 110-123

This is the speech of restrained, suppressed emotion—restrained yet adventurous and full. There is in it poetry of the most evocative sort:

> Concealment, like a worm i' th' bud
>
> She sat like Patience on a monument,
> Smiling at grief
>
> *We men* may say more, swear more

Viola has no long speeches anywhere and no other speech

at all which quite so flawlessly embodies the essence of
her sensitive feminine personality.

Othello's speeches are perhaps more consistently of the
very quality of his personality than are those of any other
Shaksperean character. Almost any one of his speeches
of any length will serve to illustrate.[3] In his case, however, there are two types of speech because there are
two aspects of Othello. There is the calm, masterful
speech which is the utterance of the great Captain of
the Wars, the master of men and of affairs and of himself. There is also the speech of a man of tumultuous
passions and of unplumbed depths of feeling:

> Of one that lov'd not wisely, but too well;
> Of one not easily jealous, but being wrought,
> Perplex'd in the extreme.
>
> V, ii, 344-346

To illustrate the first type of Othello speech we cannot do better than take the famous passage in which,
before the Venetian Senate, he undertakes his defence of
his wooing of Brabantio's daughter:

> Most potent, grave, and reverend signiors,
> My very noble, and approv'd good masters,
> That I have ta'en away this old man's daughter,
> It is most true; true I have married her.
> The very head and front of my offending
> Hath this extent, no more. Rude am I in my speech,
> And little bless'd with the soft phrase of peace;
> For since these arms of mine had seven years' pith
> Till now some nine moons wasted, they have us'd
> Their dearest action in the tented field;
> And little of this great world can I speak
> More than pertains to feats of broil and battle;

[3] I find strong support for this part of the discussion in Mr. G.
Wilson Knight's article on "The Othello Music" in *The Wheel of
Fire*, 107-132.

And therefore little shall I grace my cause
In speaking for myself. Yet, by your gracious patience,
I will a round unvarnish'd tale deliver
Of my whole course of love—what drugs, what charms,
What conjurations, and what mighty magic
(For such proceeding am I charg'd withal)
I won his daughter.

Oth., I, iii, 76-94

As illustration of the tumultuous and passionate expression of the Moor's nature we take a few lines from his speech after Iago's diabolic insinuations have delved deep beneath his confidence in his wife:

O, now for ever
Farewell the tranquil mind! farewell content!
Farewell the plumed troop, and the big wars
That make ambition virtue! O, farewell!
Farewell the neighing steed and the shrill trump,
The spirit-stirring drum, th' ear-piercing fife,
The royal banner, and all quality,
Pride, pomp, and circumstance of glorious war!
And O ye mortal engines, whose rude throats
Th' immortal Jove's dread clamours counterfeit,
Farewell! Othello's occupation's gone!

III, iii, 347-357

In this speech there is distraction but it still moves to the measured beat of high poetry. A more revealing passage, of how thoroughly disrupted is the General's habitual self-possession, is the one in which he lapses into disjointed prose as he imagines Cassio and his wife in intimate embrace:

Lie with her? lie on her?—we say lie on her when they belie her.—Lie with her! Zounds, that's fulsome.—Handkerchief—confessions—handkerchief!—To confess, and be hang'd for his labour—first to be hang'd, and then to confess! I tremble at it. Nature would not invest herself in such shadowing passion without some instruction. It is not

words that shakes me thus.—Pish! Noses, ears, and lips?
Is 't possible?—Confess?—handkerchief?—O devil!
                    Falls in a trance.
                    IV, i, 35-44

Then, when the tragedy has run its course, and Othello's mind, now cleared of the deceptions of the villain, returns once more to its steadier pace, again the measured and controlled fashion of speaking resumes. It is the speech to the Venetian emissaries:

                    I pray you, in your letters,
When you shall these unlucky deeds relate,
Speak of me as I am. Nothing extenuate,
Nor set down aught in malice. Then must you speak
Of one not easily jealous, but being wrought,
Perplex'd in the extreme; of one whose hand
(Like the base Indian) threw a pearl away
Richer than all his tribe; of one whose subdu'd eyes
Albeit unused to the melting mood,
Drop tears as fast as the Arabian trees
Their med'cinable gum. Set you down this;
And say besides that in Aleppo once,
Where a malignant and a turban'd Turk
Beat a Venetian and traduc'd the state,
I took by th' throat th' circumcised dog
And smote him—thus.
                    V, ii, 340-356

Observe the sharp caesural breaks in almost all of the lines of this, and, what is perhaps just as significant of its quality, three lines which have no break at all:

            Albeit unused to the melting mood
            Drop tears as fast as the Arabian trees . . . .
and
        I took by the throat the circumcised dog . . . .

No one else speaks as do these speeches. The poised, deliberate utterance of the self-mastered man; the wild and turbulent speech of a great mind rendered distraught and ungoverned—and the return to poise and deliberateness. These are Othello's speeches, or, if you will, these speeches are Othello.

In turning now to the speech of Imogen, we come upon a different phenomenon from that observed in the others. Her speech is not alone true to her character, it goes farther and adds a color to her presentation which we should otherwise miss. It is, nevertheless, distinctly hers. It is clipped, trenchant speech, full of suggestion, but packed and epigrammatic. And, unless the situation is too stark and tragic, there is ever an overtone of whimsical humor. Her speech lacks the balance and finish of Portia's just as it lacks the delicacy of Perdita's. It is peculiarly her own. Some of the most typical lines follow.

Posthumus, going to his exile, bids her farewell, and as he goes, she says:

> There cannot be a pinch in death
> More sharp than this is.
>   *Cym.*, I, i, 129-130

Her irate old savage of a father, chiding her for her disobedient choosing of Posthumus, cries out upon her: "Past grace? obedience?" and she answers, "Past hope, and in despair; that way, past grace" (137-138). A moment later he exclaims: "What are thou mad?" and once again her packed whimsical fashion of speech, "Almost, sir. Heaven restore me!" (148-149). When, some days later a letter is brought from her banished husband, she reads it aloud for a little way, but after a moment she breaks off and reads the rest silently, saying to her visitor:

So far I read aloud;
But even the very middle of my heart
Is warm'd by th' rest and takes it thankfully.

                    I, vi, 26-28

When Iachimo, going about to undermine her loyalty, comes to the point of reporting disparagingly of her absent lord, she almost instantly catches the bent of his treachery and fairly shouts him down:

Thou wrong'st a gentleman who is as far
From thy report as thou from honour, and
Solicit'st here a lady that disdains
Thee and the devil alike.—What ho, Pisanio!

                    145-148

Out in the Welsh mountains, cast off from her lord's troth and trust, and driven to masculine disguise to protect herself, she turns to thoughts of self-destruction as her way of escape. Presenting her bosom to her servant for the knife's stroke, she finds, in adjusting her garments, just above her heart a packet of Leonatus' love letters. The irony of it strikes her. In the immediately succeeding speech one catches the quick, whimsical chuckle as this sheerest accident restores balance, for though she talks on of dying for a little while longer, this ironic incident has turned her back to sanity:

                    Come, here's my heart—
Something's afore 't. Soft, soft! we'll no defence!—
Obedient as the scabbard. What is here?
The scriptures of the loyal Leonatus
All turn'd to heresy?

                    III, iv, 80-84

In the concluding scene, which is a most remarkable medley of explanation, the physician, who had mixed the nearly-fatal medicine at the request of the wicked Queen,

asks Imogen: "Have you ta'en of it?" and she answers,
"Most like I did, for I was dead" (V, v, 258-259). As
it dawns upon Posthumus in this scene that the supposed
boy, Fidele, who just a moment before he had thrown
violently from him, is indeed Imogen, he embraces her,
and she says earnestly, gladly, but with the old irrepres-
sible touch of whimsy:

> Why did you throw your wedded lady from you?
> Think that you are upon a rock, and now
> Throw me again.

261-263

To go no farther than a simple question may, by now, ac-
complish what analysis might otherwise be called upon
to do. This speech of Imogen, does it sound like Rosalind, or Beatrice, or Viola?

Perdita, the lost one, is Shakspere's greatest romantic
miracle. In spite of sixteen years (all the years she has
had) spent in a shepherd's cottage, she has unmistakably
the quality of a princess. She is "the prettiest low-born
lass that ever ran on the greensward," and her creator
has written into her speech a most remarkable expression
of her personality. It is delicate, dainty, maidenly speech,
coy and sweet, and, though spoken with the freshness
of the springtime meadows, yet still girlishly precise and
proper with the dignity of a princess to the manner born.

Let us note first the few lines in which she shrugs her
pretty shoulders at Prince Florizel's flattery:

> Sir, my gracious lord,
> To chide at your extremes it not becomes me;
> O, pardon that I name them!

W. T., IV, iv, 5-7

But more representative of her manner of speaking are
the lines with which she presents nosegays to Camillo
and the King:

Here's flow'rs for you;
Hot lavender, mints, savory, marjoram;
The marigold, that goes to bed wi' th' sun
And with him rises weeping. These are flow'rs
Of middle summer, and I think they are given
To men of middle age.

103-109

Then she turns to the young prince, and to the girls:

Now, my fair'st friend,
I would I had some flow'rs o' th' spring that might
Become your time of day . . . .
. . . O Proserpina
For the flowers now that, frighted, thou let'st fall
From Dis's wagon! daffodils,
That come before the swallow dares and take
The winds of March with beauty; violets—dim,
But sweeter than the lids of Juno's eyes
Or Cytherea's breath; pale primroses,
That die unmarried ere they can behold
Bright Phoebus in his strength (a malady
Most incident to maids); bold oxlips and
The crown imperial; lilies of all kinds,
The flow'r-de-luce being one! O, these I lack
To make you garlands of; and my sweet friend
To strew him o'er and o'er.

112-127

After the exposure of Florizel and the outpouring of
Polixenes' wrath, poor Perdita is left to pick up the pieces.
I think pieces have seldom been more deftly and daintily
picked up:

Even here undone!
I was not much afeard: for once or twice
I was about to speak, and tell him plainly
The selfsame sun that shines upon his court
Hides not his visage from our cottage, but
Looks on alike. [*To Florizel*] Will't please you,
    sir, be gone?
I told you what would come of this. Beseech you

Of your own state take care. This dream of mine—
Being now awake, I'll queen it no inch farther,
But milk my ewes and weep.

452-461

III

In this chapter we have been occupied with Shaksperean characters as they are revealed in the sort of speech
he has given them, and as we come to the end of it we
find ourselves inescapably driven back to the playwright
and to a paramount interest in how he worked in this
craft of his. We have felt it clear that these characters
in their speech and in subtle nuances and turns of phrase
are individualized. What was his method in this? What
his awareness of any method?

Obviously this matter of manner or tone of speech as
a characterizing device is only a small part of the whole
story of Shakspere's method as a creator of character.
Perhaps more has been written on this large subject of
characterization than on any other regarding his work.
It involves many factors; the choice of character, the
color and variety of his role, his relations to other people,
his reactions to experience, the effect he has on other
persons, his foibles, whims, convictions, and passions—
all these enter into what we call the making of a character.

And now, following upon the matter of this chapter,
there is another factor of some import to be added to this
list; it is the consideration of *how* the character will
speak. There were some conventions regarding this in
Shakspere's day as, rustic and uncouth persons speak
prose and persons of rank speak verse, but the thing we
are dealing with goes far beyond that. It is part of the
whole marvelous faculty of the poet which made him

an accurate reporter of humanity. If it is a minor matter, it is nevertheless a sort of ultimate in the realization
of character.

Perhaps it would be truer than calling this process the
making of a character to call it the *reporting* of a character or the *recording* of a character. Coleridge was
deeply impressed with this faculty of Shakspere and was
greatly pleased by Schlegel's remark that "Shakspeare
. . . gives us the history of minds: *he lays open to us, in
a single word, a whole series of preceding conditions.*"[4]
So we come again, as we consider this matter of manner
of speech, to the question: What was Shakspere's method
in this? What his awareness of any method?

Our best answer is that there is great unlikelihood that
Shakspere himself ever deliberately wrought after such
effects. His genius is too naive and common-sensical for
that. What *is* likely is that the effect came as a by-prod-
uct of the total operation of his genius as a creator of
character. His method—if method it may be called—
seems to have consisted in the taking of an idea for a
character—a name, perhaps, or a suggestion in a source
story, or a mere colorless role in a plot—but as he held
it and turned it in his hand and lifted it into its place in
the dramatic pattern, it assumed the qualities of humanity, not a mere role any longer, but a vital character, its
motives, its attitudes, its reactions to circumstances and
to other characters becoming human and personal.

And even in the case of some characters, the very tone
of their speech became harmonized and identified with
the qualities of the personality.

[4] S. T. C., *Treatise on Method*, ed. Alice D. Snyder, 1934, p. 31.
The quotation from Schlegel, Miss Snyder thinks, is from Black's tr.
(1815) of A. W. Schlegel's *Lectures on Dramatic Art and Literature*,
II, 132.

CHAPTER XIII

SOME OBSERVATIONS ON THE PROCESSES
OF THE CREATIVE MIND

As I fit this chapter into its position as end-piece to a book on Shakspere and Common Sense, I am letting it, to a large extent, speak for itself as a contribution to the total theme. I regret it if I have seemed to deprecate the careful work of scholars who have done such splendid service in reconstructing for us the society and the thought and even the very events and personalities of Shakspere's England. We are immensely in their debt and without such reconstruction we should perhaps not be able really to read Shakspere at all. My plea, however, is against the assumption that Shakspere knew all this lore and was analytically aware of his age in the way these researchers are. My notion of Shakspere is of a man alive and sensitive to all experience, intelligent without being learned, quick to listen to all report, a reader but not a scholar, and deeply endowed with common sense and a feeling for humanity.

As a final word, let me say, when we come to a problem of Shakspere interpretation the procedure is not to knit the brows and take the hardest way; the open sesame of most Shakspere problems is the easier way of common sense. At least, it is the first way to try.

So we turn to a consideration of Some Observations on the Processes of the Creative Mind. I am aware of the pretentious sound of this title and hasten to disclaim the suggestion that I have any recondite source of knowledge about the ways of genius. This is neither a psychology nor a philosophy of genius, and its limited suggestions are based to a great extent on inference, as, I believe, they must always be.

Two primary observations will occupy us. I. In its essential operation, the creative mind is a normal mind. II. During the processes of creation, the creative mind is extraordinarily sensitive and aware of itself. These observations I shall support briefly and, I hope, aptly by citations from literature.

I

Let us take, then, the first observation: the creative mind is a normal mind. I wish before undertaking its support to buttress this statement with a cautionary word. I do not mean to say that the product of the creative mind is possible to all normal minds. That, of course, is patently not true. What I mean is that, while the product is distinguished and significant beyond ordinary compass, notwithstanding, the mind which devised it was working in all essential ways as your mind or mine would work at the same task. The difference in result is in the fact that the artist's mind possesses a refined faculty of selectivity. The artist produces a play or a story or a poem, presenting characters, scenes, themes as you or I do. His is better than ours because he has a more reliable sense of the fitness of details and of their arrangement. But that is not a matter of the way the mind works; it is, rather, a matter of quality in the workman.

In returning now to pick up our first observation, I wish to present four respects in which the processes of the creative mind demonstrate its normality. (1) One interesting way in which the artist's mind betrays itself as working like the ordinary mind is in the revelation that now and again the mind of the artist may pick up and run for a time upon a manner of expression. Everyone who speaks or writes much and who observes himself at all, has caught himself overworking some word or phrase or employing with unwonted frequency some form of expression. But this is for the time only, and then it drops back into less frequent use.

There are, of course, puns and word play in Chaucer's poetry, but they are not frequent or distinctive as a mark of style. There is, however, one rather startling cluster of puns in the "Squire's Tale" within the scope of one hundred and fifty lines.

> Al be it that I kan not sowne his stile,
> Ne kan clymben over so heigh a style.
>   105-106

> As many heddes, as many wittes ther been.
> They murmureden as dooth a swarm of been.
>   203-204

> And yet nys glas nat lyk asshen of fern;
> But for they han yknowen it so fern,
> Therfore cesseth hir janglyng and hir wonder.
>   255-257

Three in this limited compass, and on each side in the same tale and in tales which precede and follow it, no such cluster, indeed, almost no puns at all. It can only mean that the artist's mind was in a sort of punning groove as he wrote this passage. He has made puns and will make more, but not with such profuseness.

In the *Tempest* there are three passages in which the participial form *beating* is used to describe the activity of the mind. The first use is by Miranda as she refers to her distress because of the storm her father has raised:

> And now I pray you, sir,—
> For still 'tis beating in my mind,—your reason
> For raising this sea-storm?
>
> I, ii, 175-177

The other two are from Prospero. After his great speech to Ferdinand explaining the pageant of the celestial figures and moving from that to the unmatched lines about the evanescence of our little lives, he excuses himself:

> If you be pleas'd, retire into my cell
> And there repose. A turn or two I'll walk
> To still my beating mind.
>
> IV, i, 161-163

And to Alonzo, who is dazed by the wonders which are taking place, he says:

> Sir, my liege,
> Do not infest your mind with beating on
> The strangeness of this business.
>
> V, i, 245-247

The concentration of the occurrences of this expression in the *Tempest* (there is only one other instance of it in all Shakspere, *Ham.*, III, i, 182) has seemed to me a particularly striking example of the point we are illustrating. It is not an ordinary or casual form of speech; it is highly suggestive and poetic. It is, indeed, one of Shakspere's better word uses—why had he not used it before, say in *Othello* or *King Lear*, where there might seem to be great use for it?

A similar example appears in Shakspere's *Coriolanus* and *Cymbeline*, plays which lie close together in the chronology, probably 1609 for *Coriolanus* and either the same year or the next for *Cymbeline*. In these plays, once in each, appears a proverb formula which Shakspere does not use elsewhere and which I have seen nowhere else in Renaissance drama. But in my own school-boy experience it was a familiar pattern. Volumnia, the hero's mother, tells the tribune Sicinius after the tribunes had cajoled the people into a repudiation of her son:

> I would my son
> Were in Arabia, and thy tribe before him,
> His good sword in his hand.
>
> Cor., IV, ii, 23-25

In *Cymbeline* the Princess Imogen, speaking of her husband Posthumus, who has been shamefully put upon by the Queen's doltish son, Cloten, rates the evil Queen and falls into the same formula:

> I would they were in Afric both together;
> Myself by with a needle, that I might prick
> The goer back.
>
> Cym., I, i, 166-169

It is a temptation to pause for a further word on this interesting formula, but our point would tarry thereby,[1] so I merely note these two close occurrences of it as another support of the point that artists' minds run oftentimes in little grooves of unconscious reiteration.

(2) A second indication that the creative mind behaves like the ordinary mind is in the fact that frequently the artist lets slip the secret of the associative processes or of the source ideas which lie behind his work. In the "Squire's Tale" once more, Chaucer is describing the arrival in Cambyuskan's court of the Stranger Knight on the brass horse; how he rode into the high hall up to

[1] The school-boy pattern was to say, when some unwelcome task confronted us, "I wish the old man Jones was here in his sock feet, and had to pick up all this trash." There is also in this Shaksperean formula a suggestion of a place out of bounds—"Somewheres east of Suez." In our school-boy parlance it was "off the school ground" or "on the way home."

the high table of the Emperor, the while the Emperor and all his retinue are struck dumb with the wonder of it. As I read, I say to myself: *What an entrance! Only one other worthy of parallel to it—the entrance of the Green Knight on the great green horse to Arthur's court to challenge Gawain*, and suddenly from Chaucer's page leaps out the name—Gawain:

> This strange knyght that cam thus sodeynly,
> Al armed, save his heed, ful richely
> Saleweth kyng and queene and lordes alle,
> By ordre, as they seten in the halle,
> With so heigh reverence and obeisance,
> As wel in speche as in his contenaunce,
> That *Gawayn*, with his olde curteisye,
> Though he were comen ayeyn out of Fairye,
> Ne koude hym nat amende with a word.
>   89-97

And now we are sure that Chaucer, too, thought of Gawain and that his mind made the same associative connection as did ours.

There is another illustration in the "General Prologue" of the *Canterbury Tales*. Chaucer in describing the Oxford Clerk, mentions his poverty and his willingness to forego other pleasures so he may satisfy his desire for books:

> For hym was levere have at his beddes heed
> Twenty bookes, clad in blak or reed,
> Of Aristotle and his philosophie,
> Than robes riche, or fithele, or gay sautrie.
>   *Gen. Prol.*, 293-296

That these details constitute for Chaucer a sort of check-list for estimating the quality of a student by an inspection of his room and its appurtenances becomes clear when we follow him into another student's room. In the "Miller's Tale" he pictures the room of "hende Nicholas," and the contrast is strong, but with such correspondence of details as to make it clear that we are in the presence of the application of a common standard of measure. Nicholas, we feel, is real, and so may have been the Pilgrim Clerk. Consider Nicholas' room as you stand on the threshold with Chaucer and peer in:

> This clerk was cleped hende Nicholas.
>
> *   *   *
>
> A chambre hadde he in that hostelrye . . . .
>
> *   *   *
>
> His Almageste, and bookes grete and smale,
>
> *   *   *
>
> On shelves couched at his beddes heed;
> His presse ycovered with a faldyng reed;
> And al above ther lay a gay sautrie,
> On which he made a-nyghtes melodie
> So swetely that al the chambre rong.
> Mil. T., 3199-3215, *passim*

The parallel is unmistakable, though the contrast is sharp. The Pilgrim Clerk went in for Aristotle rather than Nicholas' Ptolemy. He had twenty books, probably Nicholas only one. But the book shelves in both rooms were in easy reach of the reclining scholars at their "beddes heed." The Pilgrim Clerk had to forego all luxuries among which were musical instruments—no "sautrie," but not so Nicholas who had a "gay sautrie" and made use of it "a-nyghtes."

(3) Another frequent manifestation of the ordinary mind which shows itself sometimes, too, in the processes of genius is the tendency to get fixed in one's mind a mis-

taken memory of a detail, say of a bibliographical matter. In the "Nuns' Priest's Tale" the Cock relates two
stories about dreams that came true, taking them he says,
from

> Oon of the gretteste auctour that men rede.
>
> N. P. T., 4174

He relates the first story and then taking up the other,
says:

> And certes in the same book I rede,
> Right in the nexte chapitre after this . . . .
>
> 4254-4255

Modern scholarship up to twenty years ago had found
three books which contain both stories. The most likely
source, as Miss Kate Peterson maintained, is a book of
exempla by Robert Holkot, but neither in this book
nor in the other two is the second story "right in the
nexte chapitre after" the first one. But in 1932, Mr. S.
Sakanishi pointed out that the two stories are also contained in the *Expugnatio Hibernica* of Gerald of Wales
and in the order which Chaucer claims for them.[2] It is
possible that Chaucer knew Gerald's book, but it is also
possible that he did not, and that he was making the
same mistake that I make over and over. I want to find
a passage. I *know* it is in a certain book: I comb the
book in vain and a week later chance upon what I was
looking for in another book. Or I want a passage in a
book. I *know* it is at the bottom of a left-hand page, so
I leaf through the volume looking at the bottoms of all
the left-hand pages—in vain! Again. In vain! And then,
relaxing the closedness of my mind to right-hand pages,
I find it in the middle of a right-hand page.

(4) One other indication of the ordinary working of
the creative mind is in the way in which shreds of re-

---

[2] *Modern Language Notes*, XLVII (1932), 150.

minder and suggestion from a former work come out still in a later work. That is, what one has been doing is likely to be matter of talk and reflection and reference for a while after it has, for itself, been laid aside. I take a few examples as quickly as possible.

Elsewhere in this volume I have suggested that Mercutio's Queen Mab speech in *Romeo and Juliet* is a scrap left over from the materials assembled for the making of *A Midsummer Night's Dream*. It has no essential place where it is, but if Shakspere, laying it regretfully aside as not needed or appropriate for the *Dream*, returned to the workshop later and, finding it there and debating whether or not to throw it in the fire, decided to wedge it in somewhere, we, I feel sure, agree with him and approve the wedging in.

In *Hamlet* there are references to the sinister phenomena of the air which terrorized Rome the night before Caesar's murder, matters which had been played up so fully a year or two before when he was at work on *Julius Caesar*. (*Ham.*, I, i, 113-120).

In *Antony and Cleopatra* one of the fine passages is Enobarbus' description of the water pageantry provided by Cleopatra for her Roman when he came to Alexandria. In *Cymbeline*, which follows hard upon *Antony and Cleopatra*, we learn that the Princess Imogen's bed chamber

> . . . was hang'd
> With tapestry of silk and silver; the story
> Proud Cleopatra, when she met her Roman
> And Cydnus swell'd above the banks, or for
> The press of boats or pride.
>
> *Cym.*, II, iv, 68-72

And in the same order we have in *Antony and Cleopatra* the spectacular use of the serpents as Cleopatra's means

of death, and in *Cymbeline*, Imogen, cut to the heart by
her husband's baseless suspicions, says:

> No, 'tis slander,
> Whose edge is sharper than the sword, whose tongue
> Outvenoms all the worms of Nile.
>
> *Cym.*, III, iv, 35-37

Perhaps, also, a line in *Coriolanus*, which is chronolog-
ically closer to *Antony and Cleopatra* than *Cymbeline*,
is in the same chain of carry-over association. Aufidius
says to Marcius:

> We hate alike.
> Not Afric owns a serpent I abhor
> More than thy fame and envy.
>
> *Cor.*, I, viii, 3-5

Had you written *Antony and Cleopatra*, don't you feel
that for a year or so water pageants and worms of Nile
might continue doing things in the processes of your
memory, and might occasionally show up here and there
in your speech and writing?

An illustration of a kindred but opposite process is in
Macbeth (III, i, 54-57), where the playwright's mind
seems already incubating the materials of the next great
play (*Antony and Cleopatra*). It is Macbeth's notion
that Banquo is a living rebuke to him as Caesar (Octavius)
was said to be to Antony.

By these four types of process I have sought to show
something of the normal quality of the creative mind.
(1) At times it tends to run in grooves; (2) sometimes
it betrays its background associations by an unwitting
word or suggestion; (3) it may become fixed in an er-
roneus memory of a detail; and (4) marks of other recent
work are often found lingering about and even intrud-
ing upon the work in hand.

II

We take up now the second of our principal observations: during the creative process, the artist's mind is extraordinarily sensitive and aware of itself. I turn to drama for illustrations of this statement, for in the theater, because of the hurry and drive of the action on the stage, because of many divisive pulls upon attention, because of the very variety of appeals which the stage has at its command, and, all too often, because of disturbing circumstances among the spectators, fine shades of phrase and niceties of word are lost. These matters the artist has spent his powers upon and most likely in forgetfulness that they will be largely wasted on laggard and otherwise occupied attention.

Before we turn to illustrations permit me to suggest that this is most likely true of the processes of all minds which work creatively. Those of you who have taught or have dealt much in public speech have become aware many times of how much more of your material you are perceiving than is any of your hearers. Because they are your own, you follow all the connections of your thought; you observe, because you put them there, all the subleties of expression. The whole matter is in your mind, and you find your zeal bruised and torn by the discovery that your best student or your most sympathetic auditor got less than half of it and missed altogether some of your best gems of phrasing and of idea.

And yet the next time you are up you find yourself at it again, wasting your mind's best effort upon inattentive ears.

Of course, this is why the quiet concentration of the scholar in the study finds far more of the subtleties and beauties of the play than does the spectator-auditor in the theater. This, indeed, is a large part of the reason why for a hundred and fifty years *Hamlet* was taken as fine spectacle, a gripping and thrilling play, and became a puzzling challenge to psychological analysis only when it had become the object of concentrated inspection and questioning in the study. This concentration of the scholar, I submit, is not unlike the creator's own absorption with the task of creation.

Much of the lay skepticism about the scholar's efforts to interpret texts is answered here. The layman says, *Why not let the stuff alone? Shakspere, was writing a play for an audience in a crowded theater, to be given upon a swiftly changing stage. These things you are digging up are all in your mind, and no one would be more surprised than the Bard himself to be shown them.*

This, I believe, is not the full truth. Of course, Shakspere knew—no one better—how the confusions of the theater muffle the fine overtones of poetry and drown out the subtle touches of characterization, but in the processes of creation he forgot those disturbances or set them aside and went on giving finish to lines and weaving in for us beauties and turns of thought, oblivious to the prospect of their falling by the wayside in the theater. And, indeed, in Shakspere's case, if they did not come out in the theater, they did not come out, for he clearly had no feeling of his work as enduring literature, and in those years no one was bending over the plays with the scholar's insight and care.

I turn now to provide a few illustrations of this last point as I am trying to present it. In the famous speech about Queen Mab which Mercutio speaks in *Romeo and Juliet*, he tells of Mab's nocturnal mischiefmaking, and, among others, he comes to her prank upon the soldier:

Sometimes she driveth o'er a soldier's neck,
And then he dreams of cutting foreign throats,
Of breaches, ambuscadoes, Spanish blades,
Of healths five fadom deep; and then anon
Drums at his ear, at which he starts and wakes,
And being thus frighted, swears a prayer or two
And sleeps again.

Romeo, I, iv, 82-88

My point is in the phrase "*swears* a prayer or two." The picture is clear. A renaissance soldier of fortune, roused from a deep slumber by a confused dream, being aroused must say his prayers before he commits himself again to sleep. But a full-blooded man roused unpleasantly from deep sleep is, in such a moment, not in a very devout frame of mind. What he says is prayer but it sounds as much like cursing. He says *amen*, but it sounds more like *A-men!* This, I believe, is not wresting the text or forcing an interpretation. It is there because the keen creative faculty of the artist put it there. It is even more convincingly based when we recall how perfectly it meshes into the whole fabric of Mercutio's character —Mercutio: poet, yet clear-eyed realist; berater of affectations; coarse, yet tender; loyal, yet cynically bitter toward "both your houses!" just the one to pierce through an empty act of pious observance with the keen scalpel of his wit. "*Swears* a prayer or two." But the chances are twenty to one that the whole matter will be missed in the theater, and if Shakspere were called on to think about it, he would agree with that estimate of the odds.

I take a second example from the closing scene of *King John*. This is the type of detail which makes up the best of what Miss Caroline Spurgeon's studies of Shakspere's imagery have contributed to the body of

Shakspere interpretation. The passage I cite is a notable image, clear, apt, distinguished, and almost sure to be missed in the theater.

John has been poisoned and is dying terribly. His sensations are of inward burning. As his attendants carry him out of doors, he says:

> Ay, marry, now my soul hath elbow room.
> It would not out at windows nor at doors,
> There is so hot a summer in my bosom
> That all my bowels crumble up to dust.
> I am a scribbled form drawn with a pen
> Upon a parchment, and against this fire
> Do I shrink up.

> _John_, V, vi, 28-34

This last image comes home with great clearness to anyone who has burned old papers in an open fire and has stood to watch the written characters as they seem to crawl and shrink in the flame. If the writing were on oily parchment, this would be even more noticeable. And just one more timid suggestion. John doesn't say _writing_; he says a _form_, a _scribbled form_. Is Shakspere by any chance thinking of John as addicted to the practice of unconscious scribbling and drawing (the modern word is _doodling_) as he sits past midnight listening to the interminable droning of his counsellors or alone with his harassed mind? And it is a temptation to transfer this image to the experience of Shakspere by simply reasoning; how could he know this image if it had not sometime happened to him? As a writer writing far into the night, his last task was to gather up and burn the wasted scraps of paper and parchment and to stand and watch the idle scribbled forms shrink up in the flame. But as the actor in the theater declaims this passage, who gets the beauty and suggestion of this image? Yet it is there; much if not all of it is there, put there by the concentrated creativity of Shakspere.

This sort of example can be produced almost endlessly. Let me cite one more. Courtly old King Duncan, who certainly knows how to be gracious to a hostess, comes to Inverness Castle hard upon the heels of the news of her husband's advancement and is received by Lady Macbeth. After the first exchange of amenities, his question is, "Where's the Thane of Cawdor?" (I, vi, 20). That, we infer, is the first time she has heard her husband called by his new title. That's a nice courtesy, for it confirms the news of his elevation, it avows his King's trust in him, and, coming from the lips of the author of the promotion, it rings especially well, fire-new from the mint. Just so we hasten to greet our new-titled friends with their fresh dignities, and perhaps especially to greet their wives with their adherent dignities. All of this, I believe, is in the text, but I do not believe it comes across once in a hundred times in the theater.

In an earlier chapter ("The Antic Disposition: Whence?") I have developed with some fulness a motivation for Hamlet's feigned madness which I am almost sure is too involved ever to register fully on spectator-auditors in the theater. But I believe the basis for it is in the text, put there by the conscious artistic processes of Shakspere's workmanship. In like manner the splendid fabric of A. C. Bradley's analysis of the motivation of Iago's villainy is too subtle to be caught and absorbed in the theater,[3] and yet it is nevertheless in the play because Shakspere was putting more than minimum attention to its creation. So, also, no doubt, is Mr. E. E. Stoll's ra-

[3] *Shakespearean Tragedy,* "Othello."

tional and well-supported interpretation of Shylock too involved for the audience in the theater, but is clearly warranted by the text.[4]

In closing this discussion, I shall repeat the two primary observations and seek to relate to each a principle of interpretation.

I. In its working processes, the creative mind is a normal mind.

If this is true, then the best approach to the interpretation of its product is the approach of common sense. Until it is proved otherwise, the best assumption is that the mind of genius works along normal, logical lines. It may even do, failing any other measure, to ask one's self, how would my own mind have worked in such a situation?

II. During the process of creation, the creative mind is extraordinarly sensitive and aware of itself. It devotes itself to a full expression of what it conceives, oblivious, for the time, to the fact that much of what it makes will be missed by most; some of it, perhaps, never perceived by anyone at all.

If this be true, then the efforts of sane, controlled interpretation are far from vain, for, at their best, they amount to an approach to the recovery of the artist's own processes at the moment of creation. At the same time, it goes without saying that such criticism uncontrolled and on the loose is capable of ludicrous and grotesque results. But to leave Shakspere in the theater is to miss much. By all means see him there, but do not forget that his most understanding friends are in the study.

[4] *Shakespearean Studies,* "Shylock."

tradition, 53
Parody coming before serious treatment, 177-78
Parrott, Thomas Marc, 223
Pater, Walter, 33
Peterson, Kate, 298
Poins, Ned, 193
Prolixity, 269-70
Psalms 116:11, 154

Quiller-Couch, Sir Arthur, 78 n.

Ramsay, Robert Lee, 64, 66 n.
Renaissance actors must have elaborate repertoires, 182-83
Richard II, 31, 36-43, 121-22, 232, 269
Richard's (II) self-dramatization beyond the point of weakness, 32; the stopped tournament (I, iii), 35; the maudlin speech and act on returning from Ireland (III, ii), 36-38; the metaphor of weeping out a grave (III, iii), 39-40; the crown-tugging scene (IV, i), 41; likening his sorrow to Christ's (IV, i), 42; the poetizing in prison (V, v), 42. His associates sense and remark this self-dramatizing quality, 38, 40, 46. He is the first complex and psychologized Shaksperean character, 47
Richard III, 24, 248
Richard III and Macbeth: similarities in their last hours, 149-50; neither at any time considers suicide, 149
Ritson, Joseph, 161
Robinson, Edwin Arlington, 227
Rogers, Thomas, *Anatomie of the Mind*, 28
Romeo and Juliet, 65, 98, 105-8, 120, 174 n., 177-78, 200, 229 n.,

263, 266, 267, 299, 302-3

Sakanishi, S., 298
Saxo Grammaticus, 221, 222
Schiller, F., 8
Schlegel, A. W., 289
Schofield, W. H., 66
Shakspere, William, a Lancastrian, 31; repeated character types, 49; his minor figures tend to take on the integrity of characters, 52, 219-20; his great great folk not usually involved in moral problems, 85; he is no esthetician, 131. His poets: lovers, 89-100, 132; anti-poets, 101-12; bad poets, 112-15; those who get unfavorable comment, 120-26; those who get favorable comment, 126-31. His poetic power at its height in *Macbeth* and following plays, 135. His experience as a traveling player, 191. He often lets dramatic effectiveness override credibility, 224. As a creator of character, 288-89; one trait more, 219-20
Sharp, Rebecca, 44
Shelley, P. B., 131
Sheridan, R. B., 266
Sidney, Sir Philip, 131, 140
Skelton, John, *Magnifycence*, 64
Sleep images in renaissance poetic convention, 140-41
Snyder, Alice D., 289 n.
Sorrel, Hetty, 44
Speech mannerisms, 270-72
Spencer, Theodore, 43
Spurgeon, Caroline F. E., 303-4
Stauffer, Donald, 45-46
Stoll, Elmer Edgar, 305
Stratford players, 37 n.

Tarkington, Booth, *Alice Adams*,